Praise for *HTML5 Cookbook*

"Written by community experts Emily Lewis, Mark Grabanski, Christina Ramey, Kimberly Blessing, Christopher Deutsch, Anitra Pavka, Kyle Simpson, and Christopher Schmitt, the *HTML5 Cookbook* provides the breadth and depth needed to use tomorrow's technology today."

— Estelle Weyl, author of *HTML5 & CSS3 for the Real World*

"There is so much for frontend designers to remember these days, it's hard to have it all memorized. The *HTML5 Cookbook* is perfect for all of us who know what we are looking for and need a quick and reliable way to find it."

— Chris Coyier, CSS-Tricks.com

"If you're ready to learn HTML5 that works today, the *HTML5 Cookbook* is the book to buy. There are some excellent books out there if you want exposition and details, but if you want to roll up your sleeves and get to work, buy this book."

— Ben Henick, Sitebuilder at-large

"The difficulty with cookbooks has always been getting the right balance between breadth and depth. I am impressed with the *HTML5 Cookbook*. Schmitt and Simpson have got this balance just right, providing enough depth on essential topics to give you what you need for implementing HTML5 features on your sites and apps, while also going further and exploring some interesting peripheral and nascent topics that you'll want to learn about soon, if not today. Covering semantics, video, audio, Canvas, progressive enhancement and backwards compatibility, forms, accessibility, geolocation and more, you're bound to get a lot out of this book whatever web disciplines you practice."

— Chris Mills, Open Standards Evangelist, Opera Software

HTML5 Cookbook

Christopher Schmitt and Kyle Simpson

O'REILLY®

Beijing · Cambridge · Farnham · Köln · Sebastopol · Tokyo

HTML5 Cookbook

by Christopher Schmitt and Kyle Simpson

Copyright © 2012 Christopher Schmitt and Kyle Simpson. All rights reserved.
Printed in the United States of America.

Published by O'Reilly Media, Inc., 1005 Gravenstein Highway North, Sebastopol, CA 95472.

O'Reilly books may be purchased for educational, business, or sales promotional use. Online editions are also available for most titles (*http://my.safaribooksonline.com*). For more information, contact our corporate/institutional sales department: (800) 998-9938 or *corporate@oreilly.com*.

Editors: Simon St. Laurent and Courtney Nash
Production Editor: Jasmine Perez
Copyeditor: Rachel Head
Proofreader: Linley Dolby

Indexer: Lucie Haskins
Cover Designer: Karen Montgomery
Interior Designer: David Futato
Illustrator: Robert Romano

November 2011: First Edition.

Revision History for the First Edition:
2011-11-04   First release
See *http://oreilly.com/catalog/errata.csp?isbn=9781449396794* for release details.

Nutshell Handbook, the Nutshell Handbook logo, and the O'Reilly logo are registered trademarks of O'Reilly Media, Inc. *HTML5 Cookbook*, the image of a common kestrel, and related trade dress are trademarks of O'Reilly Media, Inc.

Many of the designations used by manufacturers and sellers to distinguish their products are claimed as trademarks. Where those designations appear in this book, and O'Reilly Media, Inc., was aware of a trademark claim, the designations have been printed in caps or initial caps.

While every precaution has been taken in the preparation of this book, the publisher and authors assume no responsibility for errors or omissions, or for damages resulting from the use of the information contained herein.

ISBN: 978-1-449-39679-4

[LSI]

1320353781

Table of Contents

Preface

We know you want to learn about all the wonderful and exciting developments that come with HTML5, like web forms, `canvas`, and local storage. But we also know the importance of establishing a good foundation for advanced development. Let's first put HTML5 into a bit of context.

What Is HTML5?

HTML5 is a specification (see *http://dev.w3.org/html5/spec/*) under development by the World Wide Web Consortium (W3C). As we write this book, the HTML5 specification is officially a *Working Draft*, which means it may go through additional revisions before becoming a recommendation. The recommendation will then go through a formal approval process, resulting in a specific version of the markup language.

Meanwhile, independent from the W3C, the Web Hypertext Application Technology Working Group (WHATWG) also pursues development of the HTML specification (see *http://whatwg.org/html*).

Notice I didn't mention a version number. That's because the WHATWG recently decided to change tack and drop versioning entirely. A "living standard" is now how WHATWG defines HTML (see *http://blog.whatwg.org/html-is-the-new-html5*). This new development model means that HTML is defined according to how it's evolving, not as a version tied to features in a "snapshot" of time.

Feature Support, Not Browser Versions

What does this mean for us designers and developers? It could lead to a greater focus on implementing individual features, rather than a full specification: no more "this is an HTML5 site," but instead "this site features web sockets and geolocation."

Then again, some in the industry argue that designers and developers *need* stable specifications to refer to in order to validate and maintain their sites effectively. Plus, having a stable "what is true now" version makes authoring and teaching more manageable.

In the end, it could all just be fodder for yet another geek debate (my money's on Batman over Spider-Man and Peter Davison as the best Doctor), but we mention it mostly as a point of clarification that we have *two* development models and a reminder of the rather interesting politics involved in the specification processes.

Five Alive

Even though WHATWG sees "HTML" as a living document that needs no version number, in this book "HTML5" is our preferred term. Why is that? For the purposes of your daily design/development life, understanding and implementing features is what's important.

Since the whole point of the *Cookbook* series is to provide you with practical recipes you can use today, let's talk support *for* HTML5. Generally speaking, all of today's latest browsers support HTML5 to some degree or another. But, like its predecessors, HTML5 doesn't have that 100% browser support that we sadly suspect we'll always be dreaming of.

Enter JavaScript

While HTML5 markup has plenty of exciting new features, as you'll see in this book, it also involves—more than ever before—a host of related web technologies, many of which rely on rich JavaScript APIs to expose themselves to your web pages.

In an effort to give you a full taste of what HTML5 and these related technologies have to offer, we will not shy away from the JavaScript details. This book will, at times, take a very heavy JavaScript perspective, as we discuss some of those advanced functionalities that various HTML5 APIs make available to us.

If JavaScript is a scary or unfamiliar topic for you, now's the perfect time to brush up on those skills—if you're serious about using HTML5, you'll almost certainly want to get comfortable with leveraging at least some of what JavaScript has to offer.

It's also important to note that many of these APIs are still evolving, even as this book is being written, edited, revised, and published. Some are more complete than others, and thus are likely to be more stable. Other APIs are still in a state of frequent fluctuation, so you should keep that in mind as you decide how you will employ HTML5 technologies in your pages.

What's in This Book

While we may not provide a full list of all the features of HTML5 and browser support for them—depending on the recipe—we do discuss the support for each of the individual elements and implementations covered throughout this book (for tips on finding out what browsers currently support what parts of the specification, see Recipe 2.3, "Understanding Browser Support for HTML5").

We also cover workarounds to implement when browser support is patchy, and why you may or may not need them. This way, you can decide for yourself if a particular feature works for you, your client, or your employer.

And that's our value to you, dear reader. Using HTML5 isn't an absolute proposition. You don't have to use embedded content or web sockets to use the new structural elements, and vice versa. You don't even have to use the new structural elements to have a valid HTML5 document; you just need the Document Type Definition.

 If you find yourself asking "what's a Document Type Definition?," start your adventure into HTML5 by checking out Recipe 1.1, "Specifying the DOCTYPE"!

Pick what works for you and leave the rest. Or, rather, *experiment* with the rest to see if you may find a practical implementation for yourself or your projects.

Our industry is like HTML in a lot of ways, and probably always will be: it's constantly changing.

And we, as the good web designers and developers that we are, have to continue staying on top of those latest changes and developments. We have to continue to educate our clients and employers about the benefits and compromises. We have to experiment with moving targets and constantly grow our skills.

Honestly, though, that all sounds pretty good to us. So, let's start coding some HTML5, shall we?

Audience

While it would probably suffice to say that this book is for any person interested in learning about HTML5, it was particularly designed and developed for web developers who want to transition from XHTML or HTML4 into new technologies.

The chapters toward the end of the book are geared more for developers who want to utilize some of the JavaScript APIs found in HTML5.

Assumptions This Book Makes

You don't want a rundown of the HTML5 specification. Rather, you want to make things work as they relate to your job. In each of this book's recipes, the Solution gives you the quick and dirty answer to the problem presented. Check out the Discussion for greater coverage.

You could start from the beginning of the book and make your way through it in a linear fashion without feeling lost. With one or two exceptions, the chapters' recipes are set up so that they build off of each other. One of the great things about the books in the Cookbook series, though, is that they're here to help you out when you find yourself with a specific problem—in this case, an HTML5-related problem. Simply crack open the book or the ebook on your tablet and find the right recipe for a practical, usable solution.

And one more thing: we assume that geolocation will forever be linked to HTML5. Even though we know, yes, that W3C Geolocation API Working Draft is separate from the HTML5 specification. That hasn't stopped people from writing blog posts, tutorials, and even books about putting geolocation into the same conversation as HTML5. And since it's such a great, serviceable API right now, we felt we had to include it in a book about HTML5 (see Chapter 8). If it troubles you, think of Geolocation and other technologies as "HTML5 and friends." However, this book probably isn't for you if you require hyper-technical hierarchies to be adhered to in order to obtain practical knowledge.

Conventions Used in This Book

The following typographical conventions are used in this book:

Italic
> Indicates new terms, URLs, email addresses, filenames, and file extensions.

`Constant width`
> Used for program listings, as well as within paragraphs to refer to program elements such as variable or function names, databases, data types, environment variables, statements, and keywords.

`Constant width bold`
> Shows commands or other text that should be typed literally by the user.

`Constant width italic`
> Shows text that should be replaced with user-supplied values or by values determined by context.

This icon signifies a tip, suggestion, or general note.

 This icon indicates a warning or caution.

Using Code Examples

This book is here to help you get your job done. In general, you may use the code in this book in your programs and documentation. You do not need to contact us for permission unless you're reproducing a significant portion of the code. For example, writing a program that uses several chunks of code from this book does not require permission. Selling or distributing a CD-ROM of examples from O'Reilly books does require permission. Answering a question by citing this book and quoting example code does not require permission. Incorporating a significant amount of example code from this book into your product's documentation does require permission.

We appreciate, but do not require, attribution. An attribution usually includes the title, author, publisher, and ISBN. For example: "*HTML5 Cookbook* by Christopher Schmitt and Kyle Simpson (O'Reilly). Copyright 2012 Christopher Schmitt and Kyle Simpson, 978-1-449-39679-4."

If you feel your use of code examples falls outside fair use or the permission given above, feel free to contact us at *permissions@oreilly.com*.

Safari® Books Online

 Safari Books Online is an on-demand digital library that lets you easily search over 7,500 technology and creative reference books and videos to find the answers you need quickly.

With a subscription, you can read any page and watch any video from our library online. Read books on your cell phone and mobile devices. Access new titles before they are available for print, and get exclusive access to manuscripts in development and post feedback for the authors. Copy and paste code samples, organize your favorites, download chapters, bookmark key sections, create notes, print out pages, and benefit from tons of other time-saving features.

O'Reilly Media has uploaded this book to the Safari Books Online service. To have full digital access to this book and others on similar topics from O'Reilly and other publishers, sign up for free at *http://my.safaribooksonline.com*.

How to Contact Us

Please address comments and questions concerning this book to the publisher:

O'Reilly Media, Inc.
1005 Gravenstein Highway North
Sebastopol, CA 95472
800-998-9938 (in the United States or Canada)
707-829-0515 (international or local)
707-829-0104 (fax)

We have a web page for this book, where we list errata, examples, and any additional information. You can access this page at:

http://shop.oreilly.com/product/0636920016038.do

To comment or ask technical questions about this book, send email to:

bookquestions@oreilly.com

For more information about our books, courses, conferences, and news, see our website at *http://www.oreilly.com*.

Find us on Facebook: *http://facebook.com/oreilly*

Follow us on Twitter: *http://twitter.com/oreillymedia*

Watch us on YouTube: *http://www.youtube.com/oreillymedia*

Acknowledgments

We can't see it, but time is an invisible dimension that surrounds us all.

Yet time is so very interesting in that it can be marked so well.

For instance, it can be marked by the due dates and deadlines of which a book of this sort is composed. So many, many deadlines.

When writing a book, for example, there is a deadline for the original manuscript.

Then there are the changes to the manuscript provided by many talented people like editors, technical editors, copyeditors, artists, designers, and so on.

They each give writers their deadlines, marking time.

Editorial deadline, technical edits deadline, copyedits deadline, art deadline, and so on.

Deadlines upon deadlines as time is.

Then there is another way time is marked.

The time away from loved ones.

After writing several books, I now know that writing a book is a Herculean task in that it keeps time away from other activities, like fun and family—something I wouldn't wish on anyone.

But then friends aren't just anyone, right?

Along with my co-lead author, Kyle Simpson, I congratulate and thank the contributors to the *HTML5 Cookbook*: Emily Lewis, Kimberly Blessing, Christina Huggins Ramey, Anitra Pavka, Marc Grabanski, and Christopher Deustch.

Thanks to our technical editors, Shelley Powers, Ben Henick, Dusty Jewett, Molly Holzschlag, and Helen Oliver, who diligently kept us on our toes.

Our copyeditor, Rachel Head, is a miracle worker, making our respective families proud by making them think we all are better writers than we probably are.

Many, many thanks to editors Simon St. Laurent and Courtney Nash from O'Reilly, who helped me stay sane during our time on this book.

Every once in a while I tried to count up how many total years of web development experience were brought to this project by all the talented writers and editors who contributed, but I got a bit too exhausted just thinking about it.

I'm not sure if all these talented, beautiful people knew what they signed up for when I first talked to them about the *HTML5 Cookbook*, but I'm happy with what we were able to make together. And I thank them for that.

Finally, thanks to my family and loved ones who have been there for me throughout my obsession with web design and development. Let's continue to share good times together.

Christopher Schmitt

http://christopherschmitt.com

http://twitter.com/@teleject

I would like to thank my wonderful and patient wife, Christen, for letting me be part of this project. I also want to thank my parents for their support and encouragement in all my various endeavors. Lastly, to my new son, Ethan, I hope someday you are happily coding along in HTML12 and you get to look back on this old HTML5 book with nostalgia. Just remember, I had to walk to school in the snow, uphill, both ways...

Kyle Simpson

http://blog.getify.com

http://twitter.com/@getify

Thank you to Christopher Schmitt for giving me the opportunity to contribute to this book. I'd also like to thank Rey Bango, who recommended me to Christopher and who has given me so many opportunities to write about what I love. Following the pimpage chain, I must thank Christian Heillman for recommending me to Rey in the first place and for always encouraging me to share what I know.

To my love, Jason, thank you for supporting me in everything I do and reminding me that new opportunities are never as scary as they first seem. Thank you, also, for reading everything I write and making sure I don't sound stupid. You make my life bigger and better than I ever dreamed.

To my other unofficial editors, Brian Arnold and Ian Pitts, thanks for taking the time over the months (and years) to read my work and offer critical feedback. You guys are not only brilliant developers, but you are great friends.

Thanks to my sister, Erin, for reminding me who I am and what is important in this world. And to my sista, Erin Shutes, thank you for 20 years of support through the best and worst of times.

To the readers of my blog, my social-network friends, and everyone I've met at conferences, thanks for being interested in what I have to share and for sharing back. You remind me every day why I love what I do.

Emily Lewis

http://emilylewisdesign.com

http://twitter.com/@emilylewis

I would like to thank my friend Christopher Schmitt for inviting me to contribute to this book; my students at Bryn Mawr College and my colleagues at Comcast Interactive Media for constantly challenging me; my mother and my great-aunt for their encouragement; and my cat, Punky, for her support.

Kimberly Blessing

http://www.obiwankimberly.com

http://twitter.com/@obiwankimberly

Thank you, Molly Holzschlag and Cameron Barrett, for encouraging me to share my geeky learnings.

(Of course) thank you, Christopher Schmitt, for convincing me to contribute to this book.

Thank you, Matt May, for your feedback as I considered what to write for this book.

I'd also like to thank all of the other wonderful people I've met at web conferences and networking events over the years. You are too many to name. Y'all inspire me to learn and laugh.

Thank you, Mom and Dad, for... well, everything.

I also want to thank our readers—*you*—for caring enough about your art to hone your skills. Your curiosity, knowledge, and empathy will advance the Web.

Anitra Pavka

http://anitrapavka.com

http://twitter.com/@apavka

A hearty thanks to Christopher Schmitt for continually providing me with opportunities for expanding my knowledge of web design. You've pushed me to develop my writing and coding skills far beyond my modest ambitions.

Thank you, my sweet husband, Paul Ramey, for providing support and patience while I research, code, and write. And thank you for providing welcome distractions when I've worked too long!

Christina Huggins Ramey

http://www.christinaramey.me

http://twitter.com/@fidlet

Thanks to Christopher Deutsch (*http://twitter.com/@cdeutsch*) for taking the geolocation chapter content ideas and running with them.

Marc Grabanski

http://marcgrabanski.com

http://twitter.com/@1Marc

CHAPTER 1

Fundamental Syntax and Semantics

Emily Lewis

1.0 Introduction

This chapter is designed to get you up and running with HTML5 basics. Covering the fundamental recipes, from declaring the DOCTYPE and character set to dealing with ambiguities of the new HTML5 semantics, it helps lay the groundwork for the rest of the book.

1.1 Specifying the DOCTYPE

Problem

You want to create an HTML5 page.

Solution

Specify the HTML5 DOCTYPE at the very beginning of your page:

```
<!DOCTYPE html>
<html>
    <head>
        <title>HTML5, for Fun &amp; Profit</title>
    </head>
    <body>
    </body>
</html>
```

 Note that the DOCTYPE is not case sensitive. Feel free to go CaMeL cAsE with the characters.

Discussion

The Document Type Definition, or DOCTYPE, tells browsers and validators what version of HTML the page is written in. Previous versions of HTML specified the version number, such as the DOCTYPE for XHTML 1.0 Strict:

```
<!DOCTYPE html PUBLIC "-//W3C//DTD XHTML 1.0 Strict//EN"
    "http://www.w3.org/TR/xhtml1/DTD/xhtml1-strict.dtd">
```

With HTML5, the version is dropped from the DOCTYPE. This allows HTML5 to be backward compatible in terms of syntax and hopefully makes the transition to HTML5 easier.

Let's say you have a site that is valid HTML 4.0, but you want to transition it to HTML5. All you have to do to make this a valid HTML5 site is make this DOCTYPE change.

Additionally, all browsers recognize the shortened DOCTYPE and render in strict standards mode.

 There are some elements that have changed between HTML4 and HTML5, so you will need to watch for elements that have been removed or deprecated. For example, center might not *technically* validate as HTML5.

See Also

The W3C Working Draft discussion on differences between HTML4 and HTML5 includes DOCTYPE at *http://www.w3.org/TR/html5-diff/#doctype*.

1.2 Specifying the Character Set

Problem

You need to define the character encoding of your web page.

Solution

In your document head, add a meta declaration for the character set:

```
<meta charset="UTF-8" />
```

Discussion

The *character encoding* instructs browsers and validators what set of characters to use when rendering web pages. If you do not declare the character set in your HTML, browsers first try to determine the character set from your server's HTTP response headers (specifically, the Content-Type header).

The character set declared in the response headers is generally taken in preference over the character set specified in your document, so the headers are the preferred method of communicating this information. However, if you cannot control what headers your server sends, declaring the character set in your HTML document is the next best option.

If a character set is declared neither in the document nor in the response headers, the browser might choose one for you, and it *may* be the wrong one for your site's needs. This not only can cause issues with rendering, but also poses a security risk.

 Several years ago, a cross-site scripting vulnerability was discovered at Google that demonstrated the importance of character encoding: *http://shiflett.org/blog/2005/dec/googles-xss-vulnerability*.

In previous versions of HTML, the character set needed to be declared with additional attributes and values:

```
<meta http-equiv="Content-Type" content="text/html; charset=UTF-8" />
```

But, as with the DOCTYPE, HTML5 only needs the minimum information required by browsers. Again, this helps with backward compatibility and makes it easier for authors to implement.

Special characters

Unicode (UTF-8) is a versatile encoding that covers most web builders' needs. Sometimes, though, you need to include a character that is outside the UTF-8 encoding.

 A great resource for character entities is at *http://www.digitalmediami nute.com/reference/entity/*. It includes the numeric, named, and Unicode references for many of the more common characters allowed in HTML.

You can specify such characters with Numeric Character References (NCRs) or as named entities in order to help browsers render them correctly. If you wanted a copyright symbol, for example, you could include it in your HTML as an NCR:

```
&#169;
```

or you could include it as a named entity:

```
&copy;
```

See Also

Mark Pilgrim's "Dive Into HTML5" discussion about character encoding at *http://di veintohtml5.info/semantics.html#encoding*.

1.3 Specifying the Language

Problem

You want to specify the primary language of your web page.

Solution

Add the `lang` attribute and appropriate value to your opening `html` element:

```
<html lang="en">
```

Discussion

Browsers, screen readers, and other user agents use the `lang` attribute to determine the language in which the content should be interpreted. The example above specifies English via the `en` value.

Declaring a document's primary language isn't a requirement for HTML5 (or any of the previous versions, for that matter). It is, however, a good practice for both usability and accessibility.

See Also

Mark Pilgrim's "Dive Into Accessibility" discussion about identifying your document language at *http://diveintoaccessibility.info/day_7_identifying_your_language.html*.

1.4 Optimizing <script>s and <link>s

Problem

You want to reference JavaScripts and include links to external CSS files in your web page as simply as possible.

Solution

Include `script` and `link` declarations, but *without* the `type` attribute:

```
<link rel="stylesheet" href="styles.css" />
<script src="scripts.js"></script>
```

Discussion

HTML5 requires only the minimum amount of information needed for user agents. In previous versions of HTML, both CSS `link`s and `script`s required the `type` attribute to indicate the language. If you forgot to include `type`, though, most browsers assumed the correct value.

HTML5 makes **type** *officially* optional, but still validates older documents that do include the attribute. This makes sense, as there is really only one standard scripting language and only one styling language for the Web in use today.

See Also

The W3C Working Draft discussion on differences between HTML4 and HTML5 includes changed attributes at *http://www.w3.org/TR/html5-diff/#changed-attributes*.

1.5 Adding Document Structure with HTML5's New Elements

Problem

You want to define your document structure with the new header, footer, nav, aside, section, and article elements.

Solution

Examine your content and document structure to determine which of the new elements work with your page:

header
> Is used to contain the headline(s) for a page and/or section. It can also contain supplemental information such as logos and navigational aids.

footer
> Contains information about a page and/or section, such as who wrote it, links to related information, and copyright statements.

nav
> Contains the *major* navigation links for a page and, while not a requirement, is often contained by header.

aside
> Contains information that is *related* to the surrounding content but also exists *independently*, such as a sidebar or pull-quotes.

section
> Is the most generic of the new structural elements, containing content that can be grouped thematically or is related.

article
> Is used for self-contained content that could be consumed independently of the page as a whole, such as a blog entry.

A simple blog structure, with a headline, navigation, a sidebar, blog posts, and a footer, could be marked up in HTML5 as:

```
<header>
    <h1><abbr title="Hypertext Markup Language">HTML</abbr>5, for Fun &amp;
```

```
        Profit</h1>
    <nav>
        <ul>
            <li><a href="/Archive/">Archive</a></li>
            <li><a href="/About/">About</a></li>
        </ul>
    </nav>
</header>
<article>
    <h2><code>nav</code> Isn't for <em>All</em> Links</h2>
    <p>Though the <code>nav</code> element often contains links, that doesn't mean
        that <em>all</em> links on a site need <code>nav</code>.</p>
</article>
<article>
    <h2>You've Got the <code>DOCTYPE</code>. Now What?</h2>
    <p>HTML5 isn't an all or nothing proposition. You can pick and choose what
        works best for you. So once you have the <code>DOCTYPE</code> in place, you
        should explore.</p>
</article>
<aside>
    <h2>HTML5 Elsewhere</h2>
    <p>Feed your HTML5 fix with resources from our partners:</p>
    <ul>
        <li><a href="http://lovinghtml5.com">Loving HTML5</a></li>
        <li><a href="http://semanticsally.com">Semantic Sally</a></li>
    </ul>
</aside>
<footer>
    <p>Copyright &copy; 2011 <a href="http://html5funprofit.com">HTM5, for Fun
        &amp; Profit</a>. All rights reserved.</p>
</footer>
```

And, with the right CSS and supporting HTML, this markup could render on the browser as shown in Figure 1-1.

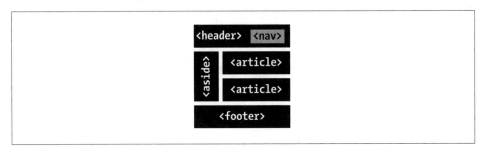

Figure 1-1. Sample rendering of a simple blog structure using HTML5's new elements

Discussion

These new structural elements were developed based on actual practices. A review of over a billion web pages (see *http://code.google.com/webstats/*) revealed the naming conventions markup authors were already using to structure and describe their content via class and id, including:

- header
- footer
- nav

The new elements in HTML5 simply attempt to reflect what authors are already doing.

Structural elements

Using these structural elements helps you make your markup more semantic, but they also help define the main landmarks in the document.

Consider how important it is for screen reader users and folks who navigate with the keyboard to be able to skip to different areas of the page, like the navigation. Previously, we've tried to provide such functionality via "skip links" and shortcuts (see *http://www.vdebolt.com/nmmug/flow.html*), but HTML5 establishes formal landmark elements that can be used instead. In fact, the Web Accessibility Initiative's Accessible Rich Internet Applications (WAI-ARIA) specification already addresses how to use HTML5 with ARIA landmark roles (see Chapter 2) for this very purpose.

That said, this is still a hypothetical. As of this writing, no browsers or assistive technologies reference the structural elements for any navigational purposes.

When to use structural elements

How do you know when to use these new elements? Again, focus on your content and consider the semantics of each element. For example, most web pages have an area considered a "header," composed of a logo, maybe the company name, and a tagline. And that certainly sounds like a good case for header. You may also have a section or aside in your document with its own set of headlines and navigation, which may also be contained in a header.

The same holds true for footer. While most pages have content appropriate for the new footer element, perhaps regarding the author, copyright, and related information, sections, articles, and asides can feature the same information—and, in turn, can also include a footer.

Finally, consider nav. You may have many groups of links on your site, some of which are for navigation, while others are external.

 nav is only appropriate for *major* site navigation, not search results links or a blogroll.

When to use <div> elements

As you can see from the blog markup example, the new structural elements can replace many of the non-semantic container divs that you may have grown accustomed to using. But div still has a place at the HTML5 party.

If you ever need a containing element *strictly for style purposes*, div is the element to use. You don't want to use one of the new structural elements just to serve as a hook for your CSS. That is not what semantic markup is about.

Just remember to focus on your content and avoid *unnecessary* use of div, such as when another element is more semantic. For example, if you have a paragraph of text, use the p element, not div. Both give you block-level formatting, but p is more semantic for that particular purpose.

Styling structural elements

All of today's browsers render the content contained by these new elements. However, some browsers don't recognize them and, as such, treat them like inline elements. This default rendering can cause some serious problems with styling.

Fortunately, it doesn't take much to fix. The current cast of browsers simply needs to be told to treat the elements as block-level elements:

```
header, footer, nav, article, aside, section {
    display: block;
}
```

With that single CSS declaration, you can happily style the structural elements—well, almost. In versions of Internet Explorer (IE) prior to IE9 you have to add a bit of Java-Script to your document so IE recognizes the elements and allows you to style them:

```
<script>
    document.createElement('header');
    document.createElement('footer');
    document.createElement('nav');
    document.createElement('article');
    document.createElement('aside');
    document.createElement('section');
</script>
```

If you want cooperation from an earlier version of IE, any time you add a new HTML5 element to your document you'll need to add the corresponding document.createEle ment. See Chapter 2 for a more detailed discussion of using JavaScript with IE.

See Also

Script Junkie's article "Using HTML5's New Semantic Tags Today" at *http://msdn.mi crosoft.com/en-us/scriptjunkie/gg454786*.

1.6 Choosing Between <article> and <section>

Problem

You don't know whether `article` or `section` is the most appropriate element to use on your web page.

Solution

Focus on your content and the semantic definitions of `article` and `section` (refer back to Recipe 1.5).

<article>

`article` can be considered a specialized form of `section`. It is intended for content that could stand on its own, outside of all surrounding content, such as "syndicatable" content like blog posts.

`article` is suitable for other types of content, including:

- Video and accompanying transcript
- News articles
- Blog comments

 Often the name of an article or a blog post is in the title of the URI. If that's the case with a page you are working on, that content should be wrapped in an **article** element.

In the code example in Recipe 1.5, we used `article` to contain the individual blog posts:

```
<article>
    <h2><code>nav</code> Isn't for <em>All</em> Links</h2>
    <p>Though the <code>nav</code> element often contains links, that doesn't mean
        that <em>all</em> links on a site need <code>nav</code>.</p>
</article>
<article>
    <h2>You've Got the <code>DOCTYPE</code>. Now What?</h2>
    <p>HTML5 isn't an all or nothing proposition. You can pick and choose what
        works best for you. So once you have the <code>DOCTYPE</code> in place, you
        should explore.</p>
</article>
```

<section>

section is the most generic of the new structural elements, intended to simply group related content. However, it is *not* a generic container element like div. The content it groups must be *related*.

Applying this definition to Recipe 1.5, we might want to add section as the parent element for both instances of article:

```
<section>
    <article>
        <h2><code>nav</code> Isn't for <em>All</em> Links</h2>
        <p>Though the <code>nav</code> element often contains links, that doesn't
            mean that <em>all</em> links on a site need <code>nav</code>.</p>
    </article>
    <article>
        <h2>You've Got the <code>DOCTYPE</code>. Now What?</h2>
        <p>HTML5 isn't an all or nothing proposition. You can pick and choose what
            works best for you. So once you have the <code>DOCTYPE</code> in place,
            you should explore.</p>
    </article>
</section>
```

This example meets the core criterion for section: the grouped content is thematically related.

But wait! The spec (see *http://www.w3.org/TR/html5/sections.html#the-section-element*) further clarifies:

> A general rule is that the section element is appropriate only if the element's contents would be listed explicitly in the document's outline.

The *document outline* refers to HTML5's new *sectioning content* model, where each of the new structural elements creates its own self-contained outline. This outline is generated by the headings (h1–h6) contained in each element (see Recipe 1.7).

So, if you want to use section, the content *should* have a natural heading. Given this additional clarification, let's modify the markup from Recipe 1.5, to include a heading for our section:

```
<section>
    <h1>Most Recent Blog Posts</h1>
    <article>
        <h2><code>nav</code> Isn't for <em>All</em> Links</h2>
        <p>Though the <code>nav</code> element often contains links, that doesn't
            mean that <em>all</em> links on a site need <code>nav</code>.</p>
    </article>
    <article>
        <h2>You've Got the <code>DOCTYPE</code>. Now What?</h2>
        <p>HTML5 isn't an all or nothing proposition. You can pick and choose what
            works best for you. So once you have the <code>DOCTYPE</code> in place,
            you should explore.</p>
    </article>
</section>
```

Discussion

The difference between `section` and `article` can be confusing, and as the spec evolves, the path doesn't seem to be getting much clearer. For the majority of use cases, though, considering these guidelines should help:

- Do not use `section` simply as a styling hook. Use `divs` and `spans` instead.
- Do not use `section` if `header`, `footer`, `aside`, or `article` is more semantically appropriate for your content (see Recipe 1.5).
- Do not use `section` unless the content has a natural heading.

See Also

HTML5 Doctor has a handy flow chart to help you choose the right HTML5 structural elements at *http://html5doctor.com/happy-1st-birthday-us/#flowchart*.

1.7 Checking Your Document Outline

Problem

You want to view your document's content outline.

Solution

Run your page through the HTML5 Outliner tool: *http://gsnedders.html5.org/outliner/*.

Discussion

HTML5 has an outline algorithm that calculates the structure of a web document. This algorithm is based on sections defined by the new structural elements.

For the main document outline, `section` and `aside` each introduce a new section in the outline, while the heading(s) within each form the outline content. This is known as *explicit sectioning*.

Let's examine the following markup example:

```
<section>
    <h1>Most Recent Blog Posts</h1>
    <article>
        <h2><code>nav</code> Isn't for <em>All</em> Links</h2>
        <p>Though the <code>nav</code> element often contains links, that doesn't
            mean that <em>all</em> links on a site need <code>nav</code>.</p>
    </article>
    <article>
        <h2>You've Got the <code>DOCTYPE</code>. Now What?</h2>
        <p>HTML5 isn't an all or nothing proposition. You can pick and choose what
            works best for you. So once you have the <code>DOCTYPE</code> in place,
            you should explore.</p>
```

```
        </article>
    </section>
```

This markup would generate the following document outline:

> 1. Most Recent Blog Posts
> 1.1 nav Isn't for All Links
> 1.2 You've Got the DOCTYPE. Now What?

Heading levels

Regardless of version, headings in HTML are ranked, with h1 being the highest and h6 being the lowest.

Before HTML5, this ranking helped structure the document outline. However, with HTML5, the importance of heading rank in determining the outline is trumped by the sectioning elements.

Let's modify the previous example to reflect h6 as the primary heading of section and h1 as the primary heading of article:

```
<section>
    <h6>Most Recent Blog Posts</h6>
    <article>
        <h1><code>nav</code> Isn't for <em>All</em> Links</h1>
        <p>Though the <code>nav</code> element often contains links, that doesn't
            mean that <em>all</em> links on a site need <code>nav</code>.</p>
    </article>
    <article>
        <h1>You've Got the <code>DOCTYPE</code>. Now What?</h1>
        <p>HTML5 isn't an all or nothing proposition. You can pick and choose what
            works best for you. So once you have the <code>DOCTYPE</code> in place,
            you should explore.</p>
    </article>
</section>
```

Because HTML5 uses the structural elements section and aside to know when a new outline section begins (not the headings), we still get the exact same outline as in the original example:

> 1. Most Recent Blog Posts
> 1.1 nav Isn't for All Links
> 1.2 You've Got the DOCTYPE. Now What?

Implicit sectioning

Since structural elements aren't *required* in HTML5, heading rank does still affect the document structure if sectioning elements aren't used. This is known as *implicit sectioning*. Further, implicit and explicit sectioning can be used together to form the document outline.

An implicit section starts with a new heading and is positioned in the document outline according to that heading's rank in relation to a previous heading. If a heading is a lower rank than its predecessor, it opens a new subsection in the outline. If a heading is a higher rank, it closes the previous section and opens a new one.

Let's create a new example to see how heading rank supports implicit sections:

```
<section>
    <h1>You've Got the <code>DOCTYPE</code>, Now What?</h1>
    <h2>Simplified <code>link</code>s and <code>script</code>s</h2>
    <p>HTML5's more flexible and simplified syntax ...</p>
    <h2>Block-Level Links</h2>
    <p>With HTML5, <code>a</code>s can contain block ...</p>
    <h3>Looking Back</h3>
    <p>In earlier versions of HTML, you had to ...</p>
    <h2>Add Structure</h2>
    <p>HTML5 gives us several new elements to add ...</p>
</section>
```

This example utilizes heading rank, rather than explicit sectioning elements, to generate the following outline:

1. You've Got the DOCTYPE, Now What?
1.1 Simplified links and scripts
1.2 Block-level Links
1.2.1 Looking Back
1.3 Add Structure

Why is this important?

Knowing what your document outline looks like can help you decide not only which heading levels to use, but also which structural elements to use. Remember how we said that a `section` should have a natural heading (Recipe 1.6)? Checking your document outline will show you if you have neglected to include a heading, which may prompt you to reconsider whether that element was the most appropriate one to use for your content. Additionally, a document outline that accurately reflects your content hierarchy can help users of assistive devices navigate your site.

Unfortunately, no browsers have implemented this outlining yet, nor do any assistive technologies utilize it for navigation. Still, checking the document outline should be a part of the development process, and it helps significantly when considering which elements and heading levels to use.

See Also

For an extremely detailed look at the outline algorithm and sectioning, the Mozilla Developer Network at *https://developer.mozilla.org/en/Sections_and_Outlines_of_an _HTML5_document* is an excellent resource.

1.8 Modifying the Document Outline

Problem

You have a primary page title and tagline marked up with headings (h1 and h2, respectively), but you don't want the tagline included in your document outline.

Solution

Contain the both headings with the hgroup element:

```
<hgroup>
    <h1>HTML5, for Fun &amp; Profit</h1>
    <h2>Tips, Tricks and Resources</h2>
</hgroup>
```

Discussion

hgroup hides all headings except the highest ranked from the document outline. In the above example, the only content that would appear in the document outline is "HTML5, for Fun & Profit" from the h1.

Even if we reverse the source order of the two headings, only the highest-ranked (h1) content will be pulled into the document outline:

```
<hgroup>
    <h2>Tips, Tricks and Resources</h2>
    <h1>HTML5, for Fun &amp; Profit</h1>
</hgroup>
```

See Also

Emily Lewis's in-depth discussion of headings, hgroup, and the HTML5 outline at *http://ablognotlimited.com/articles/the-beauty-of-semantic-markup-part-3-headings*.

1.9 Emphasizing Text

Problem

You want to add emphasis or emphatic stress to text content.

Solution

Contain the text to be emphasized with the em element:

```
<p>My name is <em>Jane</em>, not John.</p>
```

Discussion

After looking at this example, you may be wondering what is new here, since em has been around since HTML4. The difference is that HTML5 slightly redefines em for text with "emphatic stress," which I translate as any text that, when spoken, I would verbally emphasize.

Redefining <i>

Another change in HTML5's text-level semantics is that the i element is no longer considered presentational. You can now use i to indicate text that is in an alternate voice or mood, or somehow offset from the normal prose; for example, a taxonomic designation, a technical term, a thought, an idiomatic phrase, or some other text whose typical typographic presentation is italicized:

```
<p>Sally thought to herself, <i>when will IE6 die?</i></p>
```

Despite the new semantic distinction, browsers typically render both em and i in italics (see Figure 1-2). Of course, you can change the default styling of either element with CSS.

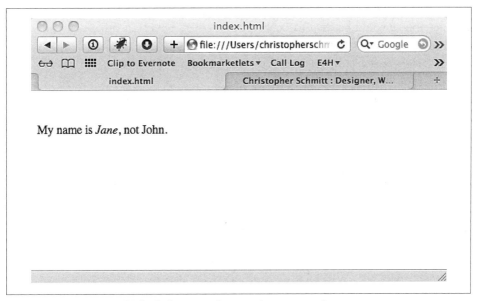

Figure 1-2. Browsers render both the <i> and <em> elements in italics

See Also

HTML5 Doctor's article "The i, b, em, & strong elements" at *http://html5doctor.com/i-b-em-strong-element/*.

1.10 Adding Importance to Text

Problem

You want to indicate a span of text that is important.

Solution

Contain the important text with the strong element:

```
<p><strong>Registration is required</strong> for this event.</p>
```

Discussion

In previous versions of HTML, strong was used to indicate strong emphasis. In HTML5, strong indicates importance and is typically used for alerts and warnings.

Redefining <b>

Like its shunned sibling i, the b element makes a comeback in HTML5. No longer considered a presentational element, b is used to stylistically offset text from the normal prose without conveying any extra importance.

For example, b could be used for keywords, product names, or other content whose text would typically be unique compared to surrounding text, such as a paragraph lead:

```
<p><b>Once upon a time,</b> there was a man who lost his mind.</p>
```

The difference between strong and b is now more semantically clear, but both are typically rendered in browsers with a heavier font weight (see Figure 1-3). Of course, CSS lets you change the default styling as needed.

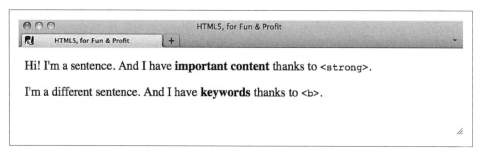

Figure 1-3. Browsers render both the <b> and <strong> elements in bold

See Also

The author's article "The Beauty of Semantic Markup, Part 2: <strong>, <b>, <em>, <i>" at *http://ablognotlimited.com/articles/the-beauty-of-semantic-markup-part-2 -strong-b-em-i*.

1.11 Highlighting Text for Reference

Problem

You want to highlight the search term(s) in a list of search results.

Solution

Contain the search term with the mark element:

```
<p>Your search for <mark>awesomesauce</mark> resulted in 923 entries:</p>
```

Discussion

mark is an entirely new element in HTML5. While the most common scenario for its use is likely for search terms, according to the spec it can be more broadly used for text that is "marked or highlighted for reference purposes, due to its relevance in another text."

mark adds no additional semantic importance or emphasis to the text it contains, but current browsers (that doesn't include IE before version 9) do display the content with a yellow background by default (see Figure 1-4), which you can change with CSS.

Figure 1-4. Browsers render the <mark> element with a yellow background by default

See Also

HTML5 Doctor's article "Draw attention with mark" at *http://html5doctor.com/draw -attention-with-mark/*.

1.12 Marking Up Small Print

Problem

You want to offset a legal disclaimer and copyright statement as small print.

Solution

Contain the small print content with the `small` element:

```
<p><small>The owner of this blog is not responsible for mind blowage. Please
    consume at your own risk.</small></p>
<p><small>Copyright &copy; 2011 Awesomest Blog. All rights reserved.</small></p>
```

Discussion

HTML5 redefined the previously presentational `small` as semantically appropriate for content typically considered "small print," such as legalese, disclaimers, terms, conditions, and copyrights. And though `small` is supposed to indicate semantics only, browsers do display this content a bit smaller by default (see Figure 1-5).

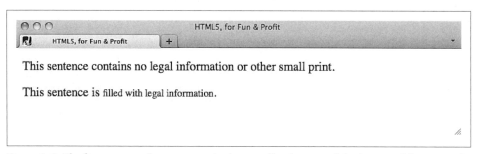

Figure 1-5. The first sentence does not contain the <small> element, while the second does; note the slightly smaller font size in part of the second sentence

See Also

The W3C Working Draft discussion of text-level semantics in HTML5 includes the `small` element at *http://www.w3.org/TR/html5/text-level-semantics.html#the-small-element*.

1.13 Defining Acronyms and Abbreviations

Problem

You want to provide expanded definitions for acronyms and abbreviations.

Solution

Contain the abbreviation or acronym with `abbr`, and include the definition as the `title` value:

```
<abbr title="Accessible Rich Internet Applications">ARIA</abbr>
```

Discussion

In previous versions of HTML we had both the `abbr` and the `acronym` elements. Not surprisingly in the always-ready-for-a-debate web world, these two elements caused much controversy.

Part of the issue is that prior to version 7, IE didn't display the `title` value of `abbr` as a tool tip (see Figure 1-6). To get around this usability limitation, authors simply started using `acronym`, regardless of whether the content was actually an acronym.

Figure 1-6. Default rendering of <abbr> tool tip in Firefox 5.0

Another part of the issue was the argument about what was an acronym versus what constituted an abbreviation.

Today, the debate is over (at least for practical purposes), as `acronym` has been dropped completely from the HTML5 specification. The reasoning is that all acronyms are shortened forms of words or phrases, which is the very definition of an abbreviation.

See Also

WHATWG's Living Standard's section on text-level semantics includes `abbr` at *http://www.whatwg.org/specs/web-apps/current-work/multipage/text-level-semantics.html#the-abbr-element*.

1.14 Adding Links to Block-Level Content

Problem

You want to wrap your site logo and main heading with a single hyperlink.

Solution

Contain both the logo image and the heading with the a element:

```
<a href="http://html5funprofit.com">
    <h1>HTML5, for Fun &amp; Profit</h1>
    <img src="logo.png" alt="HTML5 for Fun and Profit" />
</a>
```

Discussion

Previous versions of HTML restricted a to inline content. So, if you had different elements that all needed to be linked to the same resource, you had to individually specify the a for each:

```
<h1><a href="http://html5funprofit.com">HTML5, for Fun &amp; Profit</a></h1>
<a href="http://html5funprofit.com"><img src="logo.png" alt="HTML5 for Fun and
    Profit" /></a>
```

Now, with HTML5, a elements can contain block-level elements. You can also still use a as in the past, for containing inline content. The only thing you can't nest inside an a is another a.

 Wrapping links around block-level elements is justification enough for using the HTML5 DOCTYPE.

See Also

HTML5 Doctor's article "'Block-level' links in HTML5" at *http://html5doctor.com/ block-level-links-in-html-5/*.

1.15 Marking Up Figures and Captions

Problem

You want to include an illustration with a caption on your web page.

Solution

Contain the illustration image with the `figure` element, and include the caption text within `figcaption`:

```
<figure>
    <img src="chart.png" alt="Chart of increasing awesomeness" />
    <figcaption>The increasing amount of awesome that this blog
        demonstrates.</figcaption>
</figure>
```

Discussion

`figure` and `figcaption` are two new elements introduced in HTML5. Though the above example references an illustration (`img`), `figure` is not restricted to that type of content. It can be used to specify code examples, photos, charts, audio, and data tables, to name just a few of the options.

Why so many different types of content? Because the spec defines `figure` (*http://www .w3.org/TR/html-markup/figure.html*) rather broadly, as:

> a unit of content, optionally with a caption, that is self-contained, that is typically refer-
> enced as a single unit from the main flow of the document, and that can be moved away
> from the main flow of the document without affecting the document's meaning.

If you've been paying attention, it might've occurred to you that this definition sounds quite similar to that for `aside` (*http://www.w3.org/TR/html-markup/aside.html*). To know which element is most appropriate for your content, consider whether the content is essential for understanding the surrounding content. If it is not essential, only related, then use `aside`. Otherwise, `figure` is appropriate.

And keep in mind two things:

- `figcaption` is optional and can reside anywhere within `figure`, whether before or after the `figure` content.

- Just because this recipe's example uses an image doesn't mean all images need to be contained by `figure`.

See Also

HTML5 Doctor's "Simplequiz #4" on figures, captions, and `alt` text at *http://html5doc tor.com/html5-simplequiz-4-figures-captions-and-alt-text/*.

1.16 Marking Up Dates and Times

Problem

You want to encode date-time content for machines, but still retain human readability.

Solution

Wrap the human-friendly date-time information in the `time` element, and specify the machine-readable information via the `datetime` attribute:

```
<p>Published: <time datetime="2011-01-15">January 15, 2011</time></p>
```

Depending on the date and time you are trying to specify, the following approaches are also valid:

Time only

```
<p>The class starts at <time datetime="08:00">8:00 am</time>.</p>
```

Date and time (requires time zone specification)

```
<p>Registration opens on <time datetime="2011-01-15T08:00-07:00">January 15, 2011
at 8:00 am, Mountain Time</time>.</p>
```

Visible machine-readable format (no date-time required)

```
<p>Published: <time>2011-01-15</time></p>
```

Discussion

Before we discuss this new element, let's first address *machine readability*. This is simply the notion of enriching your web content with additional, semantic information that machines (search engines, user agents, etc.) can parse to glean more meaning from your content.

> We're not aware of any machines that are currently parsing the date time information from `time`, but we can imagine this soon to be on the horizon, particularly for search engines that want to accurately display time-sensitive results for news queries.

Next, let's talk date-time information on the Web. For machine readability, date-time information has to be specified in the international standard format, *ISO 8601*. For dates, the format is *YYYY-MM-DD*. For times of day, the format is *hh:mm:ss*. And when combining dates with times, you join the numeric representations with a T: *YYYY-MM-DDThh:mm:ss*.

Okay, back to the new `time` element. As you can see from the examples, you can specify dates, times, and date-times. What the human user experiences is the content contained by `time`. What machines read is the `datetime` ISO 8601 value.

> One limitation of `time` that is worth mentioning is that it can't be used for imprecise dates, such as "August 2011." It does require, minimally, the day, month, and year for dates.

What about microformats?

By this point, you may be wondering about *microformats* (*http://microformats.org*), which are HTML-based design patterns for expressing machine-readable semantics. The hCalendar (*http://microformats.org/hCalendar*) microformat, for example, is used for indicating date-time information.

 Want to learn more about microformats? Check out Emily Lewis's *Microformats Made Simple* (New Riders, *http://microformatsmadesimple.com*) for lots of practical examples and easy-to-understand explanations.

Neither HTML5 generally nor the `time` element specifically negates the use of microformats. You can still use them. In fact, the `time` element would make a great semantic hook for adding hCalendar. However, current microformats parsers don't recognize the `time` element, so the two can't be used together.

This is unfortunate for a POSH and microformats devotee, but it is the reality of this industry. As new technologies evolve, older technologies respond, and we designers and developers have to weigh the pros, the cons, and the future.

Publication dates

Another new date-related feature in HTML5 is the `pubdate` attribute for `time`. Adding this attribute indicates that the `time` is the actual publication date-time for a web page or an article (such as a blog post) on a page:

```
<p>Published: <time datetime="2011-01-09" pubdate>January 9, 2011</time></p>
```

This helps differentiate publication dates from other instances of `time` on a page or within an article.

See Also

Mark Pilgrim's "Dive Into HTML5" discussion on dates and times at *http://diveintohtml5.info/semantics.html#time-element*.

1.17 Setting the Stage for Native Expanding and Collapsing

Problem

You want to provide content that can expand and collapse with user focus (once browsers support it).

Solution

Contain the full content with the `details` element and indicate the content area that is "focusable" with `summary`:

```
<details>
    <summary>Upcoming Topics</summary>
    <p>For the new year, we have a great line up of articles!</p>
    <ul>
        <li>Understanding the Outline Algorithm</li>
        <li>When to Use <code>hgroup</code></li>
        <li>Machine Semantics with Microdata</li>
    </ul>
</details>
```

Discussion

This recipe sets up a solid semantic structure for a very common behavior that we currently have to use JavaScript to achieve. The `summary` element indicates which content is the "control" that expands or collapses the full `details` content upon user focus (see Figure 1-7). And, if you want to ensure that `details` is expanded by default (see Figure 1-8), you can add the `open` attribute:

```
<details open>
```

Only Chrome currently supports this behavior. For the other browsers you still have to use JavaScript to create expanding/collapsing content, because none of today's browsers support the functionality of `details` and `summary`.

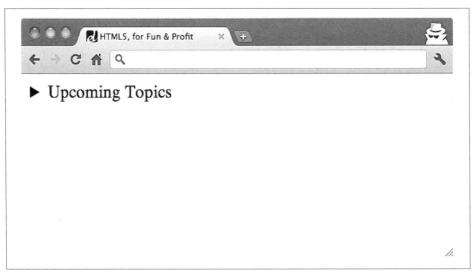

Figure 1-7. Default display of <summary> in Chrome 13 with collapsed <details> content

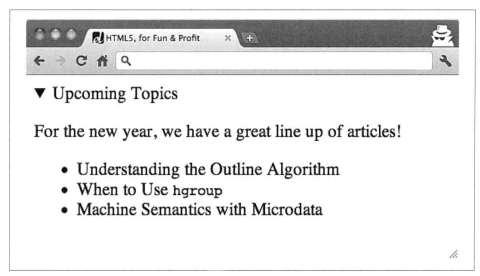

Figure 1-8. Default display of <summary> in Chrome 13 with <details open>

See Also

Remy Sharp has put together a nice little script that forces browsers to apply the expanding and collapsing behavior to details at *https://gist.github.com/370590*.

1.18 Controlling the Numbering of Your Lists

Problem

You want an ordered list to have numbering different than the default of starting with 1.

Solution

Specify one of the semantic control attributes on the ol or li. For instance, to start a numbered list at 3 (see Figure 1-9), include the start attribute in your ol and specify 3 as the value:

```
<ol start="3">
    <li>Apples</li>
    <li>Oranges</li>
    <li>Bananas</li>
</ol>
```

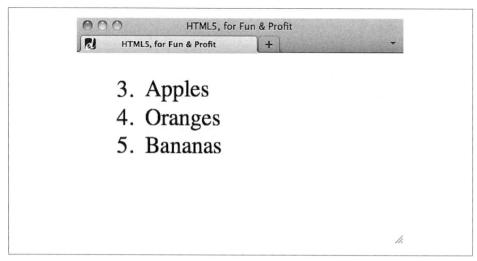

Figure 1-9. Default rendering of <ol start="3"> in Firefox 5.0

Discussion

start has been around for a while, but was deprecated as presentational. HTML5 now recognizes the semantic value of controlled numbering and welcomes it back. This "reordering" via start works the same across all browsers, IE6 included.

Reversed attribute

Another attribute for controlling the numbering of an ordered list is the reversed attribute, which reverses the order of a list (e.g., for a countdown from 10):

```
<ol reversed>
    <li>Apples</li>
    <li>Oranges</li>
    <li>Bananas</li>
</ol>
```

Unfortunately, none of the current browsers support this attribute yet.

Value Attribute

You can also specify the exact number value for each li, which can come in handy if you are ranking something and there is a "tie" (see Figure 1-10):

```
<p>The results are in for your favorite fruit, and we have a tie for first place!</p>
<ol>
    <li value="1">Bananas</li>
    <li value="1">Oranges</li>
    <li value="2">Apples</li>
</ol>
```

All current browsers support the value attribute for li.

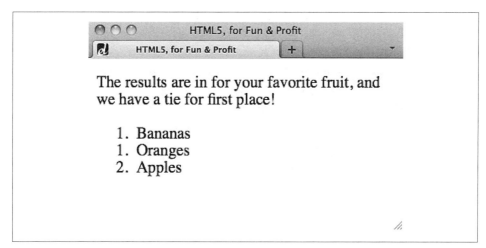

Figure 1-10. Ordered list with specified <li> values

See Also

The W3C's Working Draft about grouping content includes the ol element at *http://www.w3.org/TR/html5/grouping-content.html#the-ol-element*.

1.19 Hiding Content to Show Later

Problem

You have content that you want to hide until after a user logs in.

Solution

Add the `hidden` attribute to the element containing the content to be temporarily hidden:

```
<p hidden>As a special deal for members, use discount code AWESOMESAUCE and save
    10% off all purchases from these vendors.</p>
```

Discussion

The `hidden` attribute is one of the more controversial additions to HTML5. As the spec defines it, `hidden` should be applied to content that is *not yet or no longer relevant* to the current user view and, as such, should not be rendered by browsers.

The Document Object Model (DOM) and machines like search engines, though, can still access the content. This means that if the content does become relevant to the user view, it can be targeted via JavaScript, for example, and displayed by removing the attribute.

Where the concerns lie is in the misunderstanding and abuse of this attribute. It is *not* to be used for the temporary show/hide that you may encounter with tabbed content and the like. Further, we already have CSS solutions that address the display of content, such as `display: none` and `visibility: hidden`.

There is semantic value in `hidden`, though, especially compared to the CSS alternative. If this attribute remains in the specification, over time the concerns may prove unwarranted.

 Just remember: do *not* use `hidden` for presentational purposes and don't rely on browsers to actually *hide* the content. Use it only for semantic purposes and use CSS to control presentation.

See Also

Peter Beverloo's article "Thoughts on the HTML5 hidden attribute" at *http://peter.sh/2010/06/thoughts-on-the-html5-hidden-attribute/*.

1.20 Making Portions of a Page Editable

Problem

You want to allow users to directly edit content in the browser.

Solution

Add the `contenteditable` attribute to the element containing the content to be edited:

```
<article contenteditable>
    <h2>Stop <code>section</code> Abuse!</h2>
    <p>As the most generic of the HTML5 structural elements, <code>section</code>
        is often incorrectly used as a styling container, when <code>div</code> is
        more appropriate.</p>
</article>
```

Discussion

This attribute is well supported by today's browsers, including IE6. In fact, con tenteditable first appeared in IE 5.5 and has since been incorporated by other brows- ers. It was originally intended to support in-browser editing such as a What You See Is What You Get (WYSIWYG) editor.

However, on its own, it only allows users to edit content. It does not have any func- tionality to save those edits, nor does it generate editing controls commonly seen in WYSIWYG editors. For that type of editing, you need to incorporate JavaScript and utilize the local storage Application Programming Interface (API) (see Chapter 8).

A good example of when to use `contenteditable` is for demonstrating how text should look when styled with CSS rules or set with a certain typeface, while allowing users to edit their own text (see Figure 1-11).

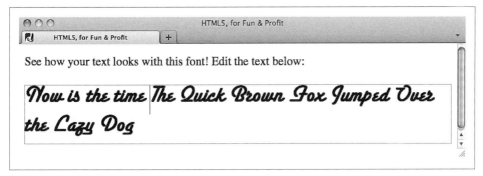

Figure 1-11. Once focus is set on an element assigned contenteditable, Firefox 5.0 displays a gray dotted line around it, indicating the area that can be edited

See Also

The W3C Working Draft discussion on user interaction includes the `contenteditable` attribute at *http://www.w3.org/TR/html5/editing.html#contenteditable*.

1.21 Setting the Stage for Native Drag-and-Drop

Problem

You want to allow users to drag and drop content on your web page.

Solution

Add the `draggable` attribute to the element that should be draggable:

```
<h2 draggable>Block-Level Links</h2>
```

Discussion

`draggable`, like `contenteditable`, has good browser support and was originally introduced for IE (by default, certain elements are already draggable: `a` and `img`). However, the simple addition of `draggable` to your elements does not create the drag-and-drop functionality on its own. `draggable` simply allows you to specify the elements that *can* be dragged.

To achieve the desired drag-and-drop functionality, you need JavaScript to:

1. Tell the browser where the draggable element can be dropped (the drop "zone").
2. Tell the browser what to do with the element once it has been dropped.

See Also

WHATWG's Living Standard addresses the `draggable` attribute at *http://www.whatwg
.org/specs/web-apps/current-work/multipage/dnd.html#the-draggable-attribute*; there is
a simple, straightforward tutorial on implementing basic drag-and-drop at *http://
html5doctor.com/native-drag-and-drop*. See Recipe 10.3 in Chapter 10 of this book for
more on implementing drag-and-drop functionality.

CHAPTER 2

Progressive Markup and Techniques

Christina Huggins Ramey

2.0 Introduction

As a web developer, you may be eager to implement HTML5's new features within your website. However, HTML5 is still a budding technology, and browser support for many of its features is spotty at best.

Your excitement at the prospect of a cutting-edge HTML5 site may be tempered by the following questions:

- How can I accommodate browsers that have yet to support many of HTML5's elements?
- What are the current best practices for coding a standards-compliant, cross-browser-compatible HTML5 website?

In this chapter you will learn how to test for supported HTML5 features within a browser, and the latest techniques for accommodating those features that aren't supported. You will learn how to get started quickly with an HTML5 boilerplate template that includes all of the latest tricks, techniques, and best practices for implementing HTML5 technologies. You'll find out how to validate your HTML5 documents, and even how to code your XHTML/HTML4 documents for future HTML5 upgradability.

The techniques presented in this chapter will give you the confidence to integrate modern HTML5 web technologies within your web pages, even as browser technology is still catching up with them.

2.1 Adding More Semantic Meaning

Problem

You want to mark up content correctly.

Solution

Apply markup in a semantic manner.

Semantic markup is markup that describes the content it contains, rather than what the content should look like. This means coding paragraphs with the p element, titles with heading elements, and so on.

Discussion

Sometimes referred to as Plain Old Semantic HTML (POSH), semantic markup eschews the use of presentational elements like font or table for layout purposes (see *http://microformats.org/wiki/posh*).

POSH focuses on content. If you have a paragraph, use p. A heading? h1. The point is to use the element that best describes the content.

Become familiar with the changes in HTML5 so that your code remains both semantic and valid. HTML5 redefined several elements like b and i (see Recipes 1.9 and 1.10) and completely dropped others, like frame, frameset, and noframes. Also gone are presentational elements and attributes, as shown in Table 2-1.

Table 2-1. Sampling of obsolete presentational features in HTML5

Elements	Attributes
basefont	align
big	background
center	bgcolor
font	border
plaintext	cellpadding
s	cellspacing
strike	height
tt	nowrap
u	valign
	width

See Also

For tips and tricks on how to style semantic markup, read *CSS Cookbook* by Christopher Schmitt (O'Reilly); visit *http://www.w3.org/TR/html5/obsolete.html* for the full list of obsolete elements and attributes.

2.2 Picking a Markup Style

Problem

You want to know what kind of syntax coding style to use.

Solution

One of the core changes HTML5 brings is a more relaxed syntax. Thanks to a simplified DOCTYPE (see Recipe 1.1), all coding styles are valid. HTML and XHTML are both welcome at the party. Some of the changes include:

- Uppercase tag names
- Optional quotes for attributes
- Optional values for attributes
- Optional closed empty elements

So, if you want to write loose and free, without concern for casing, quotes, or attribute values, you can go forth with confidence; your syntax will validate.

That being said, it is worth noting that valid syntax doesn't necessarily equal good syntax, and that many developers still tout certain "best practices" that lend clarity to your code. These best practices include the following suggestions:

- Code your tag names in lowercase. Uppercase is more difficult to read than lowercase, and distinguishing your code from your content in this manner is unnecessary: any decent text editor will color-code your HTML document so that you can visually pick out your tags with ease.

- Enclose all attribute values in quotes. There might be instances in which you need to use quotes (e.g., if there is more than one value), and doing this universally helps to eliminate coding errors and leads to a consistent look.

- Close all elements with content. Knowing where a `div` ends just makes for clearer code, and doing this consistently enhances clarity and makes your code easier to maintain.

Discussion

Whatever coding style you use, consistency is key: adhering to a strict syntax can help you more quickly identify errors in your markup.

A major benefit is that a strict syntax is easier to standardize for development teams. A standard convention can save hours in development time, particularly for large projects with distributed team members.

Ultimately, though, there is no right or wrong style in HTML5. Simply follow a style that helps you develop code consistently and troubleshoot efficiently.

See Also

For more style recommendations, see *http://www.fredzlinkz.com/webcitymaster/html5-syntax-style-recommendations*.

2.3 Understanding Browser Support for HTML5

Problem

You want to find out if a browser or specific browser version supports a feature of HTML5.

Solution

As of this writing, the HTML5 specification is still evolving. Browsers are implementing portions of the specification before it's complete, but support in modern browsers is not 100% complete (nor should it be).

As demonstrated by the chapters in this book, there is a sizable portion of the HTML5 specification that is supported and can be utilized immediately. For a breakdown of HTML5 support across browsers, see *http://caniuse.com/#cats=HTML5*. A visual representation of HTML5 as well as CSS3 can be seen at *http://html5readiness.com*, as shown in Figure 2-1.

Discussion

Generally speaking, all of today's latest browsers support HTML5 to some degree or another.

Using HTML5 isn't an absolute proposition. You don't have to use embedded content or web sockets to use the new structural elements, and vice versa. You don't even have to use the new structural elements to have a valid HTML5 document; you just need the Document Type Definition (see Recipe 1.1).

Pick the features that work for you, and leave the rest. Or, rather, *experiment* with the rest to see if you may find a practical implementation for yourself or your projects.

See Also

See *http://html5readiness.com* for a visual representation of browser support for HTML5 and CSS3.

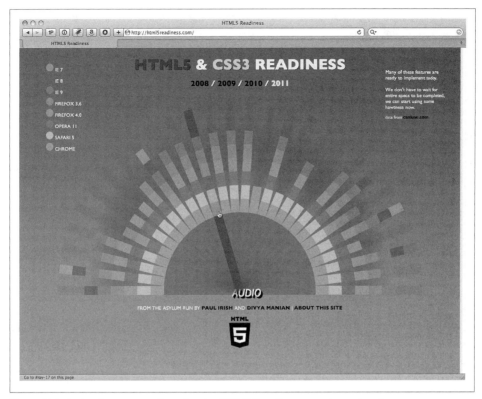

Figure 2-1. A visual representation of native HTML5 audio support in modern browsers

2.4 Making Internet Explorer Recognize HTML5 Elements

Problem

Internet Explorer doesn't apply CSS to elements it doesn't recognize. And, unfortunately, Internet Explorer (prior to IE9) doesn't yet recognize most HTML5 elements. This means implementing HTML5 is difficult, as Internet Explorer won't render any CSS that you apply to these new elements.

Solution

A clever solution to this problem, attributed to Sjoerd Visscher (see *http://intertwingly .net/blog/2008/01/22/Best-Standards-Support#c1201006277*) and known as the *shim* technique, involves creating a DOM element of the same name as the HTML5 element that you want to use. Once you create this element, Internet Explorer will apply CSS to it.

For example, let's say you create the following simple body header that includes a navigation element:

```
<header>
    <h1>Riddles of the Sphinx</h1>
    <nav>
        <ul>
            <li><a href="index.html">Home</a></li>
            <li><a href="/about/">About</a></li>
            <li><a href="/blog/">Blog</a></li>
            <li><a href="/contact/">Contact Me</a></li>
        </ul>
    </nav>
</header>
```

and then style these elements:

```
header {
    width: 600px;
    height: 25px;
    background-color: #ccffff;
    border: 2px solid #66cc99;
    padding: 10px;
}

nav {
    width: 100%;
    float: left;
    list-style: none;
}

nav li {
    float: left;
    padding-right: 7px;
}
```

When we view this page in Internet Explorer 8 or below (as shown in Figure 2-2), the CSS is not applied.

For Internet Explorer to recognize these elements, just add the following script to the head of the HTML document (make sure you add it to the head of the document, as the elements need to be declared before the page renders):

```
<script>
    document.createElement("header");
    document.createElement("nav");
    document.createElement("footer");
</script>
```

Then declare the three HTML5 elements that we've used on the page—header, nav, and footer—as DOM elements.

Now, when we view this page in Internet Explorer (as shown in Figure 2-3), the browser sees these elements and applies its CSS.

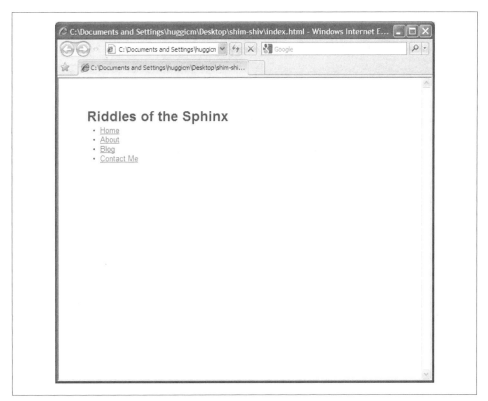

Figure 2-2. Basic rendering of the list

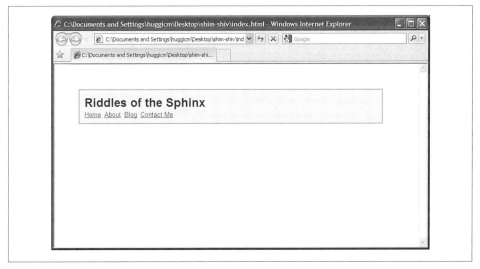

Figure 2-3. Internet Explorer recognizes the elements

Discussion

While this technique is effective, it can be cumbersome to create DOM elements for all of the HTML5 elements on a page, especially if you are making heavy use of many of them.

Web developer Remy Sharp has created a script that enables *all* of the HTML5 elements. Integrating this script into your page can be much more convenient than handcoding a script every time you want to sprinkle some HTML5 into your page. You can download the script from *http://remysharp.com/2009/01/07/html5-enabling -script/* and integrate it into the head of your HTML, or you can hotlink the script from the Google code repository:

```
<!--[if lt IE 9]>
    <script src="http://html5shim.googlecode.com/svn/trunk/html5.js"></script>
<![endif]-->
```

If you wrap this code within this conditional, it will only call the script if the browser is Internet Explorer 8 or lower (IE9 has broad-range support for HTML5 elements and technologies).

 To make the elements behave as block level elements, set the new HTML5 elements to display:block in your style sheet.

See Also

John Resig's blog post detailing the HTML shim technique (Resig calls it "shiv" in his blog post): *http://ejohn.org/blog/html5-shiv/*.

2.5 Detecting HTML5 Features with JavaScript

Problem

You want to implement HTML5 features when they're supported by the browser, but degrade to another solution when they're not.

Solution

HTML5 comes with great cutting-edge technologies that, as a designer, you may be eager to take advantage of.

Unfortunately, HTML5 currently comes with limited browser support. You might like to implement some of these new technologies, but you also want to accommodate browsers that don't yet support them.

Modernizr (see *http://modernizr.com*) is a JavaScript library that makes it very easy to do just that: it detects the availability of various HTML5 and CSS3 features within a user's browser and allows you to create fallbacks when a desired feature isn't currently supported (see Figure 2-4).

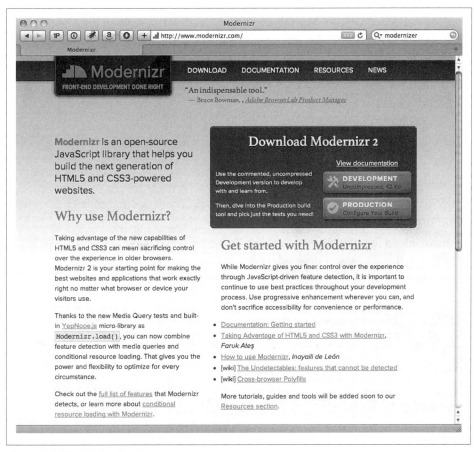

Figure 2-4. The Modernizr site

Using Modernizr

To see how Modernizr works, let's run through an example using the JavaScript library where we create an audio player using HTML5's `audio` tag. If the user is viewing the page with a browser that doesn't support the `audio` element, we want to display an error message alerting the user of the problem.

If we wanted to really make this page cross-browser compatible, we would probably use a Flash audio player as a fallback. However, for the purposes of this recipe, we want to keep this example fairly simple.

Here is our basic HTML code for our player:

```html
<img src="vscover.jpg" alt="Veil &amp; Subdue: Courtship of the Black Sultan"/>
<div id="caption">
    <div id="audio">
        <audio>
            <source src="turnthepage.ogg">
            <source src="turnthepage.mp3">
        </audio>
        <p><input type=button onclick="playPause()" value=" " tabindex="0" />
            &ldquo;Turn the Page&rdquo; / <em>Veil &amp; Subdue</em> / Paul
            Ramey</p>
    </div>
</div><!--end caption-->
```

We've included an image of the album cover art and our audio element, along with customized controls.

First, download the Modernizr JavaScript library from *http://modernizr.com*. Include a reference to this file within the head of your HTML document:

```html
<script src="js/modernizr-1.6.min.js"></script>
```

 This script must be included in the head of your document with a normal script tag; it cannot be loaded dynamically with script loader techniques.

When this script runs, it detects whether or not the browser supports the audio element and then does two things:

1. Assigns a value (true or false) to the JavaScript property Modernizr.audio.
2. Adds a class to the HTML tag. If the browser supports the audio element, it will add a class called audio. If the browser doesn't support the audio element, it will add a class called no-audio.

Now you can write a script specifying what to do if the Modernizr.audio property is true or false and code your CSS, specifying styles for elements when the audio element is supported and when it isn't.

So, let's write a small script (we can put this in the head of our document) that only runs when the audio element is supported:

```html
<script>
if (Modernizr.audio) {
    function playPause() {
```

```
            var myAudio = document.getElementsByTagName('audio')[0];
            if(myAudio.paused)
                myAudio.play();
            else
                myAudio.pause();
        }
    }
</script>
```

This script adds functionality to the custom controls we added to the page. It will only activate if the `Modernizr.audio` value is true (and thus won't waste browser resources if the browser doesn't support the `audio` element).

Next, it would be nice if we could get rid of the customized controls altogether when the browser doesn't support the `audio` element. This is easy to do with Modernizr, as we can take advantage of the class it added to the HTML tag:

```
.no-audio #audio {
    display: none;
}

.audio #audio input[type="button"] {
    width: 45px;
    height: 29px;
    background: url(button.png);
    border: 0px solid #000;
    float: left;
    margin-right: 10px;
}
```

When the `audio` element isn't supported, Modernizr adds a `no-audio` class to the `header` element. So, we can select for this class in our CSS and set the display value to `none` for any element we want to disappear. Here, it would be the `div` we labeled "audio," which encloses the controls.

When the `audio` element *is* supported, however, Modernizr adds the `audio` class to the `header` element. To cover this case we can select for this `class` instead and style our control button as we please.

The next step is to set up an error message for when the `audio` element isn't supported. First, we need to add the HTML for this error box to our HTML and then place a notice underneath the "audio" `div`:

```
<div id="error">
    <p>&ldquo;Turn the Page&rdquo; / <em>Veil &amp; Subdue</em> / Paul Ramey</p>
    <div id="error-box">
        <p>Too bad! This browser does not support the audio features on this page.
            Might I suggest installing the latest version of your browser?</p>
    </div>
</div>
```

Using the same basic technique as above, we can hide this `div` when the `audio` element is supported and style it appropriately when it is not supported:

```
.audio #error {
    display: none;
}

.no-audio #error-box {
    background-color: #ffffcc;
    padding: 1px 10px;
    color: #000;
    border: 5px solid #ffff66;

}
.no-audio #error-box a {
    color: #333;
}
```

Figure 2-5 shows the audio element supported by the browser, while Figure 2-6 shows the result in a browser that does not support the audio element.

Figure 2-5. The audio controls appear in a browser that supports the audio element

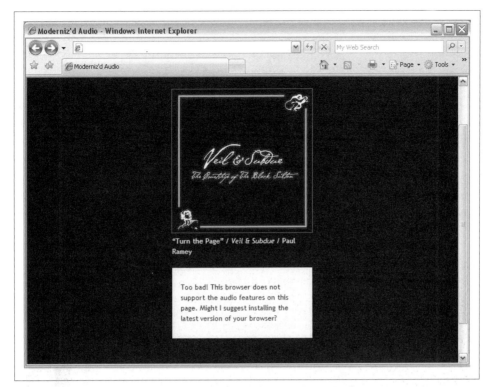

Figure 2-6. How the page looks when the audio element is not supported

Currently Modernizr checks for over 20 HTML5 and CSS3 features and also includes the shim technique covered in Recipe 2.4. Each checked feature comes with its own specific CSS classes and JavaScript property. Check out Modernizr's documentation at *http://modernizr.com/docs/*, which includes sample code for each feature that it supports.

 See Chapter 5 for more information and recipes on using HTML5 audio.

Discussion

Modernizr isn't the only tool available to assess and work around this issue: traditionally, "UA sniffing" or "browser sniffing" was used to determine which browser a user was running. Then, the designer could implement browser-specific code to customize the page.

This method, however, is unreliable in a number of ways. First of all, a browser can fake a UA string, which is the value that the browser-sniffing technique looks at to determine the browser in use. Additionally, users can switch off certain features of their browsers, so that even if you can determine the correct browser, you still can't be sure which features are supported.

Also, if the user is running a new browser, a newer version of a browser, or an alternative browser that you may not have bothered to check for, your code may fail to recognize it altogether. Not to mention that it falls on *your* shoulders to be on top of what browsers support which features.

Modernizr avoids these pitfalls, as it detects specifically which *features* are supported, rather than merely trying to detect what browser the user is viewing the page through. This is a far more reliable method if you want fine-tuned control over the user's experience of your website.

 Modernizr now supports a "production" version (see *http://www.mod ernizr.com/download/*). This version generates a custom build of Modernizr with only the HTML5 tests needed for your sites or web applications.

See Also

The documentation on the official Modernizr website at *http://www.modernizr.com/ docs/*.

2.6 Using HTML5 Boilerplate

Problem

You want to get up and running with HTML5 with a robust working template.

Solution

Use Paul Irish's HTML5 Boilerplate (as shown in Figure 2-7) as a jumping-off point for your website. Not only does it include an HTML5 template complete with an organized folder structure and CSS file, but it also incorporates current coding best practices, browser bug fixes, and popular JavaScript libraries.

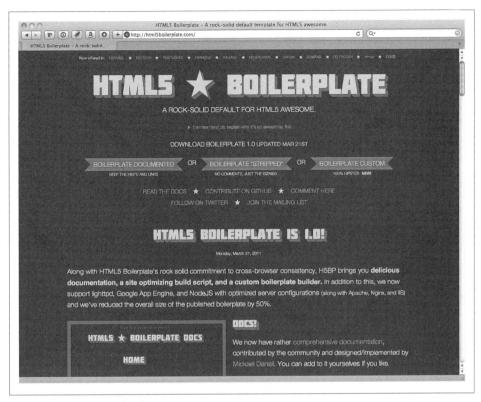

Figure 2-7. HTML5 Boilerplate site

It incorporates three years of research into current cutting-edge coding techniques, so you can just get on with building your website. In fact, HTML5 Boilerplate includes *so* much that it would be time prohibitive to mention it all. So, here are some of its highlights:

- An *index.html* file that includes:
  - Valid HTML5 markup
  - References to Modernizr and jQuery JavaScript libraries (which are included with the template)
  - Conditional statements that add classes to body tags based on what version of Internet Explorer the page is being viewed on (so you can easily create IE6- or IE7-specific styles)
  - A basic structural skeleton within the body tag
  - IE6 *.png* fix script
  - Google analytics script

- A CSS file that includes:
  - — A global reset
  - — Font normalization (so your fonts are sized the same across all browsers)
  - — Some basic styles for lists, tables, and so on
  - — A few nonsemantic classes (for image replacement and element hiding)
  - — Print styles
  - — Space for mobile browser and orientation styles (e.g., an iPad displayed horizontally versus vertically)
- A favicon and Apple touch icon (which you'll probably want to customize)
- Webserver config files

While a dizzying array of cutting-edge web technology, it's fairly simple to get started with using the boilerplate.

Using HTML5 Boilerplate

First, download the latest version of HTML5 Boilerplate from *https://github.com/pau lirish/html5-boilerplate*.

Unzip the files and place them at the root of your web project. The documentation suggests that you start off by deleting a couple of things:

1. The demo files (located in a folder called *Demo*)
2. The profiler code (located near bottom of the *index.html* file; it begins with the comment "yui profiler and profileviewer - remove for production")

Use the *index.html* file as a template for all of your HTML documents. Flesh out the basic elements and `div` containers included in the file, or start from scratch and create your own: while Paul's skeleton is a great start, feel free to take it as a starting point.

You'll also want to customize the information in the `head` of the document (the title, author, and so on).

As a last tweak to your HTML document, add your site ID to the Google Analytics code at the bottom of the file. (If you don't use Google Analytics, you'll want to delete this section.)

Then, you'll want to customize the *style.css* file. The boilerplate CSS file has a space for your primary CSS. It begins with the comment:

```
/* Primary Styles
   Author:
*/
```

Once you've added the primary CSS, feel free to add orientation styles and mobile browser styles. You'll find these under the section beginning with the comment:

```
/*
 * Media queries for responsive design
 * These follow after primary styles so they will successfully override.
 */
```

Finally, customize the favicon and Apple touch icon. That should be as easy as replacing the current icons included in the boilerplate files.

Discussion

While it's fairly simple to get a basic HTML5 site started with HTML5 Boilerplate, to really get the most out of the boilerplate you'll want to study the online documentation to understand some of what is going on with the code.

For instance, if you don't understand the classes that the boilerplate includes in the HTML (such as the IE body classes or the image-replacement class), you won't be able to take advantage of these useful bits of CSS in your site. Similarly, if you don't know how to implement the IE6 *.png* fix that's included with the boilerplate, that script will turn out to be fairly useless.

Additionally, there may be some things you'll want to get rid of, if you don't use them: you can delete the IE6 *.png* script if you don't care about supporting IE6, and you can delete the *.htaccess* file if you aren't on an Apache server. Knowing what is included in the boilerplate makes it easy to trim it down to include only what you need.

That's not to say you need to spend hours poring over the documentation to understand every bit of its inner workings. You might as well create your own boilerplate, if you go through all that trouble.

However, it will behoove you to get an overview of the pieces that make up the boilerplate; that way, if there is something you think may be useful for your site, you can study that bit in more detail.

See Also

The Official Guide to HTML5 Boilerplate at *http://net.tutsplus.com/tutorials/html-css -techniques/the-official-guide-to-html5-boilerplate/* and the HTML5 Boilerplate Documentation at *http://html5boilerplate.com/docs/*.

2.7 Validating HTML5

Problem

You want to identify and eliminate coding errors in your HTML.

Solution

Validating your code is one of the key best practices in web development and is a great first step in eliminating coding errors. While validation doesn't guarantee that your web page will look or behave like you expect, it does guarantee that any unexpected behavior is not due to a mismatched tag or unrecognized CSS selector.

Why validate? Fortunately (or unfortunately, depending on your position on web standards), most web browsers try to compensate for invalid coding. So, even a horrendous collection of tag soup consisting of mismatched tags and improper nesting will probably look okay in most browsers. However, different browsers handle errors differently.

That means that if your code isn't valid, a browser can try to compensate for errors in unexpected ways. Additionally, mobile browsers are less forgiving of erroneous code (they simply don't have the resources to compensate for errors the way that desktop browsers can). So, an invalid page that renders fine on your desktop browser may break on your mobile phone. In light of modern web technologies, it is becoming increasingly important to validate your code and eliminate errors. In doing so, you go one step further in ensuring that your web page renders as expected across multiple browsing environments.

Fortunately, validating for HTML5 is not much different than validating XHTML/HTML4. Indeed, you may find that creating a valid HTML5 document is much easier, as the HTML5 specification, in general, is much more lenient than its predecessors. If you want to capitalize your HTML tags, go ahead; the HTML will still validate. If you're too lazy to close out your li tags, you need not feel guilty for doing so. The validator won't chastise you—it will leave that job up to your colleagues.

So, let's get on to the business of validating our code. Currently, there are two popular online validators that you can use:

- The W3C's Unicorn unified validator (shown in Figure 2-8), which performs a variety of checks and can validate HTML5 and CSS3: *http://validator.w3.org/unicorn/*
- The Validator.nu HTML5 Validator: *http://html5.validator.nu/*

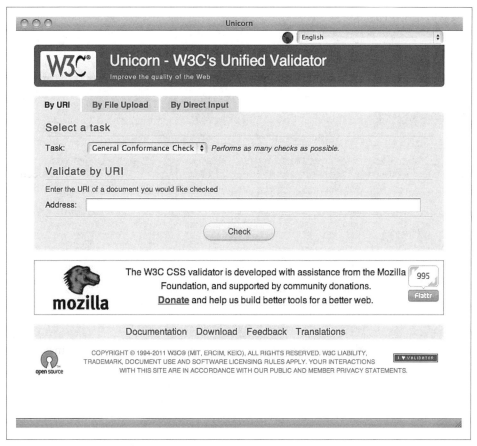

Figure 2-8. The unified validator dubbed Unicorn

To check your code, you can enter the URL, upload your HTML file, or simply paste the contents of the file into the validator. When you click Check, the validator will either verify that the code is valid HTML (and CSS, if you are checking that as well) or present you with a list of errors by line number, as shown in Figure 2-9.

Note that you will usually need to run your page through the validator more than once: many syntax errors (e.g., an improperly closed tag) can generate a cascade of further errors that are eliminated when the initial error is fixed, so you'll want to revalidate your document as you correct your errors.

Currently, the W3C's Unicorn validator checks CSS 2.1 by default, but you can customize this check to include CSS3 as well.

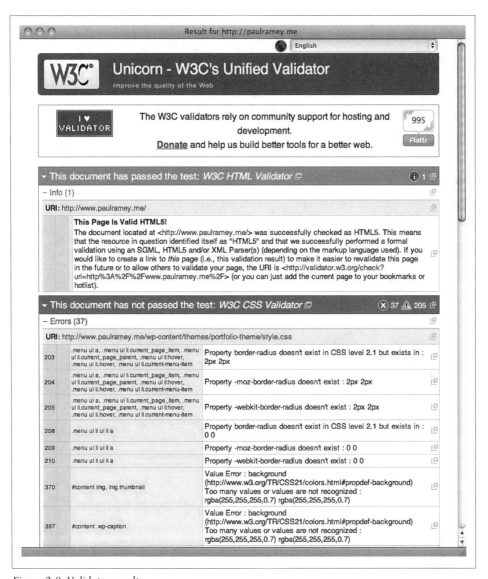

Figure 2-9. Validator results

Discussion

Validation isn't the end-all, be-all of good HTML coding. There may be instances in which you purposefully include invalid code in your HTML document. Perhaps there is a necessary hack that doesn't validate, or you want to include a piece of cutting-edge CSS that isn't yet widely supported across browsers (and thus is not recognized by modern validators).

These can be perfectly valid reasons for having a web document that doesn't validate. And while it may be controversial whether you should include said hack or CSS technique, intentionally including a piece of invalid code can still be a part of good web development practice.

Validation should be seen as one of many tools in your web development toolbox, and not the final say as to whether your page is coded correctly. That said, validating your code is a great way to find unintentional errors in coding, and, all things being equal, a valid HTML5 document is generally better than an invalid one.

See Also

The documentation for these two services at *http://code.w3.org/unicorn* and *http://about .validator.nu/*.

2.8 Mapping HTML5 Elements to ID and Class Names

Problem

You aren't ready for HTML5 yet, but you want to code your site so that upgrading to HTML5 in the future will be painless.

Solution

There may be legitimate reasons why you don't want to take the HTML5 plunge yet. Perhaps you worry about browser support. Perhaps you like to keep things simple, and you don't want to implement the myriad scripts and tweaks necessary to make an HTML5 site compatible with all modern browsers.

However, you still appreciate the semantic markup of HTML5, and you'd like to code your site so that, when all modern browsers catch up, your XHTML/HTML4 code will be as ready as possible for the transition to HTML5.

Fortunately, it's quite simple to mirror the semantic structure of an HTML5 site using `div`s labeled with HTML5-ish `id` and `class` names. Let's take a look at how this can be done. We're going to create a simple blog front page, as shown in Figure 2-10.

Looking at this site, we can pick out a few key structural elements:

- A body header, which contains the blog title and a navigation bar
- A section that contains two blog posts
- A footer

If we were coding this site in HTML5, we'd mark this up with various `header` and `footer` tags, a `nav` tag, and `article` tags. However, as we're going to mark it up with XHTML/HTML4 instead, we're going to mirror the structure and naming conventions of HTML5 as closely as possible by using `div`s with `id` and `class` names.

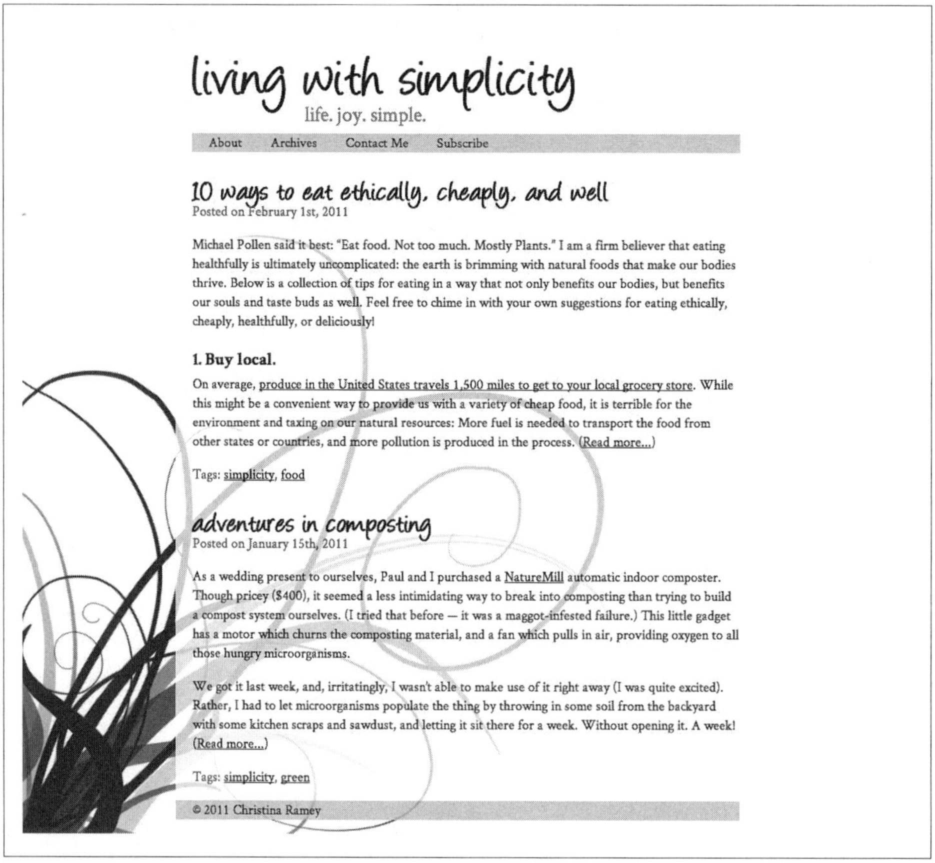

Figure 2-10. A sample web page

First, let's work on the header:

```
<div id="header">
    <h1>living with simplicity</h1>
    <div id="tagline">
        life. joy. simple.
    </div>
    <div class="nav">
        <ul>
            <li><a href="about/">About</a></li>
            <li><a href="archives/">Archives</a></li>
            <li><a href="contact/">Contact Me</a></li>
            <li><a href="subscribe/">Subscribe</a></li>
        </ul>
    </div><!--end nav-->
</div><!--end header-->
```

Ultimately, this may differ little from how you would have initially coded this page. But note that we have mirrored the HTML5 element names with the **"header"** and **"nav"** divs. In HTML5, the header tag should include a heading tag (here we have our h1 title tag) and can include the nav element as well (hence the inclusion of the navigation bar within our header).

Next, let's mark up our blog posts:

```
<div class="posts">
    <div class="article">
        <div class="header">
            <h1>10 ways to eat ethically, cheaply, and well</h1>
            <div class="meta">Posted on <span class="date">February 1st, 2011</span>
            </div>
        </div><!--end header-->
        [Post Content]
        <div class="footer">
            <div class="meta">Tags: <a href="tags/simplicity" rel="tags">
             simplicity</a>, <a href="tags/food">food</a></div>
        </div><!--end footer-->
    </div><!--end article-->
    <div class="article">
        <div class="header">
            <h1>adventures in composting</h1>
            <div class="meta">Posted on <span class="date">January 15th, 2011</span>
            </div>
        </div><!--end header-->
        [Post Content]
        <div class="footer">
        <div class="meta">Tags: <a href="tags/simplicity" rel="tags">simplicity</a>,
        <a href="tags/green/" rel="tags">green</a></div>
        </div><!--end footer-->
    </div><!--end article-->
</div><!--end posts-->`
```

Note first that we've wrapped our posts in a div we labeled **"posts"**. You may be tempted to name it "section" (along with the corresponding HTML5 section tag)— after all, a collection of blog posts does seem to account for its own generic section. Recall, however, that the HTML5 section element is not meant to stand in for any old div: something is justifiably a "section" only if it has at least one head tag (i.e., only if it can represent a level in the outline of the HTML document). This div does not have a head tag, so we have given it an alternative semantic name.

Next, we've wrapped each post within a div that we've named **"article"**. This corresponds to the article tag in HTML5. Each article div, in turn, has its own header and footer (which, again, would match up with the header and footer HTML5 tags).

Interestingly, we've also enclosed each post title in h1 tags. Prior to HTML5, having more than one h1 tag within an XHTML/HTML document was generally frowned upon. In order for your page to be outlined properly within the DOM, your head tags should follow a natural progression: h3 tags followed h2, and h2 followed the h1 tag, which enclosed the title of the page. With the advent of HTML5, this was no longer necessary: as the browser understood the article element, semantically, it could be ranked (and outlined) differently than, say, the header element.

Thus, you no longer need to rely on the head tags to do all of the ranking and outlining of the information within your document—that task is instead handled by these new semantically rich elements.

So, each of your elements (such as `header` or `article`) can begin with its own `h1` tag. While it may seem strange to mirror this new coding convention in an XHTML/HTML4 document, it will nonetheless make it easier to transition your page to HTML5 later.

Finally, we close our page with a `div` labeled `"footer"`, which maps onto the HTML5 `footer` tag:

```
<div id="footer"> <p>&copy; 2011 Christina Ramey</p> </div>
```

Now, when we are ready to switch to HTML5, it will be easy enough to change all of these `div`s to their corresponding HTML5 tags, thus saving us the headache of having to do any major restructuring of the page.

Discussion

There is no mystery to this technique of mapping of HTML5 tags to XHTML/HTML4 `div`s. Indeed, you many not need to alter your current coding technique much, if at all. However, once you decide on proper ID and class names that mirror HTML5 tags, it is best to stick with that naming convention (particularly if you are coding a lot of pages).

That way, when it does come time to translate these pages to HTML5, you won't need to recall that you named your header `"header"` in one document but `"main-header"` in another. It will also make it easier to do a quick find-and-replace with your text editor across multiple documents.

See Also

Oli Studholme's HTML5 ID and class name cheat sheet at *http://oli.jp/2008/html5-class -cheatsheet/*.

CHAPTER 3

Forms

Kimberly Blessing

3.0 Introduction

Forms are the workhorse of any web application. Whether you are updating your Facebook status, paying a bill online, or remotely programming your DVR, forms are what make the magic happen.

Currently, making that magic both robust and seamless requires some interesting and tricky uses of HTML and JavaScript. HTML5 makes much of this work far simpler—and even where browsers aren't yet supporting the new HTML5 form features, it's easy to use these as building blocks and add support with JavaScript.

HTML5 gives us new elements and new attribute values for the `input` element to yield new form fields, as well as some new attributes that allow us to remove many lines of JavaScript. However, since not all browsers yet support these new features, it is still necessary to use some JavaScript to ensure cross-browser compatibility.

3.1 Displaying a Search Input Field

Problem

You want to present a user with a search form field.

Solution

Use the `input` element with an HTML5 `type` value of `search`:

```html
<form>
    <p><label>Search <input type="search" name="query"></label></p>
    <p><button type="submit">Submit</button></p>
</form>
```

Discussion

The search input type displays a text input field that may visually differ from that of a regular text field, based on the stylistic conventions of the platform.

For example, Safari on Mac OS displays the search field with rounded (instead of square) corners, as shown in Figure 3-1. Both Safari and Chrome display an icon within the field to delete the current value, as shown in Figure 3-2.

Some user agents will display a plain text input field for the search input type, so support cannot be determined by visual appearance alone.

Testing browser support

To accurately test a browser's support of the search input type (see Table 3-1 for a listing of compatible browsers), load Mike Taylor's support test page at *http://www .miketaylr.com/code/input-type-attr.html*. The page shows not only support for the search attribute value, but for other attribute values for input as well.

Table 3-1. Browsers supporting the search input type

IE	Firefox	Chrome	Safari	Opera	iOS	Android
10 Platform Preview 2	4.0+	10+	4.0+	11.0+	✓	✓

If a user agent does not support the search input type, it will revert to displaying a text input field. What is the value in having a separate input type for search, when only some user agents will render a visually different input field? There are a few answers to this question.

First, enabling visual styles reminiscent of an operating system in the browser can make for a better user experience. Second, designating a search input field as such may help assistive devices more correctly signal users as to the purpose of the field or form.

Finally, the search input type gives us a more semantic input type value to use in our forms and gives us a better hook for our CSS, as compared to using a class or ID. The following CSS applies rounded corners to the search input field for all user agents that support the border-radius property:

```
input[type="search"] {
    border-radius: 10px;
}
```

See Also

For more information on search inputs in WebKit browsers, including Chrome and Safari, see *http://css-tricks.com/webkit-html5-search-inputs/*.

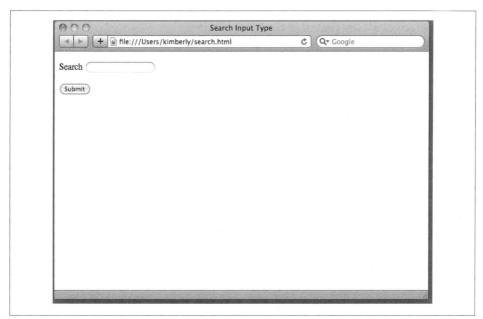

Figure 3-1. A blank search input field in Safari 5

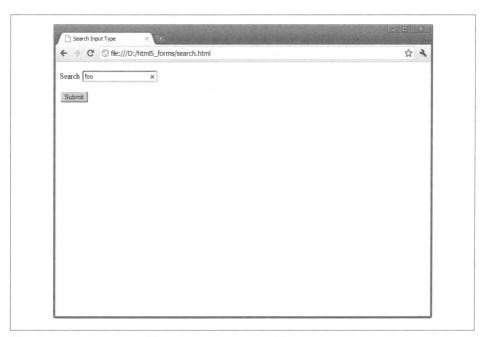

Figure 3-2. A search input field with content in Chrome 12

3.2 Contact Information Input Fields

Problem

You want to present a user with a form to provide contact information, such as an email address, a URL, and a telephone number.

Solution

Use the `input` element with HTML5 `type` values of `email`, `url`, and `tel`:

```
<form>
    <fieldset>
        <legend>Contact Information</legend>
        <p><label>E-mail address <input type="email" name="email"></label></p>
        <p><label>Web site <input type="url" name="website"></label></p>
        <p><label>Telephone number <input type="tel" name="phone"></label></p>
    </fieldset>
    <p><button type="submit">Submit</button></p>
</form>
```

Discussion

How many times have you created text input fields to collect data like an email address, and then had to write JavaScript to validate the input? You won't have to do this with the new `email` and `url` input types.

These restrict the value entered to a valid email address or absolute URL. If the user enters a value that is not valid, the user agent warns the user and the form data is not submitted (see Figures 3-3–3-6 for examples of this across various browsers).

The `tel` input type does not enforce any particular syntax, due to the variety of telephone number formats used around the world. The new `pattern` attribute can be used to enforce a particular syntax, however. For more information, see Recipe 3.12.

User agents vary in terms of the feedback provided to the users as they complete the form. At the time of this writing, some browsers are starting to visually highlight fields that do not validate on blur when the user exits the input field, but do not display the error message until the form is submitted. Other browsers provide no feedback until the form is submitted. See Table 3-2 for a browser support chart.

Table 3-2. Browsers supporting the email, url, and tel input types

IE	Firefox	Chrome	Safari	Opera	iOS	Android
10 Platform Preview 2	4.0+	10+	4.0+	11.0+	✓	✓

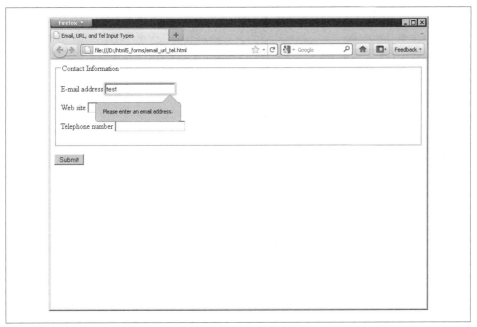

Figure 3-3. The email input field error messaging in Firefox 4

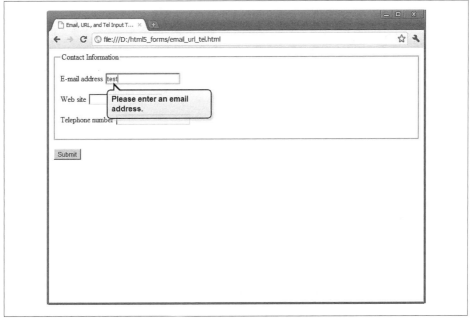

Figure 3-4. The email input field error messaging in Chrome 12

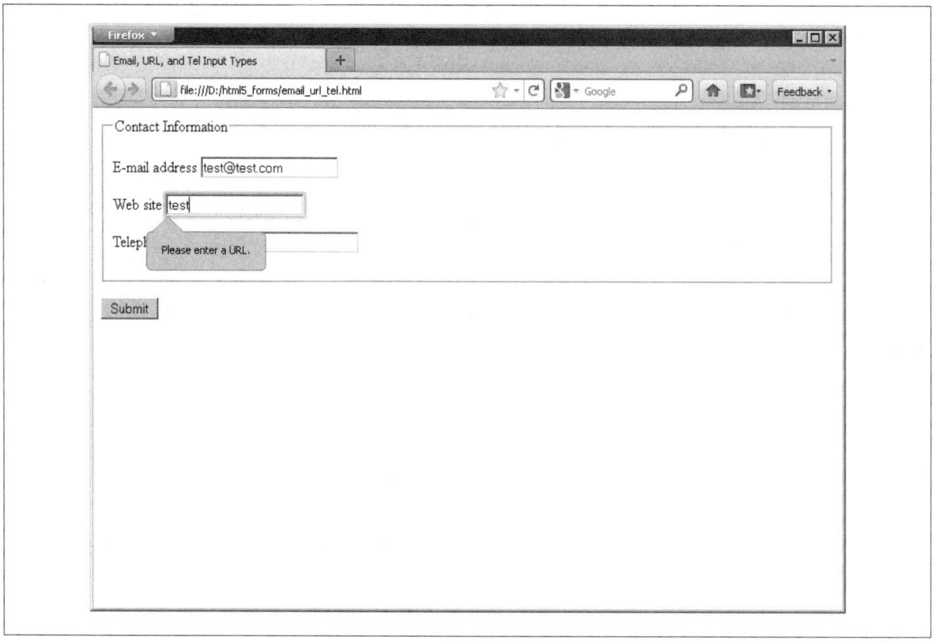

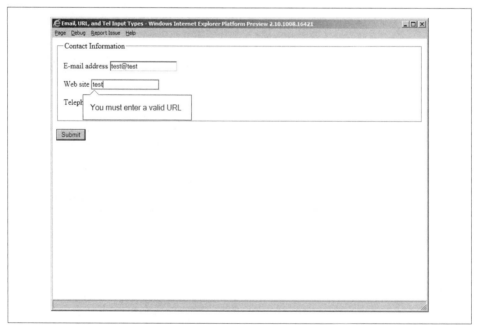

Figure 3-5. The url input field error messaging in Firefox 4

Figure 3-6. The url input field error messaging in the second Internet Explorer Platform Preview

Customizing the default error message

If you look closely at Figures 3-5 and 3-6, you'll notice that the default error message varies from browser to browser. You can specify your own language by adding a title attribute to each input field:

```
<input type="url" name="website" title="That doesn't look like a valid web
    address.">
```

As with search, it's visually difficult to determine whether or not a user agent supports email, url, or tel. Mike Taylor's support test at *http://www.miketaylr.com/code/input -type-attr.html* is useful here, too. Browsers that do not support these new input types display a text input field.

On some touch-screen devices, the user agent will display a custom on-screen keyboard for these fields. For example, if the email input field is selected, the keyboard shows not only letters but also the at sign (@) and a period, as seen in Figure 3-7. Cool, huh?

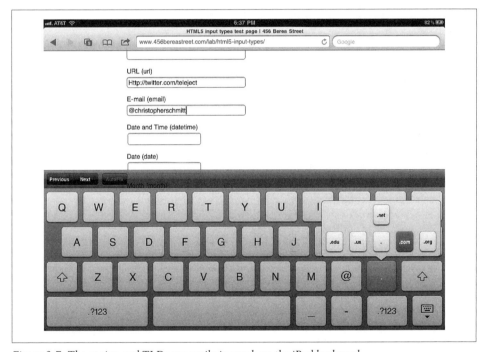

Figure 3-7. The at sign and TLDs are easily in reach on the iPad keyboard

See Also

For more about on-screen keyboard configurations for these fields, see Mark Pilgrim's "Dive Into HTML5" online book at *http://diveintohtml5.info/forms.html#type-email* and *http://diveintohtml5.info/forms.html#type-url*.

3.3 Utilizing Date and Time Input Fields

Problem

You want to provide a user with a form to specify a date and/or time—for example, when scheduling an appointment.

Solution

HTML5 provides a number of new input types to assist in date and time entry.

This first solution uses the `input` element with the HTML5 `type` value of `datetime` to display both a date-picker widget and a time spinner control in combination, as shown in Figure 3-8:

```
<form>
    <p><label>Appointment Date and Time <input type="datetime"
        name="dateAndTime"></label></p>
    <p><button type="submit">Submit</button></p>
</form>
```

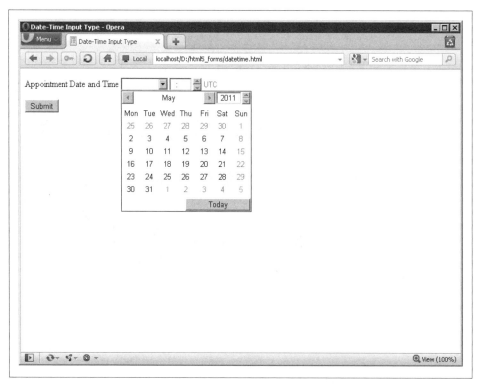

Figure 3-8. The datetime input field renders a date-picker widget and time spinner control in Opera 11.5

To present the date and time input fields separately, as shown in Figures 3-9 and 3-10, use separate input fields with the HTML5 type values date and time:

```
<form>
    <fieldset>
        <legend>Appointment Request</legend>
        <p><label>Date <input type="date" name="date"></label></p>
        <p><label>Time <input type="time" name="time"></label></p>
    </fieldset>
    <p><button type="submit">Submit</button></p>
</form>
```

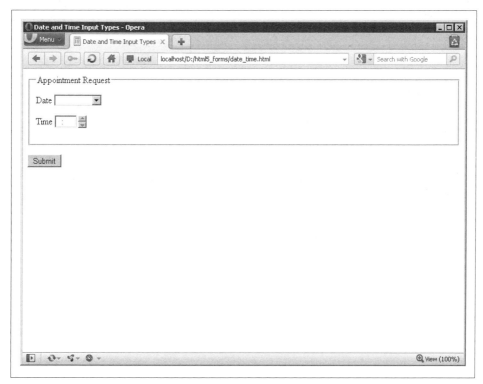

Figure 3-9. Date and time input fields in Opera 11

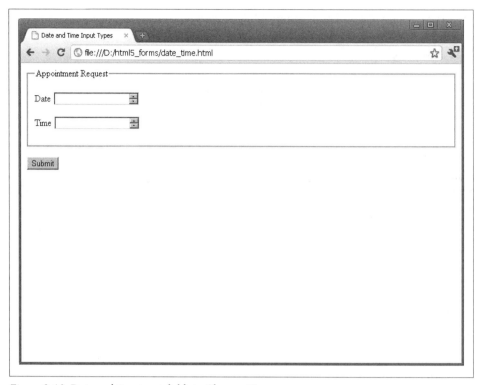

Figure 3-10. Date and time input fields in Chrome 12

Discussion

The `datetime`, `date`, and `time` family of input types, which also includes `month`, `week`, and `datetime-local`, are excellent proof that new features in HTML5 are based on what web designers and developers have been doing for years with various JavaScript libraries and other solutions.

Opera has been the leader in generating date and time controls, rendering a calendar-based date-picker control for `date` and a time spinner control for `time`, and many expect other browsers to eventually follow its lead.

Webkit-based desktop browsers recently introduced support for these input types, using spinners for both. User agents that do not support these input types revert to a text input field.

For a look at browser support for the `date` and `time` input types, see Table 3-3.

Table 3-3. Browser support for the date and time input types

IE	Firefox	Chrome	Safari	Opera	iOS	Android
-	-	10+	5.0+	9.0+	✓	✓

 For tips on delivering a more consistent cross-browser experience, see Recipe 3.13.

Like all other form inputs, you can specify a value to be displayed when the page is rendered. The value for the `date` input type must be a valid date string, such as `2010-12-31`, which represents December 31, 2010.

The value for the `time` input type must be a valid time string, such as `23:59:59`, which represents 11:59 P.M., one second before midnight.

Finally, the value for the `datetime` input type must be a valid global date and time string, such as `2010-12-31T23:59:59Z`, which represents one second before midnight UTC on December 31, 2010.

Additional features

Two new `input` element attributes, `min` and `max`, can limit the range of dates and times that users can select. This is useful in cases where you don't want users to select appointment dates or times in the past or select birthdates in the future, as shown in Figure 3-11:

```
<form>
    <fieldset>
        <legend>Appointment Request</legend>
        <p><label>Date <input type="date" name="date" min="2011-03-15"
            max="2012-03-14"></label></p>
        <p><label>Time <input type="time" name="time" min="08:00"
            max="18:00"></label></p>
    </fieldset>
    <p><button type="submit">Submit</button></p>
</form>
```

See Also

For more information on valid date and time values, see the HTML5 specification at *http://www.w3.org/TR/html5/common-microsyntaxes.html#dates-and-times*.

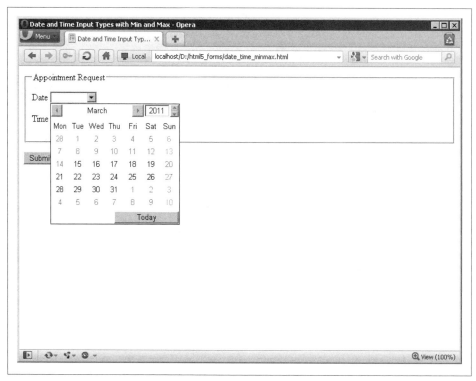

Figure 3-11. Dates prior to March 15, 2011 are not selectable when the min attribute is used in Opera 11.5

3.4 Number Inputs

Problem

You want to present a user with a form in which to enter a number—for example, to enter the quantity of an item in an order form.

Solution

Use the input element with the HTML5 type value of number:

```
<form>
    <p><label>Quantity <input type="number" name="quantity"></label></p>
    <p><button type="submit">Submit</button></p>
</form>
```

Discussion

As you may have guessed, the number input type restricts the value to a valid number—a floating-point number, to be specific.

If the user enters a value that is not valid, the user agent warns the user, and the form data is not submitted, as shown in Figure 3-12.

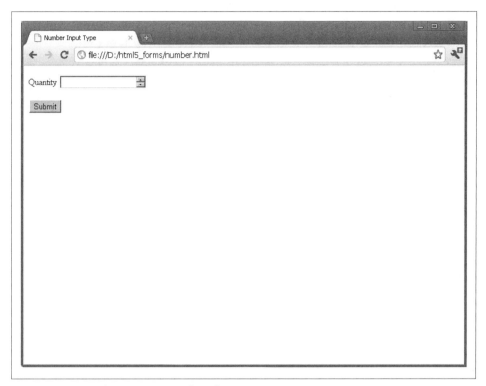

Figure 3-12. A number spinner control in Chrome 12

Some user agents display this form field with a spinner control next to the field, while others do not. On some touch-screen devices, the user agent displays a numeric on-screen keyboard for this field.

For a browser support reference on the number input type, see Table 3-4.

Table 3-4. Browser support for the number input type

IE	Firefox	Chrome	Safari	Opera	iOS	Android
10 Platform Preview 2	-	10+	4.0+	9.0+	✓	✓

User-friendly input fields

As always, it's important to think through the user experience when implementing the number input type. For example, if you're asking for a US zip code using the number input type, presenting a spinner control might confuse the user, since its purpose isn't well known yet. On the other hand, you can't rely on all browsers displaying a spinner, so take care in crafting instructional text—don't reference the spinner arrows, in case they're not there!

Load Mike Taylor's support test (see *http://www.miketaylr.com/code/input-type-attr .html*) to determine what level of support a particular browser has for this input type. If a user agent does not recognize the number input type, it will display a text input field.

Additional features

The min and max attributes can be used with the number input type to limit the values that can be entered. In addition, you can use the step attribute to specify the amount by which the value should be incremented. In this example, a customer must order in pairs, so the minimum quantity is 2 and the step value is 2, as shown in Figure 3-13:

```
<form>
    <p><label>Quantity (must order in pairs of 2) <input type="number"
        name="quantity" min="2" max="20" step="2"></label></p>
    <p><button type="submit">Submit</button></p>
</form>
```

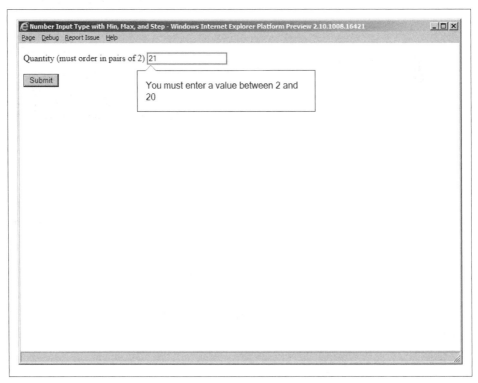

Figure 3-13. Internet Explorer 10 Platform Preview 2 uses a text entry field for the number input type, but it honors the min, max, and step attributes and will display an error if necessary

For a screenshot of an on-screen keyboard configuration for number, see Figure 3-14.

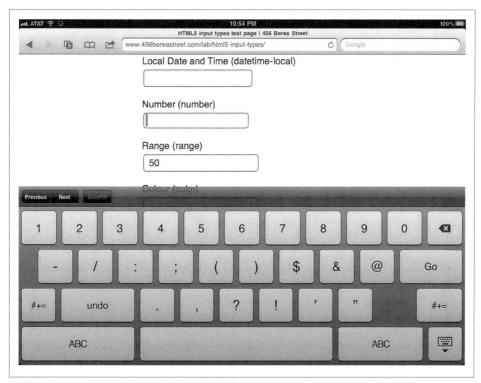

Figure 3-14. The number keyboard is displayed when number is the input value

See Also

See Mark Pilgrim's writeup on the number input type at *http://diveintohtml5.info/forms .html#type-number*.

3.5 Selecting from a Range of Numbers

Problem

You want to present a user with a form to select a number from a range—for example, to adjust the volume on a video.

Solution

Use the input element with the HTML5 type value of range:

```
<form>
    <p><label>Volume <input type="range" name="volume"
```

```
        min="0" max="10" step=".5" value="5"></label></p>
  </form>
```

Discussion

The range input type is like number in that it restricts the value to a valid floating-point number, but it has the added caveat that the exact value is not important.

Exact values are important on product order forms and the like, for values like quantity, so number should be used in those cases. The range input type is useful in cases of relative or subjective input, such as assigning a rating to an event or product. To emphasize this point, the specification requires that the control be rendered as a slider or similar control, as shown in Figure 3-15.

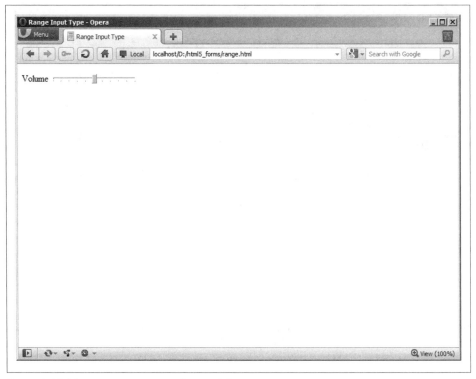

Figure 3-15. The range input type in Opera 11.5

Webkit-based browsers and Opera render a horizontal slider control for the range input type. If a user agent does not recognize this input type, it displays a text input field instead.

For a browser support reference on the range input type, see Table 3-5.

Table 3-5. Browser support for the range input type

IE	Firefox	Chrome	Safari	Opera	iOS	Android
-	-	10+	4.0+	10.0+	✓	✓

 For tips on delivering a more consistent cross-browser experience, see Recipe 3.13.

Additional features

As with the `number` input type, you can specify minimum and maximum values using the `min` and `max` attributes and an increment value using the `step` attribute. These could be used with `range` to replace the radio buttons commonly used for scaled ratings, such as satisfaction rankings.

See Also

The W3C specification on `range` at *http://www.w3.org/TR/html-markup/input.range .html*.

3.6 Selecting Colors

Problem

You want to present a user with a form to select a color—for example, to customize the look of a web page.

Solution

Use the `input` element with the HTML5 `type` value of `color`:

```
<form>
    <p><label>Background color <input type="color" name="bg"></label></p>
    <p><label>Foreground color <input type="color" name="fg"></label></p>
    <p><button type="submit">Submit</button></p>
</form>
```

Discussion

The `color` input type restricts the value to a valid RGB value in hexadecimal format, including the number sign or octothorpe, #, displayed before the six digits.

The HTML5 specification prescribes a color-well control for this input type, but so far only Opera has implemented this control. Webkit-based browsers that support `color`, like Chrome and Safari, render a text input field but successfully validate entries and prohibit form submission if the value is not valid, as shown in Figures 3-16 and 3-17.

If a user agent does not support the `color` input type, it will display a text input field instead.

For details on browser support of the `color` input type, see Table 3-6.

Table 3-6. Browser support for the color input type

IE	Firefox	Chrome	Safari	Opera	iOS	Android
-	-	10+	5.0+	11.0+	✓	✓

 For tips on delivering a more consistent cross-browser experience, see Recipe 3.13.

See Also

"Octothorpe" is a good word and bears repeated mention in polite company; see *http://en.wiktionary.org/wiki/octothorpe*.

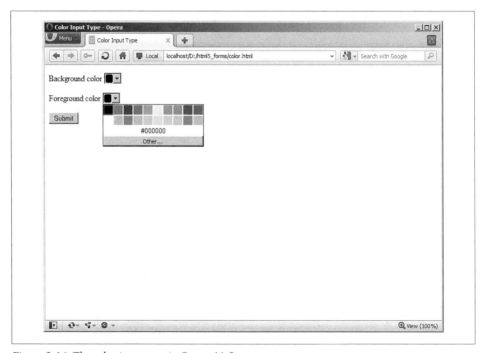

Figure 3-16. The color input type in Opera 11.5

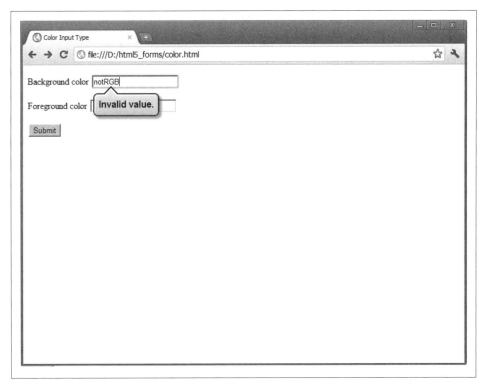

Figure 3-17. The color input type in Chrome 12

3.7 Creating an Editable Drop-Down

Problem

You want to give the user the ability to enter text but also prompt her with some suggestions to choose from. This is sometimes known as an *editable drop-down* or a combo box.

Solution

Use the HTML5 `datalist` element to create a list of suggestions using the `option` element, and associate the list with an `input` element via the `list` attribute:

```
<form>
    <p><label>Donation amount <input type="text" name="donation"
        list="donations"></label></p>
    <datalist id="donations">
        <option value="10.00">10.00</option>
        <option value="25.00">25.00</option>
        <option value="50.00">50.00</option>
    </datalist>
```

```
    <p><button type="submit">Submit</button></p>
  </form>
```

Discussion

The `datalist` element is used to define a list of suggested values for other input controls—it is not a form input or control itself.

The suggested values are specified using `option` elements, just as they would be for a `select` element, but nothing renders on the screen until the `datalist` is associated with an `input` element. Binding a `datalist` to an input field is done by specifying an `id` on the `datalist` and using this as the value of the `list` attribute on the `input` element.

The result is a control that both accepts user input and presents a list of options for the user to choose from. This is not unlike the type-ahead or autocomplete functionality implemented in many browsers and on most search websites, as shown in Figures 3-18 and 3-19.

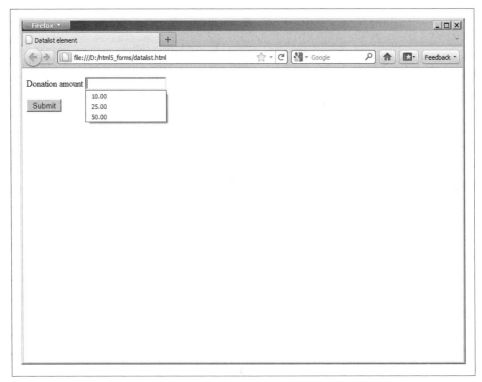

Figure 3-18. An editable drop-down rendered using input and datalist in Firefox 4

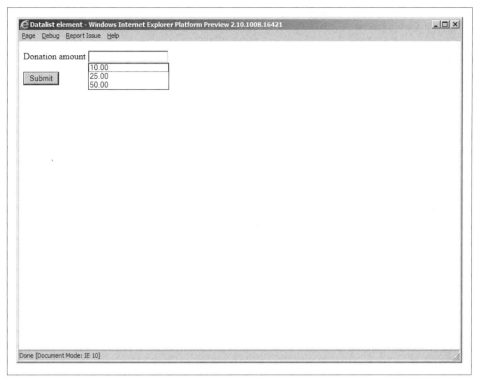

Figure 3-19. An editable drop-down rendered using input and datalist in Internet Explorer 10 Platform Preview 2

For browsers that have not yet implemented `datalist`, the above solution results in the display of the text input field, but not the list of suggestions. In a few cases, older browsers may display the option labels.

For a reference on `datalist` browser support, see Table 3-7.

Table 3-7. Browser support for the datalist element

IE	Firefox	Chrome	Safari	Opera	iOS	Android
10 Platform Preview 2	4.0+	-	-	10.0+	-	-

A datalist workaround

Web developer Jeremy Keith has proposed the following implementation, which works with both modern browsers that support the HTML5 `datalist` element and those that do not:

```
<form>
    <p><label for="donation">Donation amount</label>
    <datalist id="donations">
        <select name="donation">
```

```
                <option></option>
                <option value="10.00">10.00</option>
                <option value="25.00">25.00</option>
                <option value="50.00">50.00</option>
                <option>Other</option>
            </select>
            If other, please specify:
        </datalist>
        <input type="text" id="donation" name="donation" list="donations"></p>
        <p><button type="submit">Submit</button></p>
    </form>
```

The result is valid, semantic, and elegant: in the former case, the editable drop-down is rendered, but in the latter case, a select drop-down is rendered next to the text input field, as shown in Figure 3-20.

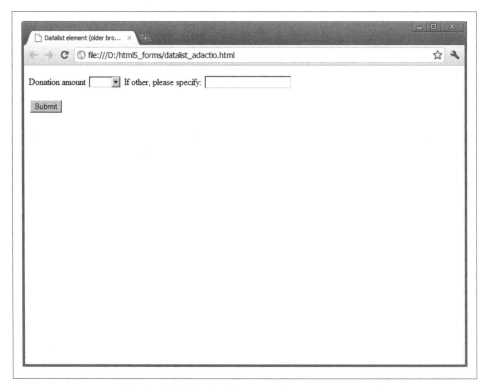

Figure 3-20. Jeremy Keith's datalist fallback solution in Chrome 12

See Also

Read Jeremy Keith's full post on the datalist solution at *http://adactio.com/journal/ 4272/*. For updated information on datalist support, see *http://caniuse.com/datalist*.

3.8 Requiring a Form Field

Problem

You want to require a form field's completion prior to form submission.

Solution

Apply the HTML5 `required` attribute on any form field that must be completed in order to submit the form:

```
<form>
    <fieldset>
        <legend>Login</legend>
        <p><label>Username <input type="text" name="username" required></label></p>
        <p><label>Password <input type="password" name="pwd" required></label></p>
    </fieldset>
    <p><button type="submit">Submit</button></p>
</form>
```

Discussion

The `required` attribute may be specified on zero or more form elements in a form.

When the user submits the form, any required field that has been left blank will cause the browser to stop the submission and an error message will be displayed. The visual display of the error varies from browser to browser, as shown in Figures 3-21–3-24.

If a user agent does not recognize the `required` attribute, it will be ignored. You can still craft JavaScript to perform this validation using this attribute, however. See Recipe 3.14, for details.

For a reference on `required` attribute support in browsers, see Table 3-8.

Table 3-8. Browser support for the required attribute

IE	Firefox	Chrome	Safari	Opera	iOS	Android
10 Platform Preview 2	4.0+	10+	5.0+	10.0+	✓	✓

See Also

Check browser support for form field validation at *http://caniuse.com/form-validation*.

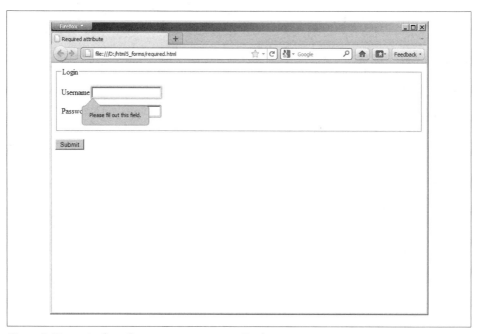

Figure 3-21. required attribute error messaging in Firefox 4

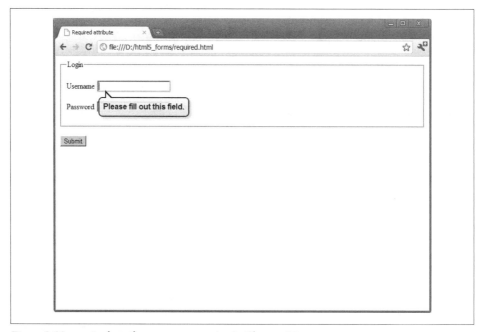

Figure 3-22. required attribute error messaging in Chrome 12

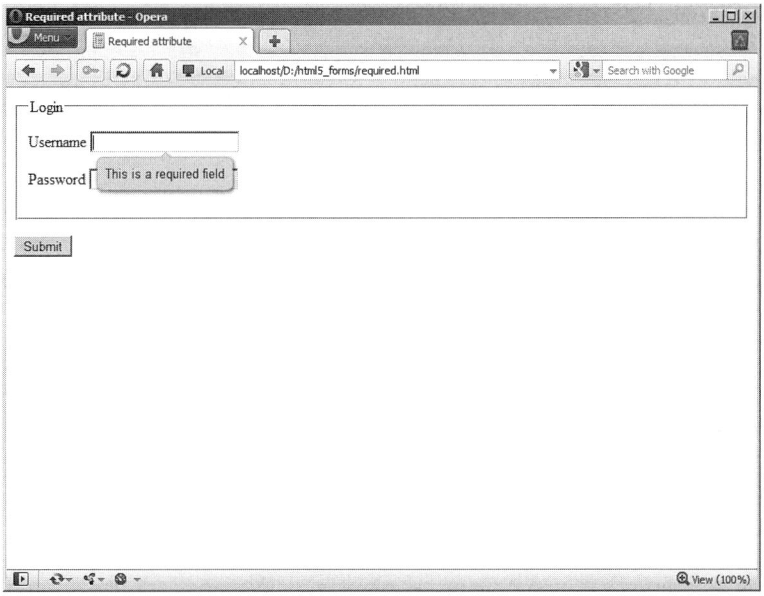

Figure 3-23. required attribute error messaging in Opera 11.5

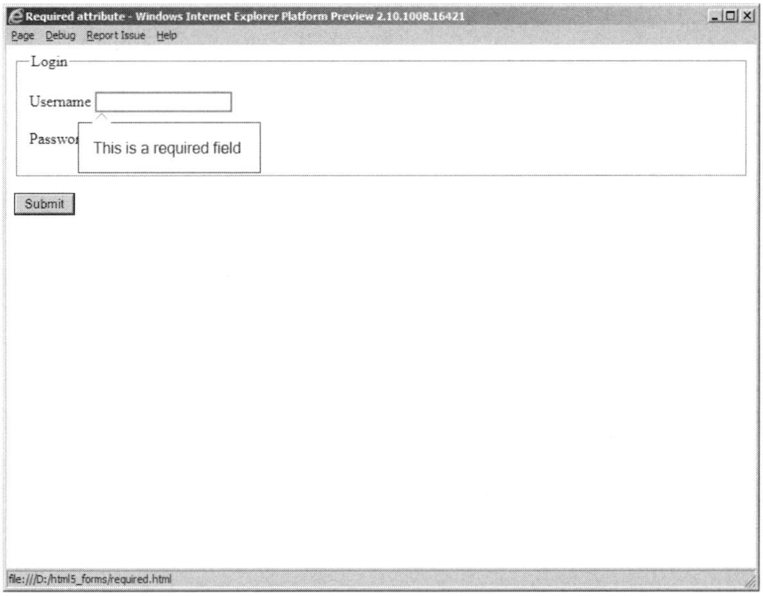

Figure 3-24. required attribute error messaging in IE 10 Platform Preview 2

3.9 Autofocusing a Form Field

Problem

You want to place the focus in a particular form field when a page loads.

Solution

Apply the HTML5 `autofocus` attribute to only one form field:

```
<form>
    <p><label>Search <input type="search" name="query" autofocus></label></p>
    <p><button type="submit">Submit</button></p>
</form>
```

Discussion

Autofocus behavior on the Web is alternately loved or hated. It's great when the search box on Google is autofocused, but it's roundly hated when the user expects to be able to scroll a page by pressing the down arrow key but the page has autofocused in a field.

A native solution both eliminates the need to write JavaScript and is potentially more accessible. When implementing the `autofocus` attribute, remember that it may be specified only once per *document*, not per form! To maintain accessibility, a user agent may honor a user setting or action that would override the focus action.

If a user agent does not recognize the `autofocus` attribute, it will be ignored. You can still use JavaScript to autofocus a field.

For a browser support reference of `autofocus`, please see Table 3-9.

Table 3-9. Browser support for the autofocus attribute

IE	Firefox	Chrome	Safari	Opera	iOS	Android
10 Platform Preview 2	4.0+	3.0+	4.0+	10.0+	✓	✓

See Also

See Recipe 3.14, for details.

3.10 Displaying Placeholder Text

Problem

You want to display some hint or help text within a form field.

Solution

The HTML5 `placeholder` attribute is used to specify instructional text when the user is not focused in the form field:

```
<form>
    <fieldset>
        <legend>Contact Information</legend>
        <p><label>E-mail address <input type="email" name="email"
            placeholder="user@domain.com"></label></p>
        <p><label>Web site <input type="url" name="website"
            placeholder="http://www.domain.com/"></label></p>
        <p><label>Telephone number <input type="tel" name="phone"
            placeholder="123-123-1234"></label></p>
    </fieldset>
    <p><button type="submit">Submit</button></p>
</form>
```

Discussion

Usability experts and user interface designers have been trying to solve the problem of displaying unobtrusive instructional text to users in forms for a long time.

Over the past five years, placeholder text within an input field has become a standard design pattern, and now we have a standard way of implementing this solution. When a `placeholder` attribute is specified on an input element, a user agent will display the value of the `placeholder` attribute in the rendered form field.

The placeholder text can then be toggled off and on, depending on which page element has focus and whether or not there is data in the form field: when the user is focused on the field, the placeholder text will disappear; if the user leaves the form field blank and leaves the field, the placeholder text will reappear, as shown in Figure 3-25.

While the `placeholder` attribute helps make a form more usable, its purpose is to provide an additional hint to the user. Do not omit the `label` element, which properly captions a form control.

If a user agent has not implemented support for the `placeholder` attribute, the attribute will be ignored.

For a reference chart on `placeholder` attribute support, see Table 3-10.

Table 3-10. Browser support for the placeholder attribute

IE	Firefox	Chrome	Safari	Opera	iOS	Android
10 Platform Preview 2	4.0+	4.0+	4.0+	11.0+	✓	✓

See Also

To deliver a more consistent experience to both browsers that support it and those that do not, see Recipe 3.13.

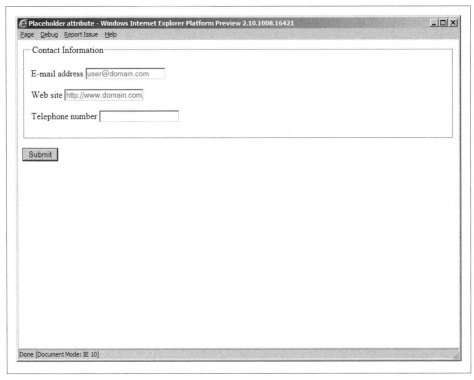

Figure 3-25. Placeholder text in Internet Explorer 10 Platform Preview 2

3.11 Disabling Autocomplete

Problem

You want to prevent autocompletion tools from populating a form field.

Solution

Set the HTML5 `autocomplete` attribute to `"off"` for any individual input field, such as
a password field:

```
<form>
    <fieldset>
        <legend>Login</legend>
        <p><label>Username <input type="text" name="username"></label></p>
        <p><label>Password <input type="password" name="pwd"
            autocomplete="off"></label></p>
    </fieldset>
    <p><button type="submit">Submit</button></p>
</form>
```

Discussion

The `autocomplete` attribute was introduced by Microsoft Internet Explorer in 1999 and was adopted by other browsers, although it was not part of any previous HTML or XHTML specification.

By default, `autocomplete` is enabled (`on`) for all form fields. You may currently rely on your browser's ability to remember your passwords and autocomplete functionality to log in to many of the websites you visit. If, however, you specify a value of `off` for this attribute, you will disable this functionality.

In addition to disabling `autocomplete` at the individual input field level, you can also disable it at the form level. If you disable `autocomplete` at the form level, you can re-enable it for an individual form field by setting `autocomplete="on"`.

While many security experts suggest applying `autocomplete="off"` to form fields that contain sensitive data, you should keep in mind that this is *not* a particularly effective security measure. Some browsers do not yet support `autocomplete`, and since so many tools exist to circumvent `autocomplete="off"`—tools that still auto-inject a user's stored password—it's often security theater or simply a false security measure.

Those browsers that do not support `autocomplete` simply ignore the attribute altogether.

For a browser support reference on `autocomplete`, see Table 3-11.

Table 3-11. Browser support for the autocomplete attribute

IE	Firefox	Chrome	Safari	Opera	iOS	Android
Yes*	4+	Yes*	Yes*	10.0+	Yes*	Yes*

> In Table 3-11, "Yes" indicates that the browser has implemented auto complete in a pre-HTML5, nonstandard way. Use Mike Taylor's input and attribute support page at *http://www.miketaylr.com/code/input-type -attr.html* to determine when a browser has implemented it per the HTML5 standard.

See Also

The `autocomplete` attribute in the WHATWG HTML specification at *http://www .whatwg.org/specs/web-apps/current-work/multipage/forms.html#attr-form-autocom plete*.

3.12 Restricting Values

Problem

You want to restrict the value of an input field according to a set of rules you specify.

Solution

Use the HTML5 `pattern` attribute to specify a regular expression that will be used to validate the user's input:

```
<form>
    <p><label>Telephone number <input type="tel" name="phone"
        pattern="[2-9][0-9]{2}-[0-9]{3}-[0-9]{4}"
        title="North American format: XXX-XXX-XXXX"></label></p>
    <p><button type="submit">Submit</button></p>
</form>
```

Discussion

For years, web professionals have been writing validation scripts to check user data prior to form submissions—and most of us would likely say that we have hated it.

With HTML5, we have a method for checking form input that doesn't rely on JavaScript: *regular expressions*.

 Regular expressions are very powerful and fun to write, once you get the hang of them. You don't need to pore over a big book like O'Reilly's *Mastering Regular Expressions*, by Jeffrey Friedl. Instead, the *Regular Expressions Cookbook* (also from O'Reilly) will help you to figure out how to define some common expressions. Then you'll be ready for that big book in no time.

The HTML5 `pattern` attribute allows you to specify a regular expression for an input field. On blur of the input field or on submit of the form (browser implementations vary), the user's input will be validated against the pattern; if it does not match, an error will be displayed and the form will not be submitted, as shown in Figure 3-26.

Regular expressions for `pattern` must use the same syntax as in JavaScript. Keep in mind that the `pattern` attribute must match the entire value, or else the user will see the error message.

When the `pattern` attribute is used, you should also specify a `title` attribute to describe the pattern. The user agent may display this text to the user as a tool tip or as an error if the submitted value does not match the pattern, as shown in Figure 3-27.

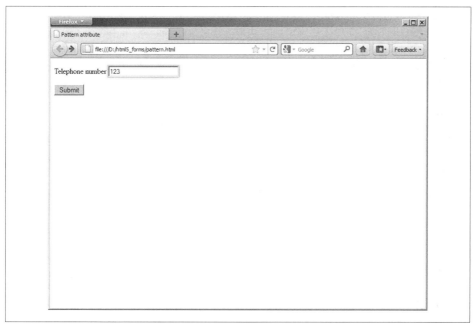

Figure 3-26. Pattern mismatch on blur of input field in Firefox 4: an error "bubble," similar to those seen elsewhere in this chapter, will be displayed on form submit

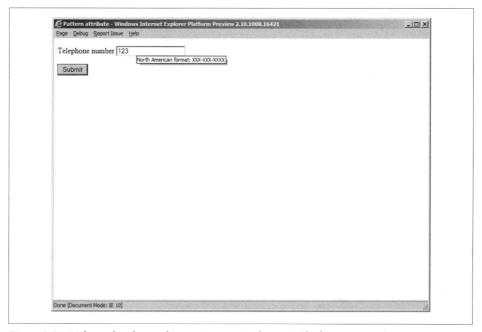

Figure 3-27. Title rendered as tool tip in Internet Explorer 10 Platform Preview 2

If a user agent cannot compile the regular expression, it is ignored and no validation will happen on that input. If a user agent does not recognize the `pattern` attribute, it, too, is ignored.

For a browser reference chart for `pattern` attribute support, see Table 3-12.

Table 3-12. Browser support for the pattern attribute

IE	Firefox	Chrome	Safari	Opera	iOS	Android
10 Platform Preview 2	4+	10+	5+	11+	-	-

 For tips on delivering a more consistent cross-browser experience, see Recipe 3.14.

See Also

As with the `required` attribute, to keep up with browser support for `pattern`, check *http://caniuse.com/form-validation*. For a list of commonly used regular expressions, see *http://html5pattern.com*.

3.13 Making HTML5 Work in Older Browsers

Problem

You want to make HTML5 input types and attributes work in browsers that do not support HTML5.

Solution

Use the Modernizr JavaScript library (see *http://www.modernizr.com*) to detect support for specific HTML5 attributes, then develop or use alternate solutions, such as jQuery UI (see *http://jqueryui.com*), for instances where features are not supported.

 Modernizr is a small, open source JavaScript library that detects native implementations of HTML5 and CSS3 features in browsers. Instead of performing browser detection in order to determine support, Modernizr performs individual feature detection. Modernizr is a very reliable way to detect support for HTML5 form features.

jQuery UI is a library of user interface design pattern implementations. It is based on and requires the jQuery JavaScript library, which is used by many of the top sites on the Web, including Google, Amazon, Twitter, and Microsoft. jQuery makes manipulating the DOM easy, and jQuery UI gives you easy-to-implement, themeable widgets.

Example 1: Supporting the autofocus attribute

Save Modernizr locally and call it in the head of your document:

```
<head>
    <script src="modernizer.js"></script>
</head>
```

Code your form using the autofocus attribute:

```
<form>
    <p><label>Search <input type="search" name="query" id="query"
        autofocus></label></p>
    <p><button type="submit">Submit</button></p>
</form>
```

Write a script to detect support for autofocus and, if it is not available, use JavaScript to focus on the element. This script can appear immediately after your form, to trigger the focus event as quickly as possible:

```
<script>
    if (!Modernizr.input.autofocus) {
        document.getElementById("query").focus();
    }
</script>
```

Example 2: Supporting the placeholder attribute

Call Modernizr and jQuery in the head of your document:

```
<head>
    <script src="modernizer.js"></script>
    <script src="jquery.js"></script>
</head>
```

Code your form using the placeholder attribute:

```
<form id="search">
    <p><label>Search <input type="search" name="query" id="query" value=""
        placeholder="Enter query"></label></p>
    <p><button type="submit">Submit</button></p>
</form>
```

Write a script to detect support for placeholder and, if it is not available, use JavaScript to toggle the display of the placeholder text in the input field:

```
<script>
    if (!Modernizr.input.placeholder) {
        $("#query").focus(function() {
            if ($("#query").val() == $("#query").attr('placeholder')) {
                $("#query").val("");
            }
        });
        $("#query").blur(function() {
            if ($("#query").val() == "") {
                $("#query").val($("#query").attr('placeholder'));
            }
        }
```

```
        });
        $("#query").blur();
        $("#search").submit(function() {
            if ($("#query").val() ==
        $("#query").attr('placeholder')) {
            return false;
            }
        });
    }
</script>
```

Even if you've never seen jQuery before, the above code is probably very easy to read. jQuery uses CSS selector syntax to refer to elements in the DOM, so $("#query") refers to the search input field with an id of query. The focus() and blur() methods are chained onto the search field, thus creating event handlers for when the field gains and loses focus. Finally, when the search form is submitted, the value of the search field is checked to ensure it's not the same as the placeholder copy; if it is, the form is not submitted.

When the blur event is triggered, the value (val) of the search field is set to the place holder attribute value, provided the value was empty.

When the focus event is triggered, the value of the search field is set to an empty string— but only if the previous value was the same as the placeholder attribute text.

This script can appear immediately after the form, or it can be combined with other scripts at the bottom of the body of your document.

 This techniques works well with all input types except password. Because browsers obscure the value of a password control, using the above solution results in your placeholder text appearing in an obscured manner. If you need to display placeholder text for a password input field, use JavaScript to insert the copy somewhere other than the value of the input.

Example 3: Supporting the date input type

Call Modernizr, jQuery, and jQuery UI in the head of your document (don't forget the CSS for jQuery UI!):

```
<head>
    <script src="modernizr.js"></script>
    <script src="jquery.js"></script>
    <script src="jquery-ui.js"></script>
    <link href="jquery-ui.css" rel="stylesheet">
</head>
```

Code your form using the date input type:

```
<form>
    <p><label>Date of Birth <input type="date" name="dob" id="dob"></label></p>
```

```
    <p><button type="submit">Submit</button></p>
</form>
```

Write a script to detect support for date and, if it is not available, trigger jQuery UI's date-picker widget:

```
<script>
    if (!Modernizr.inputtypes.datetime) {
        $("#dob").datepicker();
    }
</script>
```

I bet you're surprised at how little code is needed for this example, as compared to the previous one! This is the beauty of adopting a reusable solution, like jQuery UI. Figure 3-28 shows the result for a browser that does not natively support the date input type.

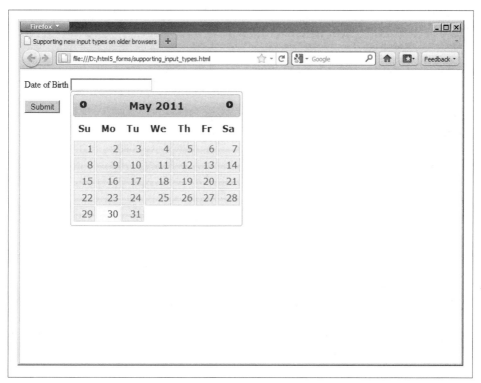

Figure 3-28. The jQuery UI date picker is triggered since Firefox 4 does not support the date and time input types

As in the previous example, this script can appear immediately after the form, or it can be combined with other scripts at the bottom of the **body** of your document.

Discussion

Remember that the new input types in HTML5 are derived from the solutions that developers have been creating with HTML and JavaScript for quite a while. This means it is fairly easy to find UI libraries that provide substitute functionality for browsers that do not yet support HTML5 forms.

In the future, when all of your users have upgraded to browsers that support HTML5 elements, input types, and attributes, you'll be able to quickly and easily remove the scripts without needing to change your markup.

See Also

For a list of fallback solutions or polyfills, see *https://github.com/Modernizr/Modernizr/wiki/HTML5-Cross-browser-Polyfills*.

3.14 Validating Form Data in Older Browsers with JavaScript

Problem

You want to validate form data in browsers that do not support HTML5.

Solution

Use the Modernizr JavaScript library (see *http://www.modernizr.com*) to detect support for specific HTML5 attributes and script alternate solutions when features are not supported. (Refer back to Recipe 3.13, for information on Modernizr and other JavaScript libraries.)

Save Modernizr locally and call it in the head of your document. We'll also call jQuery (see *http://www.jquery.com*) to make it easy to reference the form element and to attach an event handler:

```
<head>
    <script src="modernizer.js"></script>
    <script src="jquery.js"></script>
</head>
```

Code your form using HTML5 form validation attributes, such as required and pattern:

```
<form>
    <fieldset>
        <legend>Login</legend>
        <p><label>Username <input type="text" name="username" required></label></p>
        <p><label>Password <input type="password" name="password" required
            pattern="[0-9a-zA-Z]{12}" title="Must be 12 alphanumeric
            characters"></label></p>
    </fieldset>
    <p><button type="submit">Submit</button></p>
</form>
```

Write a script to detect support for **required** and **pattern** and define alternate form handling if support is not available:

```
<script>
if (!Modernizr.input.required || !Modernizr.input.pattern) {
    $('form').submit(function() {
        var validData = true;
        $('[required], [pattern]').each(function() {
            if (($(this).attr('required') !== false) && ($(this).val() == "")){
                $(this).focus();
                alert("The " + $(this).attr('name') + " field is required!");
                validData = false;
                return false;
            }
            if ($(this).attr('pattern')){
                var regexp = new RegExp($(this).attr('pattern'));
                if (!regexp.test($(this).val())){
                    $(this).focus();
                    alert("The data in the " + $(this).attr('name') +
                        " field isn't in the right format!");
                    validData = false;
                    return false;
                }
            }
        });
        return validData;
    });
}
</script>
```

Discussion

We've been validating forms with JavaScript for about 15 years, so there are plenty of ways to require form field completion and to validate data. What's new about this solution is that it leverages the HTML5 form attributes **required** and **pattern** to establish the rules for validation, and the JavaScript simply keys off of them. In the recent past, developers have used the **rel** attribute to perform a similar style of validation, but this is no longer necessary (nor is it valid HTML5).

Again, when all of your users have upgraded to browsers that natively support HTML5 form validation, you'll be able to quickly and easily remove the scripts without needing to change your markup.

See Also

Smashing Magazine's listing of best practices and tutorials for web form validation at *http://www.smashingmagazine.com/2009/07/07/web-form-validation-best-practices -and-tutorials/*.

3.15 Example: Sample Form

Problem

You want to present a user with an appointment scheduling form, for example, for scheduling a doctor's appointment.

Solution

```
<!DOCTYPE html>
<html>
<head>
<title>Appointment Scheduler</title>
</head>

<body>
<h1>Appointment Scheduler</h1>

<form>

    <fieldset>
        <legend>Personal Information</legend>
        <p><label>Name <input type="text" name="name" required></label></p>
        <p><label>Telephone number <input type="tel" name="phone" required
            pattern="[2-9][0-9]{2}-[0-9]{3}-[0-9]{4}" title="North American format:
            XXX-XXX-XXXX"></label></p>
        <p><label>E-mail address <input type="email" name="email"></label></p>
        <p><label>Date of birth <input type="date" name="dob"></label></p>
    </fieldset>

    <fieldset>
        <legend>Appointment Request</legend>
        <p><label for="reason">What is the reason for your visit?</label></p>
        <datalist id="reasons">
            <select name="reason">
                <option>Annual physical</option>
                <option>Cold or flu symptoms</option>
                <option>Blood test</option>
                <option>Post-operative</option>
                <option>Other</option>
            </select>
        If other, please specify:
        </datalist>
        <input id="reason" name="reason" list="reasons"></p>
        <p><label>Current pain level <input type="range" name="pain" min="0"
            max="10" step=".5" value="5" title="0 is no pain, 10 is worst pain
            imaginable"></label></p>
        <p><label>Preferred date <input type="date" name="date" required
            min="2011-03-15" max="2012-03-14"></label></p>
        <p><label>Preferred time <input type="time" name="time" required
            min="08:00" max="18:00" step="1:00"></label></p>
    </fieldset>
```

```
    <p><button type="submit">Submit</button></p>
</form>

</body>
</html>
```

Discussion

This is the future of form markup, my friends! When rendered in a browser that fully supports HTML5 forms, the only thing this form will want for is some CSS—no JavaScript necessary! It will render nicely across a variety of devices and be much more accessible than what we use today, as shown in Figure 3-29.

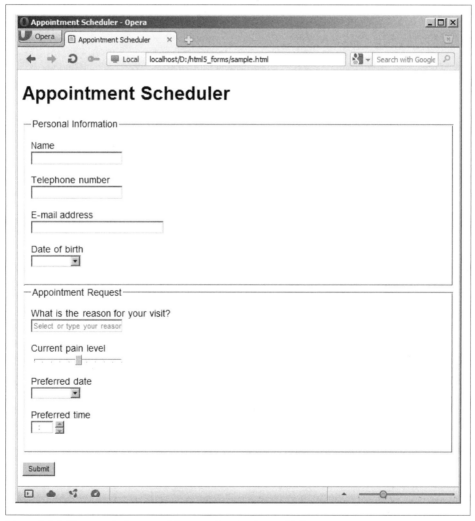

Figure 3-29. The sample form, with basic styling, in Opera 11.5

When will we have full support in the majority of browsers for HTML5 forms? Opera is leading the way in support, but Firefox and Chrome are on rapid release cycles and are catching up quickly.

The second Internet Explorer Platform Preview was released during the writing of this chapter and it, too, shows good progress.

See Also

Chapter 8 of *CSS Cookbook* by Christopher Schmitt (O'Reilly), for a discussion of styling forms.

CHAPTER 4

Native Audio

Emily Lewis

4.0 Introduction

You already deal with *embedded content*—content that is imported or inserted into a web page—almost every day (see *http://www.w3.org/TR/html5/content-models .html#embedded-content-0)*. Think about the `img` element. It inserts content—the image—into your web page via the `src` attribute.

With HTML5, we now have many more options for embedded content, including native audio via the new `audio` element (see *http://dev.w3.org/html5/markup/audio .html)*.

Native? Yes. That means no more ungainly `object` and `embed`. No more need to deliver audio with a third-party plug-in and, as such, no more design headaches with dynamic layouts or drop-down menus.

With `audio` in our arsenal, not only can we deliver audio files directly through the browser, but we can style and manipulate the element and its attributes via CSS and JavaScript.

4.1 Adding HTML5 Audio

Problem

You want to play native audio on your web page.

Solution

Add the `audio` element, with the `src` attribute referencing the location of your audio file and fallback content for older browsers:

```
<audio src="audio.ogg" controls>
    Download <a href="audio.ogg">episode 42 of Learning to Love HTML5</a>
</audio>
```

Also be sure to include the `controls` attribute if you want browsers to display a default control interface for your audio (see Figure 4-1):

```
<audio src="audio.ogg" controls>
```

Figure 4-1. Default audio controls in Chrome 9 include play/pause, a progress bar, and volume/mute

The audio file in this example uses Ogg Vorbis (*.ogg*), which is a royalty-free, open source codec (see *http://www.vorbis.com*). However, there are many other audio formats for the Web (see Table 4-1), which is one of the biggest challenges in implementing HTML5 audio.

A *codec* is a technology used for compressing and decompressing data. *Audio* codecs compress and/or decompress digital audio data into different formats that aim to retain the highest level of quality with the minimum bit rate.

Multiple audio codecs

The HTML5 specification does not dictate or make any recommendations about what audio codecs should be supported. And since it would make far too much sense for browser makers to agree (see *http://lists.whatwg.org/pipermail/whatwg-whatwg.org/2009-June/020620.html*), there isn't a single format that works in all browsers, as you can see in Table 4-1.

Table 4-1. Current browser support for HTML5 audio formats

Browser	AAC (.aac)	MP3 (.mp3)	Ogg Vorbis (.ogg)	WAV (.wav)	WebM (.webm)
Chrome 6+		X	X		X
Firefox 3.6+			X	X	X
IE9+	X	X		X	
Opera 10.5+			X	X	
Safari 5+	X	X		X	

Let's take a closer look at these formats:

.aac
> Lossy compression scheme developed as an improvement over MP3, with similar bit rates but better sound quality

.mp3
> Patented yet popular format that uses lossy compression to achieve file sizes one-tenth of noncompressed

.ogg
> Open source alternative to *.mp3* that also uses a lossy compression format

.wav
> Proprietary format for audio that does not utilize any compression

.webm
> Google's open, royalty-free media format, which relies on the Vorbis audio codec for compression

Integrating multiple sources

In terms of which format to choose, the reality is that if you want your content to reach the widest possible audience you have to encode and include *multiple* audio files in your HTML5 `audio` element. Fortunately, HTML5 does allow this.

> When using the `source` element in `audio`, the `src` attribute is dropped. `src` only comes into play (pun intended) if you are referencing a *single* audio format.

In terms of best practices, it's recommended that you minimally include the *.ogg* royalty-free format *and* either the *.mp3* or *.wav* format. This type of approach should cover your bases with the latest browsers:

```
<audio controls>
    <source src="audio.ogg">
    <source src="audio.mp3">
    Download <a href="audio.ogg">episode 42 of Learning to Love HTML5</a>
</audio>
```

Preloading the audio

`audio` has several attributes that allow you to configure your audio implementation.

> For a full description of the attributes available for HTML5 media elements, see the WHATWG standard: *http://www.whatwg.org/specs/web-apps/current-work/multipage/video.html#media-element-attributes*.

The `preload` attribute allows you to hint to the browser when it should begin buffering the audio:

```
<audio controls preload>
```

While `preload` currently has limited browser support, it seems useful for optimizing the download process. You can simply specify `preload` and leave it to the browser to decide the appropriate action, or you can choose from three defined `preload` values:

preload="auto"
> Is the same as a Boolean `preload`, and suggests that the browser should begin downloading the file but leaves the ultimate action up to the browser. So, if it is a mobile situation or a slow connection, the browser can decide not to preload in order to save bandwidth.

preload="metadata"
> Hints that the browser shouldn't buffer the audio itself until the user activates the controls, but that metadata like duration and tracks should be preloaded.

preload="none"
> Suggests that the audio shouldn't be downloaded until the user activates the controls.

Discussion

In addition to the browser inconsistencies with audio formats, there is a bit of inconsistency in the support for `audio` itself. There are browser bugs, quirks, and oddities that will hopefully be addressed by the browser makers in the near future, but until they are it is up to us designers and developers to remain informed.

 24Ways provides a list of some of these browser issues: *http://24ways .org/2010/the-state-of-html5-audio*.

Creating fallback content

As you saw in the first example of this recipe, `audio` allows us to include *fallback* content. What this means is that if a user is on a browser that doesn't support HTML5 `audio`, he will instead see some replacement content (see Figure 4-2).

Download <u>episode 42 of Learning to Love HTML5</u>

Figure 4-2. Fallback content displayed in IE8, which lacks HTML5 <audio> support

The HTML5 specification says that all child elements of audio other than source should be ignored. This means that providing additional fallback content won't result in any negative consequences for a user on an HTML5-capable browser.

For example, you could include fallback Flash:

```
<audio controls>
    <source src="audio.ogg">
    <source src="audio.mp3">
    <object data="player.swf?audio=audio.mp3">
        <param name="movie" value="player.swf?audio=audio.mp3">
        Video and Flash are not supported by your browser.
    </object>
</audio>
```

Or you could simply describe what the audio file contains and include a link to the file for a user to download and play on his device's media player (along with some gentle encouragement to upgrade to a new browser):

```
<audio controls>
    <source src="audio.ogg">
    <source src="audio.mp3">
    Your browser does not support HTML5 audio. You should upgrade. In the
    meantime, download <a href="audio.ogg">episode 42 of Learning to Love
    HTML5</a>.
</audio>
```

Accessible alternatives

Another challenge with HTML5 audio is that alternative content for multimedia doesn't quite exist in practice. *Theoretically*, accessibility would be delivered through two steps: first, multimedia authors include a subtitles file in the container *.ogv* or *.mp3*, and then browsers give users an interface to access those subtitles and captions.

 Using the alt attribute with img isn't a practical solution. It isn't what the HTML5 specification intends, and, more important, assistive technologies don't process audio fallback content in that fashion.

For now, there's not much more than a few experimental approaches you can try:

- Accessible HTML5 Video with JavaScripted captions: *http://dev.opera.com/articles/view/accessible-html5-video-with-javascripted-captions/*
- HTML5 and Timed Media: *http://www.bbc.co.uk/blogs/rad/2009/08/html5.html*
- Demos of HTML5 Video and Audio Tag Accessibility: *http://www.annodex.net/~silvia/itext/*

You may note that some of these resources reference video. That's because HTML5 audio and video are so similar that the approaches described can be applied to both (as discussed in Chapter 5).

Beyond issues with captioning, audio support in general is inconsistent among assistive technologies. For example, some screen readers don't recognize the element at all and simply skip it.

Further, audio accessibility, like keyboard support, is inconsistent among browsers. As this is the case for HTML5 across the board, we recommend staying updated at *http:// html5accessibility.com*.

Intellectual property rights

You may have already figured out that HTML5 audio isn't a "one size fits all" solution. But it isn't just the need for multiple file formats or inconsistent browser support that's at issue: *HTML5 does not offer any copy protection.*

audio (and video, see Chapter 5) is as easy to save to a user's hard drive as img and, therefore, isn't a good fit for all use cases. If Digital Rights Management (DRM) is needed, a plug-in, not audio, is likely a better solution with how copy protection stands today.

See Also

For more about HTML5 multimedia accessibility, the W3C wiki offers an in-depth view of known issues and proposed solutions: *http://www.w3.org/html/wg/wiki/Multi mediaAccessibilty*.

4.2 Manipulating the Audio Stream

Problem

You want to be able to control and manipulate how your HTML5 audio plays in the browser.

Solution

As part of the specification, audio has a few attributes that give you simple and instant control over your playback:

autoplay
> Tells the browser to start playing the audio as soon as the page loads.

> I hesitate to even mention this attribute because it does exactly what it says, and is one of the most annoying, non-user-friendly things on websites (*http://www.punkchip.com/2009/04/autoplay-is -bad-for-all-users*). So, while autoplay is available, don't use it. Seriously. Don't.

loop

Another self-descriptive attribute, loop tells the browser to loop the audio when playing forward.

 This is less offensive than the autoplay attribute, but it should still be used with discretion.

Like controls, both autoplay and loop are Boolean attributes, so you simply include them in the opening audio tag when you want them:

```
<audio controls loop>
```

Discussion

What if you want more control than these basic attributes provide? Fortunately, audio and video have attributes, events, and methods you can manipulate with JavaScript to create custom controls, including:

canplaytype(*type*)
Returns a string indicating whether the browser can play a particular type of media

currentTime
Indicates the current playback position, denoted in seconds

duration
Gives the length of the audio file in seconds

play();
Starts playback at the current position

pause();
Pauses playback if the audio is actively playing

For example, suppose you want to include controls that allow the user to jump to a specific time in the audio file. You can add this functionality with a button and a dash of JavaScript to manipulate the play() method based on the read/write property currentTime:

```
<audio>
    <source src="audio.ogg">
    <source src="audio.mp3">
</audio>
<button title="Play at 30 seconds" onclick="playAt(30);">30 seconds</button>
<script>
    function playAt(seconds){
        var audio = document.getElementsByTagName("audio")[0];
        audio.currentTime = seconds;
        audio.play();
    }
</script>
```

There is no stop method, but using the same approach as in the example above, stop functionality can be mimicked by using the `pause()`; method to return to the beginning of the audio file via `currentTime`:

```
<audio>
    <source src="audio.ogg">
    <source src="audio.mp3">
</audio>
<button title="Play at 30 seconds" onclick="playAt(30);">30 seconds</button>
<button title="Stop Audio" onclick="stopAudio();">Stop Audio</button>
<script>
    function playAt(seconds){
        var audio = document.getElementsByTagName("audio")[0];
        audio.currentTime = seconds;
        audio.play();
    }
    function stopAudio(){
        var audio = document.getElementsByTagName("audio")[0];
        audio.currentTime = 0;
        audio.pause();
    }
</script>
```

 Note that when creating your own custom controls, you drop the controls Boolean attribute from `audio`.

For more information on creating custom controls, see Recipe 4.5.

See Also

For a much less rudimentary approach to manipulating the audio playback with custom controls, see Opera's "Everything You Need to Know About HTML5 Video and Audio" at *http://dev.opera.com/articles/view/everything-you-need-to-know-about-html5-video-and-audio/*.

4.3 Generating <audio> Using JavaScript

Problem

You want to generate real-time audio on your web page.

Solution

You can generate audio on the browser without the `src` attribute or `source` elements by using methods defined by the Mozilla Audio Data API (*https://wiki.mozilla.org/Audio_Data_API#Writing_Audio*):

```
mozSetup(channels, sampleRate)
```
Defines the channels and sample rate for the generated audio stream

```
mozWriteAudio(buffer)
```
Writes the samples, from an array, for the generated audio

```
mozCurrentSampleOffset()
```
Gets the current playback position of the audio, denoted in samples

Discussion

This particular implementation of audio has somewhat limited support. In fact, only Firefox 4+ and Chrome Beta currently support it. As such, it is more an experimental approach than something geared for mainstream use.

If you happen to be the experimental type, though, check out this short video presentation of what is possible with the Mozilla Audio Data API: *http://www.youtube.com/watch?v=1Uw0CrQdYYg*.

See Also

The transcript for the "jasmid—MIDI synthesis with JavaScript and HTML5 audio" talk from Barcamp London 8 provides a very high-level discussion about the challenges and practical implications of generating audio on the fly, in the browser: *http://matt.west.co.tt/music/jasmid-midi-synthesis-with-javascript-and-html5-audio/*.

4.4 Visualizing <audio> Using <canvas>

Problem

You want to create a visualization of your HTML5 audio using canvas.

Solution

This example delivers a rudimentary canvas implementation that visualizes audio with waveforms (see Figure 4-3):

```
<audio src="audio.ogg"></audio>
<canvas width="512" height="100"></canvas>
<button title="Generate Waveform" onclick="genWave();">Generate Waveform</button>

<script>
    function genWave(){
        var audio = document.getElementsByTagName("audio")[0];
        var canvas = document.getElementsByTagName("canvas")[0];
        var context = canvas.getContext('2d');
        audio.addEventListener("MozAudioAvailable", buildWave, false);
        function buildWave (event){
            var channels = audio.mozChannels;
            var frameBufferLength = audio.mozFrameBufferLength;
```

```
            var fbData = event.frameBuffer;
            var stepInc = (frameBufferLength / channels) / canvas.width;
            var waveAmp = canvas.height / 2;
            canvas.width = canvas.width;
            context.beginPath();
            context.moveTo(0, waveAmp - fbData[0] * waveAmp);
            for(var i=1; i < canvas.width; i++){
                context.lineTo(i, waveAmp - fbData[i*stepInc] * waveAmp);
            }
            context.strokeStyle = "#fff";
            context.stroke();
        }
        audio.play();
    }
</script>
```

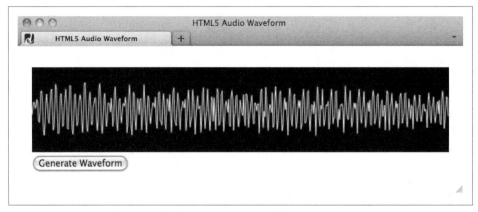

Figure 4-3. Wave visualization of audio via canvas in Firefox 5

In this solution, we combine what is discussed about canvas in Chapter 9 with some methods from the Mozilla Audio Data API. Let's break it down piece by piece, starting with the core audio element, canvas, and a button to trigger the visualization:

```
<audio src="audio.ogg"></audio>
<canvas width="512" height="100"></canvas>
<button title="Generate Waveform" onclick="genWave();">Generate Waveform</button>
```

 For brevity's sake, I'm using the src attribute for audio in this example, but this would also work with multiple source elements.

Next, add a background color via CSS to indicate a simple presentation for the canvas:

```
<style>
    canvas {background: #000;}
</style>
```

 Note that the width and height values in canvas are DOM attributes, not style attributes. As such, you need to specify them in the markup, not the CSS, so that the browser knows the dimensions of its drawing space. See Chapter 9 for more on canvas.

And now for the JavaScript. First, set up an overall function to generate the wave:

```
<script>
    function genWave(){
```

Inside that function, get both the audio and canvas elements:

```
var audio = document.getElementsByTagName("audio")[0];
var canvas = document.getElementsByTagName("canvas")[0];
```

Then set up canvas with its drawing context (see *http://diveintohtml5.info/canvas.html #shapes*):

```
var context = canvas.getContext('2d');
```

Next, add an event listener to gather data about the audio file using methods from the Mozilla Audio Data API (*https://developer.mozilla.org/en/Introducing_the_Audio_API _Extension#section_2*):

```
audio.addEventListener("MozAudioAvailable", buildWave, false);
```

Then, include a private function to build the canvas wave drawing, and get the number of channels and frameBufferLength:

```
function buildWave (event){
    var channels = audio.mozChannels;
    var frameBufferLength = audio.mozFrameBufferLength;
```

 Note that you need to divide frameBufferLength by channels because frameBuffer contains an array of audio samples that are not separated by channels, but are all delivered together.

Get the frameBuffer data:

```
var fbData = event.frameBuffer;
```

Set the step increment:

```
var stepInc = (frameBufferLength / channels) / canvas.width;
```

and set the wave amplitude:

```
var waveAmp = canvas.height / 2;
```

Next, reset `canvas` so the strokes don't build on top of each other:

```
canvas.width = canvas.width;
```

Finally, build the stroke and set stroke properties:

```
context.beginPath();
context.moveTo(0, waveAmp - fbData[0] * waveAmp);
for(var i=1; i < canvas.width; i++){
    context.lineTo(i, waveAmp - fbData[i*stepInc] * waveAmp);
}
context.strokeStyle = "#fff";
```

Add the stroke to `canvas`:

```
        context.stroke();
    }
```

and play the audio:

```
        audio.play();
    }
</script>
```

Discussion

Just as generating real-time audio with JavaScript (see Recipe 4.3) is limited to Firefox 4+, so is this method of `audio` visualization with `canvas`. This is because only the Mozilla Audio Data API allows you to access the key audio data (in this example, `frame Buffer`) necessary to create the `canvas` drawing.

Further, this method of audio visualization must run on a web server, and it requires that the audio file reside on that *same server* due to Firefox security measures (*https://wiki.mozilla.org/Audio_Data_API#Security*).

 While this recipe makes use of the Mozilla Audio Data API, browsers (including Firefox) may support the Web Audio API from the W3C. For more information, see the specification at *https://dvcs.w3.org/hg/audio/raw-file/tip/webaudio/specification.html*.

See Also

For a far more sophisticated and interactive use of `audio` and `canvas`, see the project from 9elements at *http://9elements.com/io/projects/html5/canvas/*.

4.5 Sample Design: Custom Audio Player

Problem

You want to design your own custom audio player.

Solution

In this sample design, we'll extend the concepts of Recipe 4.2, to create a custom audio player (see Figure 4-4), rather than relying on the default controls attribute.

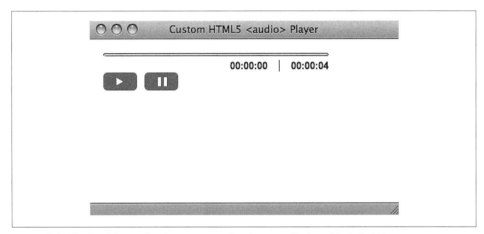

Figure 4-4. The final design for the custom audio player as displayed in Safari 5

Define <audio> and player structure

We'll start with the markup for our HTML5 audio and player controls:

```
<div id="player">
    <audio src="media/audio.mp3"></audio>

    <div class="playerControls">
        <button id="audioPlay" title="Play"
            onclick="playPause();">&#x25ba;</button>
        <button id="audioPause" class="hidden" title="Pause"
            onclick="playPause();">&#x2590;&#x2590;</button>
        <button id="audioStop" title="Stop" onclick="playStop();">&#x25a0;</button>

        <div id="audioSeek">
            <div id="audioLoaded"></div>
        </div>

        <ul id="audioTimes">
            <li id="audioElapsed">00:00:00</li>
            <li id="audioDuration">00:00:00</li>
        </ul>
```

```
    </div>
  </div>
```

For the purposes of simplicity, this example includes only a play/pause toggle, a stop button, and a progress bar.

 The choice of the `button` element for the player controls is simply a semantic and accessibility preference, not a requirement.

JavaScript API

Next, we turn to the powerful DOM API to deliver functionality to the player markup.

 For a more usable, accessible experience, you can also use detection (see *http://diveintohtml5.info/everything.html*) for HTML5 `audio`. Then, only if it *is* supported will the player markup and `audio` element be inserted. This means browsers that don't support HTML5 `audio` won't see a player they can't use. Modernizr (see *http://modernizr.com*) can aid in this detection.

First, declare the `audio` element and player controls, making sure the `script` appears after the `audio` element in the source:

```
<script>
    audio = document.getElementsByTagName("audio")[0];
    audioDuration = document.getElementById("audioDuration");
    audioElapsed = document.getElementById("audioElapsed");
    audioPlay = document.getElementById("audioPlay");
    audioPause = document.getElementById("audioPause");
    audioStop = document.getElementById("audioStop");
    audioLoaded = document.getElementById("audioLoaded");
```

Then determine eventful information about the audio file:

```
    audio.addEventListener("loadedmetadata", setDuration, false);
    audio.addEventListener("timeupdate", setElapsed, false);
```

Next, define the functions driving the progress bar:

```
    function setDuration(event) {
        audioDuration.innerHTML = timeFormatter(audio.duration);
    }

    function setElapsed(event) {
        audioElapsed.innerHTML = timeFormatter(audio.currentTime);
        amountLoaded = (audio.currentTime/audio.duration)*100;
        audioLoaded.style.width = amountLoaded + 'px';
    }
```

and the function to toggle play and pause:

```
function playPause() {
    if (audio.paused){
        audio.play();
        audioPlay.className = 'hidden';
        audioPause.className = '';
    } else {
        audio.pause();
        audioPlay.className = '';
        audioPause.className = 'hidden';
    }
}
```

Then define the function for the stop, which is based on Recipe 4.2:

```
function playStop() {
    audio.pause();
    audio.currentTime=0;
    audioPlay.className = '';
    audioPause.className = 'hidden';
}
```

and the function to format the time for the progress bar:

```
function timeFormatter(seconds){
    function zeroPad(str) {
        if (str.length > 2) return str;
        for (i=0; i<(2-str.length); i++) {
            str = "0" + str;
        }
        return str;
    }
    var minute = 60,
        hour = minute * 60,
        hStr = "",
        mStr = "",
        sStr = "";

    var h = Math.floor(seconds / hour);
    hStr = zeroPad(String(h));

    var m = Math.floor((seconds - (h * hour)) / minute);
    mStr = zeroPad(String(m));

    var s = Math.floor((seconds - (h * hour)) - (m * minute));
    sStr = zeroPad(String(s));

    return (hStr + ":" + mStr + ":" + sStr);
}
</script>
```

CSS for style

Finally, we'll style our player so it doesn't look quite so plain (see Figure 4-5). We'll start with styles for the dimensions of the player and how the buttons should appear:

```css
#player {
    height: 50px;
    padding: 10px;
    position:relative;
    width: 300px;
}

button {
    background: #666;
    border:1px;
    -moz-border-radius: 5px;
    border-radius: 5px;
    bottom: 10px;
    color: #fff;
    padding: 5px;
    position:absolute;
    width:45px;
}

#audioStop {
    font-size:22px;
    left: 65px;
    line-height: 11px;
}
```

Then we'll add styles that help with the play/pause toggle:

```css
#audioPlay.hidden,
#audioPause.hidden { display:none; }

#audioSeek {
    background: #ccc;
    border: 1px solid #000;
    -moz-border-radius: 10px;
    border-radius: 10px;
    display:block;
    height:2px;
}
```

and styles for the green progress bar:

```css
#audioLoaded {
    background: #0c0;
    border: 1px solid #0c0;
    -moz-border-radius: 10px;
    border-radius: 10px;
    display:block;
    height:1px;
}
```

And, finally, styles for the time counters:

```
#audioTimes {
    float:right;
    list-style:none;
    margin: 5px 0 0;
}

#audioTimes li {
    font:bold 13px Arial, Helvetica sans-serif;
    float: left;
}

#audioTimes li:first-child {
    border-right: 1px solid #000;
    margin-right: 15px;
    padding-right: 15px;
}
```

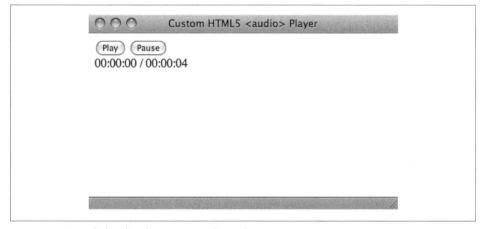

Figure 4-5. Unstyled audio player as viewed in Safari 5

Discussion

Not into rolling your own? There are a few prebuilt solutions you can consider for customized player controls, including playlist features:

- jPlayer jQuery plug-in: *http://www.jplayer.org*
- MooTools HTML5 Audio Player: *http://simulacre.org/mootools-html5-audio-player*

See Also

The "Creating Your Own Accessible HTML5 Media Player" tutorial at *http://terri llthompson.blogspot.com/2010/08/creating-your-own-accessible-html5.html*.

CHAPTER 5

Native Video

Emily Lewis

5.0 Introduction

HTML5's new embedded content elements offer designers and developers more options for including media in our sites.

Similar in nature to audio, the video element shares many of the same attributes, has a similar syntax, and can be styled and manipulated with CSS and JavaScript. And just like audio, video has some implementation challenges.

5.1 Adding HTML5 Video

Problem

You want to play native video on your web page.

Solution

Use the video element with the addition of a src attribute that references the location of your video file:

```
<video src="video.ogv"></video>
```

To display default video player controls (see Figure 5-1), add the Boolean controls attribute:

```
<video src="video.ogv" controls></video>
```

Native player controls look different in different browsers. Style your own controls with JavaScript and CSS (see Recipe 5.6).

Figure 5-1. Default video player controls in Firefox 4

Preloading

The `preload` attribute allows you to *suggest* to the browser whether and how it should download the video:

```
<video src="video.ogv" controls preload></controls>
```

You can skip the attribute and let the browser decide, or give browsers a "hint" with specific values (refer back to Recipe 4.1, for details):

- `preload="auto"` or, simply, `preload`
- `preload="metadata"`
- `preload="none"`

Fallback content

You should also make it standard practice to include *fallback content* with `video`:

```
<video src="video.ogv" controls>
    Your device does not support HTML5 video. <a href="video.ogg">Download the
    Learning to Love HTML5 introductory video</a>.
</video>
```

Note that providing fallback content is not the same as ensuring accessibility or providing accessible content.

Fallback content is content that displays on browsers that don't support video. It does two things: informs the user that her browser doesn't support HTML5 video and provides a link to download the video.

For a good overview of the state of HTML5 video accessibility, see *http://john.foliot.ca/accessibility-and-html5-today/*.

Along with different video formats, Flash video can be inserted as a fallback alternative.

In fact, you can nest fallback content for lack of support for both the `object` and `video` elements:

```
<video src="video.ogv" controls>
    <object type="application/x-shockwave-flash"
            data="player.swf?file=video.mp4">
        <param name="movie" value="player.swf?file=video.mp4">
        <a href="video.mp4">Download the Learning to Love HTML5
            introductory video</a>
    </object>
</video>
```

Discussion

Unfortunately, `video` is not as straightforward to implement as it might seem, because not all browsers support the same set of video file formats.

Multiple video codecs

As with audio (see Recipe 4.1), the HTML5 specification doesn't specify which video codecs should be supported.

Instead, the browser makers decide which format to support (see Table 5-1). This is fine, but getting browser vendors to agree on any one thing is nearly impossible. Getting them to agree on which video formats—much less a single video format—to support is going to be next to impossible. To work around this situation, video needs to be encoded and published in multiple formats in order to display across the broadest range of browsers.

While the `blink` element is almost universally disliked, it's still supported in browsers. Go figure.

Table 5-1. Current browser support for video formats

Browser	H.264 (.mp4)	Ogg Theora (.ogv)	VP8 (.webm)
Chrome 6+	R	Y	Y
Firefox 3.6+		Y	Y
IE9+	Y		D
Opera 10.5+		Y	Y
Safari 5+	Y		

In Table 5-1, R indicates "removed," D indicates "download required," and Y indicates "yes (supported)." Note that Google removed support for H.264 from the Chrome browser with version 11. IE9 supports VP8, but only if the user installs the codec on Windows.

As you can see from Table 5-1, if you want to reach all of the latest browsers you need to include *at least* the *.mp4* and *.ogv* formats. Briefly, the supported formats are:

.mp4
> The container format for the proprietary H.264 codec that encodes video for a full range of devices, including high definition.

.ogv
> The free, open source container format for the open source Theora codec. Results in lower quality than H.264.

.webm
> Another open source container format, which is used by the new, royalty-free VP8 codec from Google.

Google pulled support for H.264 in Chrome (see *http://blog.chromium .org/2011/01/html-video-codec-support-in-chrome.html*), while VP8 is supported by Microsoft's IE9 with the installation of a decoder (see *http: //windowsteamblog.com/windows/b/bloggingwindows/archive/2010/05/ 19/another-follow-up-on-html5-video-in-ie9.aspx*).

Why is there such a messy situation with video codecs? Intellectual property and licensing fees are a large factor. Browser makers who want to use certain formats (and therefore codecs) natively are subject to the intellectual property rights of the codecs and formats.

Apple and Microsoft have paid the licensing fees to allow the H.264 video codec to play natively in their respective browsers. The vendors that produce the Firefox and Opera browsers, meanwhile, opt to support free, open source formats.

For a more in-depth explanation of why there are so many codecs and formats for video, check out this great introductory video from Stephanie Sullivan Rewis on HTML5 video: *http://tv.adobe.com/watch/adc-presents/videoandhtml5part2gettingstarted/*. You will need Flash installed on your Internet-enabled device in order to see it, though.

Browser support

Aside from the challenges of dealing with multiple codecs and format containers, `video` has full support in all of the latest browsers. However, `video` is not supported in Internet Explorer 8 and below. For these earlier versions, you'll need to rely on fallback content.

See Also

For some open source videos on developing and experimenting with HTML5 `video` support, search the Internet Archive (see *http://www.archive.org/details/movies*).

5.2 Ensuring Multi-Browser Video Support

Problem

You want to make sure your native video plays on the broadest range of browsers possible.

Solution

Use the `source` child element of `video` to specify each of your video formats:

```
<video controls>
    <source src="video.mp4" />
    <source src="video.ogv" />
    Your device does not support HTML5 video.
</video>
```

Note that you must remove the `src` attribute and value from the `video` element, as seen in Recipe 5.1.

As we saw in Table 5-1, using *.mp4* and *.ogv* covers all browsers that support HTML5. But order matters, too. List your source formats from most to least desirable, as browsers will play the first format they recognize.

The Video for Everybody site provides comprehensive details about bugs and device nuances with HTML5 video: *http://camendesign.com/code/video_for_everybody/*.

Discussion

Beyond specifying the video files themselves, it is good practice to also specify the *MIME type* for your video files:

```
<source src="video.mp4" type="video/mp4" />
<source src="video.ogv" type="video/ogg" />
```

 Firefox does not play Ogg video if the MIME type is wrong.

Since file formats are simply containers for different codecs, you should also specify the compression used:

```
<source src="video.ogv" type="video/ogg; codecs='theora'">
```

Including this information speeds up rendering of the video since it indicates what kind of content the browser is utilizing without the browser having to download a portion of the file to make its own determination.

Here are some examples of MIME types with codecs:

```
type="video/ogg; codecs='theora, vorbis'"
type="video/mp4; codecs='avc1.42E01E'"
type="video/webm; codecs='vp8, vorbis'"
```

Unfortunately, even if you declare your MIME types with the proper codec in your HTML, there can also be challenges related to the MIME types supported by your *server*. If your server isn't configured to support the MIME types your video uses, there will be playback issues.

You can, however, configure your server to support video MIME types. Information about Ogg media from the Mozilla Developer Center (*https://developer.mozilla.org/en/Configuring_servers_for_Ogg_media*) can equally be applied to *.webm* and *.mp4*.

See Also

If you have your own video but want to convert it to other formats, check out these tools:

- Miro VideoConverter: *http://www.mirovideoconverter.com/*
- WebM Tools: *http://www.webmproject.org/tools/*
- MPEG StreamClip: *http://www.squared5.com/*

- TinyOgg: *http://tinyogg.com/*
- OggConvert: *http://oggconvert.tristanb.net/*

5.3 Setting Video Dimensions

Problem

You want to specify the width and height of your video player.

Solution

Add the `width` and `height` attributes, and their corresponding values, to `video`:

```
<video controls width="640" height="360">
    <source src="video.mp4" type="video/mp4" />
    <source src="video.ogv" type="video/ogg" />
    Your device does not support HTML5 video.
</video>
```

Discussion

Browsers render the video player according to the dimensions you assign, not the resolution of your actual video. Using different dimensions might lead to a loss in quality by expanding a video beyond its native resolution; the same goes for scaling down a large video simply to fit into a small space.

So, when possible, use the *same* dimension values for the `video` element as for the video file itself, and don't resize your video with `width` and `height`.

Technically speaking, the width and height of a `video` element do not need to be set as browsers default to inheriting the dimensions of the video file itself. The drawback to this approach is that if the dimensions are not set, browsers won't know what space to reserve for your video and may have to redraw your page after downloading the video data.

The `width` and `height` values need to be set in CSS pixels as integers and not as percentages or other values. Adding dimension values helps browsers more efficiently render your pages, which usually results in a better user experience.

Since you probably don't want to use `width` and `height` to resize your video to something other than its native dimensions, you can instead use encoding software to specify the resolution.

See Also

Mark Pilgrim's "Dive Into HTML5" (see *http://diveintohtml5.info/video.html*), which provides very detailed instructions about using many of the encoding tools available, and CSS Pixel at *http://www.emdpi.com/csspixel.html*.

5.4 Displaying a Placeholder Image Before Video Plays

Problem

You want to display a still frame, or poster image, before the user starts the video.

Solution

Add the `poster` attribute with the placeholder image file path as the value:

```
<video controls width="640" height="360" poster="video_still.png">
    <source src="video.mp4" type="video/mp4" />
    <source src="video.ogv" type="video/ogg" />
    Your device does not support HTML5 video.
</video>
```

Discussion

Poster images can be a nice user enhancement, especially when the video doesn't load or can't be displayed.

Consider a single-source *.mp4* video viewed in Firefox, as shown in Figure 5-2.

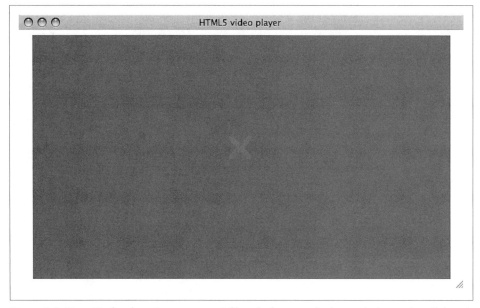

Figure 5-2. Since Firefox doesn't support .mp4 files, the browser displays a dark gray box if there is no poster image specified

Unfortunately, different browsers handle poster images differently:

- Firefox stretches the image to fill the dimensions of the player (see Recipe 5.3).
- Chrome keeps the image at its original size.
- Safari displays the poster image until the video data is loaded, at which point it displays the first frame from the video. If the poster image is a different size from the video, the video is resized to match the aspect ratio of the poster image (see Figure 5-3).

Figure 5-3. Safari 5 resizes the video to match the aspect ratio of the poster image, making it important to ensure your images are sized correctly

See Also

John Foliot points out the lack of accessibility of the **poster** attribute in a blog post at *http://john.foliot.ca/the-current-problem-with-the-poster-attribute-of-the-video-element/* . Keep this limitation in mind when using **poster**.

5.5 Making Video Loop

Problem

You want your video playback to loop automatically.

Solution

Add the `loop` Boolean attribute to `video`:

```
<video controls width="640" height="360" loop>
    <source src="video.mp4" type="video/mp4" />
    <source src="video.ogv" type="video/ogg" />
    Your device does not support HTML5 video.
</video>
```

Discussion

As of this writing, Firefox does not support `loop` unless the user has the Media Loop add-on (*https://addons.mozilla.org/en-US/firefox/addon/media-loop-45730/*) installed. All other browsers will loop natively.

That said, use `loop` *thoughtfully*. Consider how your users will experience a video that loops and whether that experience will be appropriate for your particular video and pleasant for your audience.

autoplay

Another `video` attribute you should judiciously consider before implementing is the Boolean `autoplay`. Just as when it is used with `audio` (see Recipe 4.2), `autoplay` starts playing the video as soon as the page loads. This can make for an extremely unpleasant user experience.

See Also

Not all Firefox users will know about the Media Loop add-on, much less have it installed. If you desperately need looping to work across all browsers, you can consider a JavaScript-based solution: *http://forestmist.org/2010/04/html5-audio-loops/*.

5.6 Sample Design: Manipulating Video with <canvas>

Problem

You want to embed a video from YouTube, but you want a better preview of how the video might appear than the default selection key (see Figure 5-4).

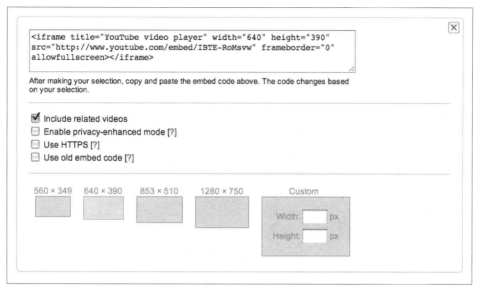

Figure 5-4. When selecting which size video you want to embed, YouTube offers static illustrations that lack context

Solution

In this Sample Design, we use canvas (see Chapter 9) to create a better and more contextual preview of what video may look like at different sizes (see Figure 5-5).

Add <video> and <canvas>

To start, reuse the markup used in this chapter for video, and add a button to trigger the drawing, as well as two canvas elements: one for a medium preview and one for a small one.

To each element, assign a unique id:

```
<video id="origVideo" width="640" height="360">
    <source src="video.mp4" type="video/mp4" />
    <source src="video.ogv" type="video/ogg" />
    Your device does not support HTML5 video.
</video>

<button title="Generate Preview" onclick="generatePreview();">Generate
    Preview</button>

<canvas id="previewMed"></canvas>
<canvas id="previewSm"></canvas>
```

Figure 5-5. Using scaling, different sizes of the single video instance are drawn on the canvas in Firefox

Generate preview

Next, create a function to generate the preview and set the JavaScript variables for the video and canvas elements:

```
<script>
    function generatePreview(){
        var video = document.getElementById('origVideo');
        var canvas1 = document.getElementById('previewMed');
        var context1 = canvas1.getContext('2d');
        var canvas2 = document.getElementById('previewsSm');
        var context2 = canvas2.getContext('2d');
```

Note that the variables to specify the 2D context for each canvas drawing state are also declared.

Set preview dimensions

Next, define the dimensions for each of the canvas drawings in the function:

```
canvas1.width = 320;
canvas1.height = 180;
canvas2.width = 160;
canvas2.height = 90;
```

Add an event listener

Then add an event listener to trigger the canvas drawing upon video play:

```
video.addEventListener('play', function(){
    drawVideo(this,context1,context2);
},false);
```

and close out the function:

```
    video.play();
}
```

Draw previews

Lastly, add the function that draws each of the canvas previews:

```
function drawVideo(video,canvas1,canvas2) {
    if(video.paused || video.ended) return false;
    canvas1.drawImage(video,0,0,320,180);
    canvas2.drawImage(video,0,0,160,90);
    setTimeout(drawVideos,25,video,canvas1,canvas2);
}
</script>
```

This function first checks to see if the video is playing:

```
if(video.paused || video.ended) return false;
```

If so, we use drawImage with scaling to draw a canvas image that is half the size of the original video:

```
canvas1.drawImage(video,0,0,320,180);
```

and a second canvas that is half the size of previewMed:

```
canvas2.drawImage(video,0,0,160,90);
```

The scaling parameters in these examples are:

```
object.drawImage(source,x,y,width,height);
```

where *x* and *y* represent the top-left corner of the image on the target canvas, and *width* and *height* are the image's size on the target canvas.

Finally, tell drawPreviews to call itself every 25 milliseconds, which roughly equals 40 frames per second (1000ms / 40fps = 25):

```
setTimeout(drawVideos,25,video,canvas1,canvas2);
```

Discussion

Here's the complete markup and script for this example:

```
<video id="origVideo" width="640" height="360">
    <source src="video.mp4" type="video/mp4" />
    <source src="video.ogv" type="video/ogg" />
    Your device does not support HTML5 video.
</video>

<button title="Generate Preview" onclick="generatePreview();">Generate
    Preview</button>

<canvas id="previewMed"></canvas>
<canvas id="previewSm"></canvas>

<script>
    function generatePreview(){
        var video = document.getElementById('origVideo');
        var canvas1 = document.getElementById('previewMed');
        var context1 = canvas1.getContext('2d');
        var canvas2 = document.getElementById('previewsSm');
        var context2 = canvas2.getContext('2d');

        canvas1.width = 320;
        canvas1.height = 180;
        canvas2.width = 160;
        canvas2.height = 90;

        video.addEventListener('play', function(){
            drawVideo(this,context1,context2);
        },false);

        video.play();
    }

    function drawVideo(video,canvas1,canvas2) {
        if(video.paused || video.ended) return false;
        canvas1.drawImage(video,0,0,320,180);
        canvas2.drawImage(video,0,0,160,90);
        setTimeout(drawVideos,25,video,canvas1,canvas2);
    }
</script>
```

With native video offered through HTML5, web developers now have the ability to dive deep into a video file and make enhancements to the user experience that were once the domain of proprietary technologies.

See Also

HTML5 Doctor offers demos and detailed descriptions of other ways to use canvas and video together at *http://html5doctor.com/video-canvas-magic/*.

CHAPTER 6

Microdata and Custom Data

Kimberly Blessing

6.0 Introduction

One of the primary benefits of web standards, promoted for over 10 years by standards evangelists, was that more semantic markup would provide greater context and meaning to content.

By the mid 2000s, web standards were catching on, but the "standardistas" recognized that semantic markup alone was not enough to convey all meaning related to content—for example, that some content is personal data or that links may represent relationships.

To solve this problem, first came XFN (XHTML Friends Network, see *http://gmpg.org/xfn/*), and then microformats (see *http://microformats.org*). Both of these solutions relied on the `class` and `rel` attributes—both valid (X)HTML—but, because those attributes had more appropriate uses, some web professionals felt that using them to convey additional semantics was somewhat of a hack.

At about the same time, the W3C XHTML 2 Working Group created the RDFa specification, based on the Resource Description Framework, to enable reuse of existing XHTML attributes—and the addition of some new ones—to support structured machine-readable data.

Microformats, in particular, caught on quickly with web professionals. Web builders started using them to mark up personal information, resumes, event data, and even cooking recipes. Search engines picked up on this and began parsing the additional data found in microformats and RDFa to improve search results.

With HTML5, the web community has a renewed focus on strictly adhering to the specification. Rather than continuing to extend—some would say abuse—the `class` and `rel` attributes, HTML5 (at least via the WHATWG spec) introduces *microdata*, which gives us a new syntax for marking up these additional structured semantics.

In addition, HTML5 allows for *custom data attributes*, which further give web professionals a standards-compliant way for embedding additional data in their markup.

The markup aspects of these features work in browsers today, but the associated DOM APIs to interact with them are not yet (microdata) or widely (custom data) supported by user agents. Still, given that it is possible to write JavaScript to interact with the additional data, there's little reason *not* to use them.

When to Use Microdata Versus Custom Data

Similar to microformats and RDFa, microdata is used to mark up structured data. It introduces new attributes that can be applied to any element in order to identify scoped name/value pairs. As with microformats, shared vocabularies are emerging to standardize how data is marked up, so microdata can be used to share data across websites and applications.

Custom data attributes are just that: *custom*. You, the programmer, create attributes using the `data-` prefix and assign them values. The name/value pairs are related to the displayed content, but are not themselves displayed. Because you define the attributes according to the needs of your website or application, these are not to be used to exchange data with another site, nor do public search engines consume them.

 Should you use microdata or RDFa for your structured data? Ongoing W3C discussions about whether or not two overlapping standards should exist have some concerned about the future of these specifications. Google, Microsoft, and Yahoo!, meanwhile, are promoting microdata and have teamed up to create Schema.org, a shared vocabulary of data structures that allows their search engines to extract more meaning from your data.

For an excellent comparison of microdata, RDFa, and microformats, read Manu Sporny's detailed analysis at *http://manu.sporny.org/2011/uber-comparison-rdfa-md-uf/*.

6.1 Adding Microdata to Markup

Problem

You want to add microdata to convey additional meaning or semantics about your content so that machine-parsing tools can access this information.

Solution

Use the `itemscope` and `itemprop` attributes, along with descriptive property names, to label your content:

```
<p itemscope>
    <span itemprop="inventor">Tim Berners-Lee</span> created the
    <span itemprop="invention">World Wide Web</span>.
</p>
```

Discussion

The `itemscope` attribute is used to identify the scope of the microdata item—an *item* being a set of name/value pairs. The `itemprop` attribute values define the property names and their associated values—in this case, the contents of the `span` tags. Thus, this example yields the following name/value pairs:

- Inventor: Tim Berners-Lee
- Invention: World Wide Web

This is a very basic example. In the next recipe, we'll look at an example that implements a standardized vocabulary.

See Also

The `itemprop` attribute in the HTML5 specification at *http://www.w3.org/TR/html5/ microdata.html#names:-the-itemprop-attribute*.

6.2 Using Microdata and Schema.org

Problem

You want to convey additional meaning about your content—for example, that the content identifies a person—so that popular search engines can extrapolate this data.

Solution

In addition to using the `itemscope` and `itemprop` attributes, specify an `itemtype` and apply the appropriate property names from the Schema.org vocabulary:

```
<section itemscope itemtype="http://schema.org/Person">
    <h1 itemprop="name">Tim Berners-Lee</h1>
    <img itemprop="image"
        src="http://www.w3.org/Press/Stock/Berners-Lee/2001-europaeum-eighth.jpg">
    <p>
        <span itemprop="jobTitle">Director</span>,
        <span itemprop="affiliation" itemscope
            itemtype="http://schema.org/Organization" itemprop="name">World Wide
            Web Consortium</span>
    </p>
```

```
    <p itemprop="address" itemscope itemtype="http://schema.org/PostalAddress">
        <span itemprop="addressLocality">Cambridge</span>,
        <span itemprop="addressRegion">MA</span>
    </p>
    <a itemprop="url" href="http://www.w3.org/People/Berners-Lee/">Website at
        W3C</a>
</section>
```

Discussion

The start of this microdata item is again indicated by the use of `itemscope` on the `section` element, but also added to this element is the `itemtype` attribute. Use `item type` with a URL in order to identify the item data type. In this case, we're using the Schema.org structure to identify a person.

As in the previous recipe, the `itemprop` attribute is applied with property names to give meaning to the content in the markup. By looking at the properties and pairing them with the content, we can tell that "Tim Berners-Lee" is a person's name and that this person's job title is "Director."

The use of `itemprop` for both the image and URL properties works a bit differently: the corresponding values in these cases are the `src` and `href` attribute values, respectively. If you've worked with microformats in the past, this concept won't be new to you.

A final special case in this example can be seen with the affiliation and address `item prop` attributes. Here, new items are nested inside of the main item. In both cases, the `itemprop` not only identifies the property that is directly related to the person item but, within the same tag, also establishes the property as an item itself with the `itemscope` attribute. Going one step further, `itemtype` is also applied to indicate the URL that describes the item data type.

While this might seem a bit complicated at first, it's not much different from combining multiple microformats (like hCard and hCalendar on a resume) or creating an XML object to represent nested data.

Whether you've worked on projects like this before or not, there is an easy way to check to see that you're making progress in applying the Schema.org vocabularies: you can use the Google Rich Snippets Testing Tool (available at *http://www.google.com/web masters/tools/richsnippets*) to validate that your structured data markup can be parsed, as shown in Figure 6-1.

> Before Google, Microsoft, and Yahoo! created Schema.org, Google was promoting Rich Snippets based on its own vocabulary at *http://data-vo cabulary.org*. Google's documentation for Rich Snippets is still live, but every page features a link to Schema.org.

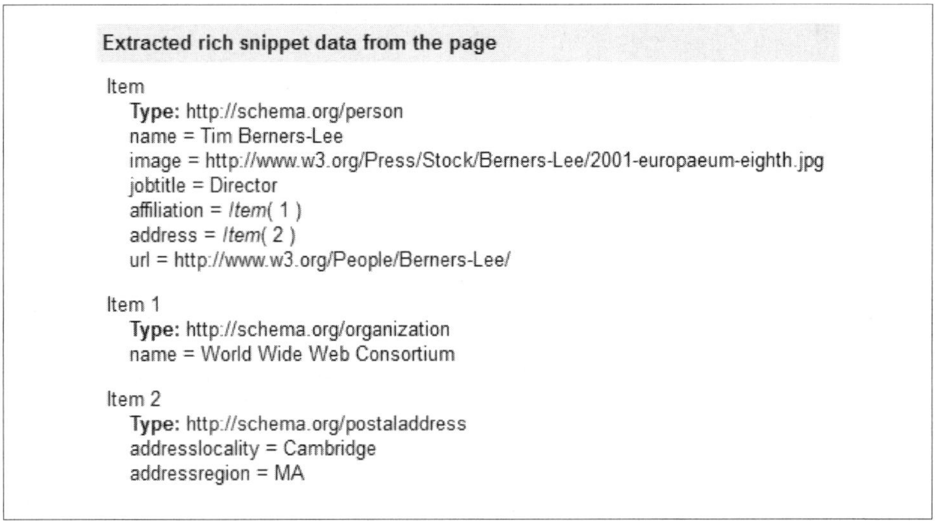

Figure 6-1. Google Rich Snippets Testing Tool results

See Also

For additional data types that are recognized by search engines, along with sample code, see *http://schema.org*. To learn more about microdata, see HTML5 Doctor's Microdata article (*http://html5doctor.com/microdata/*) and Mark Pilgrim's chapter from "Dive Into HTML5" (see *http://diveintohtml5.info/extensibility.html*), which also details Google Rich Snippets.

6.3 Adding Custom Data to Markup

Problem

You want to attach additional data to your content that is not displayed to the user.

Solution

Define your own `data-` attributes to name and store the information:

```
<h1>My Volkswagens</h1>
<ul>
    <li data-year="1996" data-color="white" data-engine="VR6">Cabrio</li>
    <li data-year="1993" data-color="purple" data-engine="VR6">Corrado</li>
    <li data-year="2008" data-color="red" data-engine="2.0T">Eos</li>
    <li data-year="2003" data-color="blue" data-engine="W8">Passat</li>
</ul>
```

Discussion

Since not everyone cares about VWs or cars, there's a lot of detail we need not provide—like the year, color, and engine type of each VW. With custom data attributes, we can include such extraneous data in the markup without requiring readers to look at it.

> The data is now stored in the HTML; read the subsequent recipes in this chapter to learn what else you can do with this data.

In order to store the year, color, and engine type of each car, in this example we created three custom data attributes: `data-year`, `data-color`, and `data-engine`.

As you can see, they all start with `data-` followed by at least one character. The name you define may not include uppercase letters, but it can include hyphens. You could, for example, define a `data-model-year` attribute, but `data-modelYear` would not be allowed.

> If your custom data attributes have additional hyphens in the name, you need to convert them to camel case names when using the dataset API—for example, `data-foo-bar` would be referred to as `dataset.fooBar`. But if you're using `getAttribute()` or `setAttribute()`, you will still reference it as `data-foo-bar`.

Even though we use the three custom attributes consistently in this example, we haven't created any special relationships by using them together—for example, we could list another car and apply only a `data-color` attribute, or we could go on to list airplanes that we've flown and reuse the `data-engine` attribute. It's up to you, the programmer, to maintain structure or define the namespace you need for your website or application.

See Also

HTML5 Doctor's discussion about custom data attributes at *http://html5doctor.com/html5-custom-data-attributes/*.

6.4 Accessing Custom Data with JavaScript

Problem

You want to access the custom data in your page and execute some logic based on the data.

Solution

Start with the same markup as that in Recipe 6.3, but add a paragraph for JavaScript output:

```
<h1>My Volkswagens</h1>
<ul>
    <li data-year="1996" data-color="white" data-engine="VR6">Cabrio</li>
    <li data-year="1993" data-color="purple" data-engine="VR6">Corrado</li>
    <li data-year="2008" data-color="red" data-engine="2.0T">Eos</li>
    <li data-year="2003" data-color="blue" data-engine="W8">Passat</li>
</ul>
<p></p>
```

Access the custom data using the **dataset** API:

```
<script>
    var cars = document.getElementsByTagName("li");
    var output = "What color are Kimberly's cars? ";

    for (var i=0; i < cars.length; i++) {
        output += cars[i].dataset.color;
        if (i != (cars.length-1)) {
            output += ", "
        }
    }

    document.getElementsByTagName("p")[0].innerHTML = output;
</script>
```

Discussion

With the introduction of custom data attributes, HTML5 also defines the dataset DOM API. This is a simple and easy way of accessing any custom data associated with any element.

The JavaScript is straightforward: we create an array of all list items (**cars**), and we create a string that is inserted into the paragraph (**output**). As we iterate over the **cars** array, we use **dataset.color** to access the value of each **data-color** attribute and append it to the **output** variable. The end result is the phrase "What color are Kimberly's cars? White, purple, red, blue" being added to the paragraph at the end of the list.

Not all browsers yet support the dataset API (see Table 6-1), but accessing custom data attributes in all browsers is easy. Where dataset is not supported, simply use getAttribute(). Here's the `for` loop using fallback logic and getAttribute() when necessary:

```
for (i=0; i < cars.length; i++) {
    if (cars[i].dataset) {
        output += cars[i].dataset.color;
    } else {
        output += cars[i].getAttribute("data-color");
    }
    if (i != (cars.length-1)) {
        output += ", "
    }
}
```

Table 6-1. Dataset API support

IE	Firefox	Chrome	Safari	Opera	iOS	Android
—	6+	7+	5.1+	11.1+	—	—

 To keep up with dataset API support, check *http://caniuse.com/dataset* regularly.

See Also

The `itemprop` attribute in the HTML5 specification at *http://www.w3.org/TR/html5/microdata.html#names:-the-itemprop-attribute*.

6.5 Manipulating Custom Data

Problem

You want to manipulate existing custom data in your page or add custom data to your page.

Solution

Let's build on the code from Recipe 6.4. We'll use the same markup to start:

```
<h1>My Volkswagens</h1>
<ul>
    <li data-year="1996" data-color="white" data-engine="VR6">Cabrio</li>
    <li data-year="1993" data-color="purple" data-engine="VR6">Corrado</li>
    <li data-year="2008" data-color="red" data-engine="2.0T">Eos</li>
    <li data-year="2003" data-color="blue" data-engine="W8">Passat</li>
</ul>
<p></p>
```

and use the dataset API to modify and create our custom data, along with `setAttri bute()` for fallback support:

```
<script>
    var cars = document.getElementsByTagName("li");
    for (var i=0; i < cars.length; i++) {
        if (cars[i].dataset) {
            cars[i].dataset.color = "yellow";
            cars[i].dataset.rating = "awesome";
        } else {
            cars[i].setAttribute("data-color", "yellow");
            cars[i].setAttribute("data-rating", "awesome");
        }
    }

    var output = "What color are Kimberly's cars? ";

    for (var i=0; i < cars.length; i++) {
        if (cars[i].dataset) {
            output += cars[i].dataset.color;
        } else {
            output += cars[i].getAttribute("data-color");
        }
        if (i != (cars.length-1)) {
            output += ", "
        }
    }

    document.getElementsByTagName("p")[0].innerHTML = output;
</script>
```

Discussion

Once you know how to access custom data, manipulating it is pretty easy. If you can use the dataset API, just assign the new value to the desired attribute; otherwise, fall back to using `setAttribute()`. This same method allows you to add new custom data attributes, as well.

In this example, we've decided to repaint all of the cars yellow using JavaScript. Looping through the list items, we access `dataset.color` (or use `setAttribute()` to access `data-color`) and assign a new value of `"yellow"`.

We also use JavaScript to add a rating for each of the cars. In that same loop, we create `data-rating` by applying a value of `"awesome"` to `dataset.rating` (or use `setAttri bute()` to do the same).

If you need to remove a custom data attribute, you can do so by setting its value to `null`. You can verify that the DOM is being manipulated by using a tool such as Opera Dragonfly, as shown in Figure 6-2.

See Also

The `dataset` specification at *http://dev.w3.org/html5/spec/Overview.html#dom-dataset*.

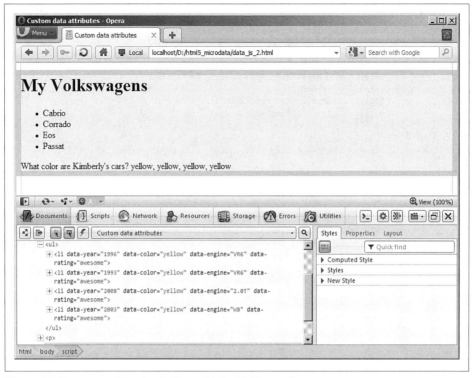

Figure 6-2. Dataset modification in Opera 11.1 with Dragonfly

6.6 Example: Creating a Map Application Using Custom Data

Problem

You want to generate markers on a map using custom data attributes.

Solution

Store the latitudes and longitudes of the locations you wish to show on the map in separate custom data attributes. Then write JavaScript to access those datasets and render markers on the map:

```
<!DOCTYPE html>
<html>
<head>
    <title>Map example</title>
    <script type="text/javascript"
            src="http://maps.google.com/maps/api/js?sensor=false"></script>
    <style type="text/css">
        #map { height:500px; width:500px; border:1px solid #000; }
    </style>
```

```
</head>
<body>
<h1>Ice Cream in Philadelphia</h1>
<ul>
    <li><a data-lat="39.9530255" data-long="-75.1596066"
        href="http://www.bassettsicecream.com/">Bassetts Ice Cream</a></li>
    <li><a data-lat="39.949888" data-long="-75.161717"
        href="http://www.capogirogelato.com/">Capogiro Gelateria</a></li>
    <li><a data-lat="39.949556" data-long="-75.1428795"
        href="http://www.franklinfountain.com/">Franklin Fountain</a></li>
</ul>

<div id="map"></div>

<script>
    var map_options = {
        zoom: 15,
        center: new google.maps.LatLng(39.95, -75.152),
        mapTypeId: google.maps.MapTypeId.HYBRID
    };

    var map = new google.maps.Map(document.getElementById("map"), map_options);

    var locations = document.getElementsByTagName("a");
    for (var i=0; i < locations.length; i++) {
        var latitude, longitude;
        if (locations[i].dataset) {
            latitude = locations[i].dataset.lat;
            longitude = locations[i].dataset.long;
        } else {
            latitude = locations[i].getAttribute("data-lat");
            longitude = locations[i].getAttribute("data-long");
        }
        locations[i][i] = new google.maps.Marker({
            position: new google.maps.LatLng(latitude, longitude),
            title: locations[i].innerHTML,
            map: map
        });
    }
</script>
</body>
</html>
```

Discussion

You already know how to define custom data, so the list of anchors containing data-latitude and data-longitude attributes should be old hat by now.

Creating a Google Map using the Google APIs is very easy—just call the API in the document head, create an element to house the map in the body, then call a script that defines your map options and triggers its rendering.

After the script triggers the drawing of the map, it then accesses the latitude-longitude positions and uses them to render markers on the map.

Example: The jQuery data() method

The jQuery library has provided support for accessing and manipulating custom data since version 1.4.3. This support was updated in jQuery 1.6 to conform to changes in the HTML5 specification; use this version of jQuery if possible (see *http://www.web monkey.com/2011/05/jquery-update-improves-html5-data-tools/*).

Using the jQuery data() method is straightforward. Let's return to an earlier example to see how it works:

```
<ul>
    <li data-year="1996" data-color="white" data-engine="VR6">Cabrio</li>
</ul>

<script>
    alert($("li").data("year"));   // alerts "1996"
    alert($("li").data("engine")); // alerts "VR6"

    // let's repaint the car again
    $("li").data("color", "yellow");

    // and add the rating data
    $("li").data("rating", "awesome");
</script>
```

The jQuery data() method successfully reads the data-year and data-engine attributes defined in the markup, but if you access data-color via the dataset API or examine the DOM object, you neither see its value turn yellow nor find a data-rating attribute, as you did in Recipe 6.5:

```
<script>
    alert($("li").data("color")); // alerts "yellow"
    alert(document.getElementsByTagName("li")[0].dataset.color); // alerts "white"
</script>
```

While jQuery reads in the data from the custom data attributes, it does not write this data back to the DOM; instead, it stores the data in a JavaScript object. This speeds up applications where a lot of data access or manipulation is performed. However, if you forget this difference and try to also use the dataset API in your application, you will encounter some unexpected results.

See Also

A small sampling of applications utilizing microdata:

- PaintbrushJS by Dave Shea: *http://mezzoblue.github.com/PaintbrushJS/demo/inde7 .html*
- Dynamic Google Analytics Tagging by Jason Karns: *http://jasonkarns.com/blog/ 2010/03/10/google-analytics-tagging/*
- SXSW 2010 Parties site by Christopher Schmitt, Kyle Simpson, Stephanie Sullivan, and Zoe Gillenwater: *http://www.sxswcss3.com*

CHAPTER 7

Accessibility

Anitra Pavka

7.0 Introduction

"Disability" is a broad term. Major categories of disabilities that affect use of the Web include visual, hearing, cognitive, speech (especially on mobile devices), and motor disabilities. A single category of disability may manifest in many forms. For example, *visual disability* includes, but is not limited to, red-green color blindness.

 About 7 to 10% of all men have trouble differentiating between red and green colors.

People may have varying degrees of disability and even multiple disabilities. Like a broken wrist or an amputation, disabilities can be temporary or permanent. And permanent disabilities may be present from birth or start later in life.

In short, anyone can become disabled.

The Purpose of Accessibility

Web accessibility is about removing barriers that prevent people from using the Web. In fact, one could say accessibility is at the heart of the Web in that its goal is to break down barriers of communication.

According to the World Wide Web Consortium (see *http://www.w3.org/standards/web design/accessibility*):

> The Web is fundamentally designed to work for all people, whatever their hardware, software, language, culture, location, or physical or mental ability. When the Web meets this goal, it is accessible to people with a diverse range of hearing, movement, sight, and cognitive ability.

Web coding and markup is a critical part of removing barriers. But done incorrectly, it can erect more barriers.

The hardware and software used to access web content constitute the rest of the solution. The user agent, such as a browser, and any assistive technology, such as a screen reader that reads aloud web content, must be able to accurately interpret and present to users the web content or functionality that you have coded.

Accessibility Guidelines

Fortunately, there are published guidelines to provide direction to web designers and developers. If you work on government or publicly funded websites, you may implement local or federal guidelines such as U.S. Section 508.

You may also be familiar with phrases like the W3C Web Accessibility Initiative (WAI) or W3C Web Content Accessibility Guidelines (WCAG). The W3C WAI updated the original WCAG. WCAG 2.0 became a W3C recommendation in December 2008, nine years after the first version was released. These guidelines provide an international set of recommendations on how to make web content more accessible and usable to people with a variety of disabilities.

WCAG 2.0 uses the acronym POUR to summarize the four principles of web accessibility. POUR stands for Perceivable, Operable, Understandable, and Robust:

Perceivable
> Means that the content is available to the senses, usually sight or hearing. That means you've done things like provide text alternatives for images, provide captions for audio and video, and include sufficient contrast between the text and the background.

Operable
> Ensures that people can use or interact with the website, including navigation, content, forms, and dynamic controls.

Understandable
> Means that the text is legible and the site behaves in consistent, predictable ways.

Robust
> Defines the page's markup and coding as working in a variety of user agents and assistive technologies.

The W3C WAI also authored WAI-ARIA 1.0 (Accessible Rich Internet Applications). ARIA provides a way to add semantic meaning to Ajax-like, dynamic web content and custom widgets by defining a set of roles and the states and properties of those roles.

In other words, ARIA allows you to programmatically communicate to assistive technologies what is displayed to sighted users as the page changes in response to user actions, rather than just what is present in the original page markup.

This is becoming increasingly important: a SecuritySpace Technology Penetration Report found that as of January 2010 over 64% of websites included JavaScript (see *http://www.securityspace.com/s_survey/data/man.200912/techpen.html*).

The work of ARIA specification is still being done, and while support is fairly robust and always improving, there are bugs and incomplete support in user agents to contend with.

The good thing is that *implementing* ARIA doesn't have to be hard. It's definitely not harder than building cross-browser, custom JavaScript widgets. And you're already doing that, right?

7.1 Writing Appropriate alt Text Descriptions

Problem

You want to add a text alternative for an image.

Solution

Add the text alternative programmatically using the `alt` attribute of the image.

If an image deserves a text alternative that can be summed up in one to two sentences (or about 75 words or less), set that text as the value of the `alt` attribute:

```
<img src="next_button.jpg" alt="Go to the next page.">
```

Alternative text should not exceed 150 characters.

How do you know how well the alternative text works? A good rule of thumb is, "If you replace every image on the page with its text alternative, the page conveys the same meaning as when the images are displayed."

If the image is complex, like a chart or diagram, and cannot be simply summarized, include the additional information adjacent to the image or link the image to a longer, more detailed text alternative:

```
<a href="diagram_desc.html"><img src="diagram.jpg" alt="Diagram that shows how
    to assemble the item with a link to the assembly instructions"></a>
```

If providing additional information beyond an `alt` attribute, ensure that the text is updated whenever changes are made to the associated image.

Multiple images

If you need to reference multiple text alternative sources for an image to make sense and all of that content is on the same web page, use the ARIA `aria-labelledby` or `aria-describedby` attributes to reference the text alternatives, as these ARIA attributes can accept multiple references.

In this example, the `aria-describedby` attributes in the `img` element reference its associated values to `id` attributes in the descriptive `h1` and `p` elements:

```
<h1 id="johnny1">Johnny throwing cake at his Mom while Dad ducks behind her</h1>
<p id="johnny2">Johnny's poor Mom is smeared with cake. Well, that shirt is
    ruined!</p>
...
<img src="johnny_1st_bd.jpg" aria-describedby="johnny1 johnny2" alt="Johnny's
    first birthday party">
```

Until user agents and assistive technologies better support `figure` and `figcaption` elements, use the `aria-labelledby` attribute to associate an image enclosed in the `figure` element with its caption.

Add the `aria-labelledby` attribute to the `img` element and add its associated value to an `id` attribute of the `figcaption` element:

```
<figure>
    <img src="ceremony_photo.jpg" aria-labelledby="figcaption123">
    <figcaption id="figcaption123">
        Opening ceremony for the new library building at the state university.
    </figcaption>
</figure>
```

Discussion

A text alternative for a nontext element such as an image is not necessarily a *description*. Instead, a text alternative should strive to serve the same purpose and present the same information, serving as a replacement for the nontext element.

Providing a text alternative for nontext elements is required to comply with WCAG 2.0. However, at the time of writing, the `alt` attribute is not technically required in HTML5.

Regardless, it's recommended to use the `alt` attribute whenever possible for images. Any decision to remove it, make it a null value, or use another method of providing text alternatives must be a conscious and carefully considered one.

Apply these best practices when writing the text alternatives for images:

- Include all content (text) that appears in the image.
- Consider the context of the image to help determine what is important about it.
- If it is relevant, convey the purpose or function of the image.
- Avoid including information that is available as text near the image.

- Avoid including phrases such as "image of" or "picture of."
- Be concise.

Null alt attribute

A null `alt` attribute is an `alt` attribute whose value contains no spaces or content. It is not the same as omitting the `alt` attribute:

```
<img src="border_decoration.jpg" alt="">
```

Adding a null or empty `alt` attribute to an image is appropriate in the following situations:

- The image is purely decorative.
- A text alternative is available immediately adjacent to the image. However, this is not a valid suggestion if the image is also a link.
- The image is one of a group of images that form a larger picture, and one of the other images already has the text alternative for the entire picture.
- The image is not meant to be seen by users (e.g., a 1-pixel image that counts page views).

 Alternative text is also not necessary when you use `background-image` CSS properties to add a purely decorative image to the web page instead of using an `img` element.

The following CSS rule associates an image with a custom class, but the CSS could be associated with an HTML element, such as the `div` or `body` element:

```
.border {
    background-image: url(border_decoration.jpg);
    background-repeat: repeat-x;
}
```

Since assistive technology may completely ignore images that have a null `alt` attribute, assistive technology users will not be made aware of the existence of such images—which might be exactly what you want, since the image might be, as discussed, purely decorative without any substantive relation to the web page's message.

However, if you omit the `alt` attribute altogether from the `img` element, the same assistive technologies announce that an image exists on the page and do their best to provide information about it, even if that information is only the filename. Keep in mind when considering whether to use a null `alt` attribute or omit the `alt` attribute that there is a difference in how some assistive technologies handle them.

Be advised that the `longdesc` attribute (see *http://www.w3.org/TR/REC -html40/struct/objects.html#adef-longdesc-IMG*) will likely be cut from HTML5. In its place, either link to a page with a longer text alternative or provide that content adjacent to the image, as described earlier in this recipe.

Using figcaption

In HTML5, an image may be enclosed in a `figure` element and the `figcaption` element may either provide the entire text alternative or supplement the text alternative provided in the image's `alt` attribute.

In practice, the `alt` attribute has and will continue to provide a more generic method for providing information about an image until such time that the `figcaption` element is well supported in browsers and assistive technologies.

As mentioned previously, some assistive technologies completely ignore images with an empty `alt` attribute. To make an image discoverable, omit the `alt` attribute if you do not plan to include a value for it:

```
<figure>
    <img src="ceremony_photo.jpg">
    <figcaption>
        Opening ceremony for the new library building at the state university.
    </figcaption>
</figure>
```

See Also

"HTML5: Techniques for providing useful text alternatives" at *http://dev.w3.org/html5/ alt-techniques/*.

7.2 Identifying Abbreviations and Acronyms

Problem

You want to identify to users what an abbreviation or an acronym represents.

Solution

Include the *full* expansion of the abbreviation in the page content.

Usually, one encloses the abbreviation in parentheses after the full expansion. Include this at least the first time that the abbreviation appears on the page:

Web Content Accessibility Guidelines **(WCAG)** 2.0 was released as a World Wide
Web Consortium **(W3C)** recommendation in December 2008.

Using abbr

Use the abbr element to programmatically associate the full expansion with the abbreviation. The abbr element is an inline element that can be used within block elements
or other inline elements:

```
<p><abbr title="Web Content Accessibility Guidelines">WCAG</abbr> 2.0 was
released as a <abbr title="World Wide Web Consortium">W3C</abbr> recommendation
in December 2008.</p>
```

If the abbreviation is plural or possessive, ensure that the content within the abbr element matches what is included in the title attribute, as shown in Figure 7-1:

```
<p><abbr title="National Aeronautics and Space Administration">NASA</abbr>'s
mission <abbr title="Space Transportation System">STS</abbr>-133 is the last
flight scheduled for Space Shuttle Discovery.</p>
```

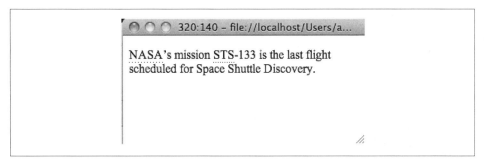

Figure 7-1. Abbreviations with a bottom border

Discussion

As noted in Recipe 1.13, the acronym element is deprecated in HTML5. This eliminates
the XHTML quandary of when it is appropriate to use the abbr or the acronym element:
the abbr element simply covers both.

Styling abbr

It's recommended to style the abbr element so that sighted users have a visual cue that
there is additional content available to them. The default styling for abbr in the Opera
and Firefox browsers displays an underline (a dotted bottom border) beneath the text.
You can add this effect in Safari, Chrome, and Internet Explorer 8 with a single line of
CSS:

```
abbr { border-bottom: 1px dotted black;}
```

When the user hovers the mouse over the abbreviation, most browsers display the full
expansion of the abbreviation.

An *abbreviation* is the shortened form of a word or phrase, such as "CSS" or "etc." An *acronym* is a type of abbreviation: it's a new word that's formed from the initial letters of a series of words. You pronounce those letters as a single word, such as "NASA" or "NATO."

See Also

For IE8 and below, see the WHATWG Blog's "Supporting New Elements in IE" workaround at *http://blog.whatwg.org/supporting-new-elements-in-ie*.

7.3 Identifying Sections of a Page Using ARIA Landmark Roles

Problem

You need a way to distinguish common sections of web content.

Solution

Add ARIA "landmarks" to enhance recognition of HTML5 elements in assistive technologies.

Since HTML5 is not supported by most assistive technologies (as of the printing of this book), you can add ARIA landmark roles to help provide meaning to these new HTML elements, as shown in Figure 7-2. The ARIA roles and HTML5 elements that are often associated together are listed below. These are *not* hard and fast rules, but helpful suggestions. Use your best judgment.

ARIA roles

Add the `banner` role to the page `header` (which typically contains the logo/name and other site-specific information). Use this role only once per document or web application:

```
<header role="banner">
```

Add the `complementary` role to the `aside` element. Both are designed to mark up content that is somewhat related to the main content. Do not use this role or element for content that is completely separate and unrelated:

```
<aside role="complementary">
```

Add the `navigation` role to each `nav` element:

```
<nav role="navigation">
```

Add the `form` role to any `form` element, unless the form contains search functionality:

```
<form role="form">
```

Add the search role to a site's search form:

```
<form role="search">
```

The contentinfo role identifies information about the page content, such as copyright and privacy terms. Use this role only once per document or web application. If your footer contains only this type of information, associate the role with the footer element:

```
<footer role="contentinfo">
    <p>Copyright 2011</p>
</footer>
```

If you have a "fat footer" with lots of other content or links, enclose the contentinfo material in a container element (like a div or a p) and assign the contentinfo role to the container:

```
<footer>
...
    <p role="contentInfo">Copyright 2011</p>
...
</footer>
```

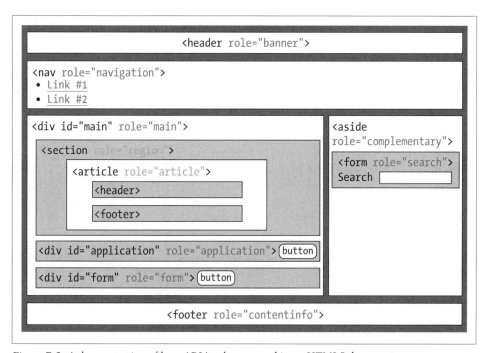

Figure 7-2. A demonstration of how ARIA roles are used in an HTML5 document

Roles for web apps

Some ARIA landmark roles, such as application and main, are unique and do not map directly to specific HTML5 elements.

Add the `application` role to an HTML element that contains a web application instead of normal web content. Ensure that the HTML element associated with this role encompasses the entire web application. This role may instruct assistive technology to enter a mode that is more appropriate for interacting with web application functionality. You may add the `document` role to the page after the application to indicate where nonapplication web content resumes:

```
<div role="application">
...
</div>
```

Add the `main` role to an HTML element that contains the primary content of the document, such as `article`s, `div`s, etc.:

```
<div role="main">
```

In the future, this solution might provide an alternative to "skip to main content" or "skip navigation" links. In other words, this role may provide a way for assistive technology users to jump directly to the page's primary content and avoid going through long lists of links and content that are repeated on every page in the site.

If an article is the central content on a page, add the `main` role to the `article` element:

```
<article role="main">
```

Discussion

ARIA extends the accessibility of HTML. Assistive technologies can use ARIA landmark roles to identify and navigate to sections of content. These roles help provide a more reliable and consistent user experience.

While you are allowed to have more than one `nav` element per page, only main blocks of navigational links should be enclosed in a `nav` element. The `footer` element is an example of where links may exist that do not need a `nav` element—the `footer` element alone may be sufficient. Of course, if you create a "fat footer" like that on the W3C site (*http://www.w3.org*), it would be appropriate to use the `nav` element in the footer.

 For more information about "fat footer" design, see the UI Patterns website at *http://ui-patterns.com/patterns/FatFooter*.

See Also

Summary of screen reader bugs with HTML5 elements combined with ARIA landmark roles at *http://www.accessibleculture.org/research/html5-aria* and workarounds for some assistive technology bugs at *http://www.accessibleculture.org/blog/2010/11/html5 -plus-aria-sanity-check/*.

7.4 Creating More Accessible Navigation Links

Problem

You want to mark up your navigational links in a way that will benefit the most users.

Solution

Enclose the list of navigational links inside the HTML5 nav element. Use an unordered list for the links if they can be visited in any order:

```
<nav role="navigation">
    <ul>
        <li><a href="#">Home</a></li>
        <li><a href="#">About</a></li>
        <li><a href="#">Blog</a></li>
        <li><a href="#">Portfolio</a></li>
    </ul>
</nav>
```

Or, if the sequence of the links is important, use an ordered list to mark up the navigational links:

```
<nav role="navigation">
    <ol>
        <li><a href="#">Chapter 1</a></li>
        <li><a href="#">Chapter 2</a></li>
        <li><a href="#">Chapter 3</a></li>
    </ol>
</nav>
```

Next, add a "skip navigation" link:

```
<div id="offscreen"><a href="#maincontent">Skip to the main content</a></div>
...
<nav role="navigation">
    <ul>
        <li><a href="#">Home</a></li>
        <li><a href="#">About</a></li>
        <li><a href="#">Blog</a></li>
        <li><a href="#">Portfolio</a></li>
    </ul>
</nav>
...
<article id="maincontent" role="main">
...
```

This link may be placed before the navigation or closer to the top of the page, depending on how much content appears before the navigation. Its purpose is to provide keyboard and assistive technology users a way to go directly to the main content on the page.

Discussion

A list, whether unordered or ordered, is generally considered the most appropriate HTML element to use for groups of navigational links. This has been the case ever since Christopher Schmitt first did it (see *http://www.alistapart.com/articles/practicalcss/*).

This markup can convey to assistive technology users how many navigational items are in the list and how far down the list the user is.

In the future, you might not need to add an ARIA role or skip links. The user agent and assistive technology should recognize each section element and allow users to jump between page sections. That is, in that future, all you would need is this:

```
<nav role="navigation">
    <ul>
        <li><a href="#">Home</a></li>
        <li><a href="#">About</a></li>
        <li><a href="#">Blog</a></li>
        <li><a href="#">Portfolio</a></li>
    </ul>
</nav>
...
<article>
```

Purpose of skipping links

The skip links prevent users from repeatedly going through the content and links that are listed on every page of a site. This is a critical addition to sites with long lists of links, such as news or ecommerce sites.

The easiest way to add a skip link is to add an anchor text link. The exact location on the screen doesn't matter, as long as the link is the first element in the page's tab order and the link anchor is placed where the main content of the page begins.

Hiding skip to main content links

If you need to "hide" the skip link from sighted users, use CSS to position the text off the screen (before you do this, consider that sighted keyboard users may be confused because the text for the link will not be visible but the user will be able to tab to the link):

```
.offscreen {
    left: -9999em;
    position: absolute;
    top: auto;
    overflow: hidden;
    width: 1px;
    height: 1px;
}
```

Avoid using `display:none` for hiding skip links as screen readers might ignore the links altogether.

Instead of hiding the skip link, consider using CSS to stylize the link to match your design. Or, better yet, have your skip link become visible with keyboard focus (see *http://webaim.org/temp/skipcss3.htm*).

See Also

Recipe 7.3, and the article on using "skip navigation" links at *http://webaim.org/techniques/skipnav/*.

7.5 Associating Form Fields with Their Labels

Problem

You need to identify the text label associated with each form field.

Solution

Use the `label` element to programmatically associate text with its form field. The value of the label's `for` attribute must match the value of the form field's `id` attribute. This `id` value must be unique on each page:

```
<label for="fName">First Name</label>
<input type="text" id="fname">
```

Do not include label elements for form fields of the type `hidden`.

Multiple labels

Add the ARIA `labeledby` or `describedby` attributes if the form field needs multiple labels or descriptions for it to make sense. Both of these attributes can accept references to multiple values. Add a space between each value:

```
<form>
    <fieldset>
        <legend>Account Logout</legend>
        <span id="labelAutoLogout">Automatically log out after</span>
        <input id="autoLogout" type="text" value="30"
                aria-labelledby="labelAutoLogout labelAutoLogoutTime"
                aria-describedby="autoLogoutDesc">
        <span id="labelAutoLogoutTime">minutes of inactivity</span>
        <p id="autoLogoutDesc">Allows you to customize the timeout period for
            each of your accounts.</p>
    </fieldset>
</form>
```

Discussion

The label element provides a caption for the associated form field. The label element is best for simple forms, while ARIA is better suited to form fields that need multiple labels or whenever the label element isn't an option.

Keep in mind that a main difference between aria-labelledby and aria-describedby is that labels are intended to be *concise* while descriptions may be *wordier* and include more detail.

See Also

The HTML5 label specification at *http://dev.w3.org/html5/markup/label.html.*

7.6 Grouping Form Fields Logically

Problem

You need to group related fields within a form.

Solution

Add the fieldset element around each group of related form fields, and add a legend as the first element within the fieldset. The legend represents a caption or title for the group of fields:

```
<form>
    <fieldset>
    <legend>Movie Rating</legend>
    <p><input type="radio" name="rating" id="rating1">
    <label for="rating1">Excellent</label></p>
    <p><input type="radio" name="rating" id="rating2">
    <label for="rating2">Good</label></p>
    <p><input type="radio" name="rating" id="rating3">
    <label for="rating3">Fair</label></p>
    <p><input type="radio" name="rating" id="rating4">
    <label for="rating4">Poor</label></p>
    </fieldset>
</form>
```

Do your best to keep the legend text brief.

Some assistive technologies announce the legend before the label for every field in the fieldset. That could get quite repetitive.

Discussion

Using the `fieldset` element to organize form fields helps users understand the purpose of the form and what's related. A `fieldset` may also be used to group sets of radio buttons or checkboxes.

The `legend` and `fieldset` can both be styled using CSS. By default, most browsers display a solid one-pixel border around the `fieldset` and the legend appears in the upper-left corner of the container, overlaying the border, as shown in Figure 7-3.

Figure 7-3. The default appearance of fieldset and legend in Opera 11

Another benefit of grouping form fields using the `fieldset` element is that the flow, or ordering, of the form should make sense to keyboard users. Unless you do something like modify the `tabindex` values, the tab order of a form usually follows the order that the fields appear in in the source code.

The field order used to be more of a problem when tables were used for form layout. The use of CSS for layout has greatly mitigated this problem because the fields can be listed in a logical order in the source code and then positioned on the screen, independent of the code order.

See Also

"Making Elements Focusable with Tabindex" at *http://snook.ca/archives/accessibility_and_usability/elements_focusable_with_tabindex* and the HTML5 `fieldset` specification at *http://dev.w3.org/html5/markup/fieldset.html*.

7.7 Enabling a fieldset Dynamically

Problem

You want to disable the fields in a `fieldset` and dynamically enable them when some other condition is met, such as the user selecting a radio button or checkbox.

Solution

Add the `fieldset` and `legend` elements around a group of related form fields that will be hidden. Note that `fieldset`s can be nested.

Add the `disabled` attribute on the two nested `fieldset` elements. Add an `onchange` event to each radio button to trigger the change:

```
<form>
    <fieldset>
        <legend>Store Credit Card</legend>
        <p><label>Name displayed on your card:<input name="fullName"
            required></label></p>
        <fieldset name="accountNum" disabled>
            <legend>
                <label>
                    <input type="radio" name="accountType"
                        onchange="form.accountNum.disabled = !checked;
                        form.accountLetters.disabled=checked">My account is a
                        12-digit number
                </label>
            </legend>
            <p><label>Store card number: <input name="cardNum"
                required></label></p>
        </fieldset>
        <fieldset name="accountLetters" disabled>
            <legend>
                <label>
                    <input type="radio" name="accountType"
                        onchange="form.accountLetters.disabled = !checked;
                        form.accountNum.disabled=checked">My account includes
                        letters and numbers
                </label>
            </legend>
            <p><label>Store card code: <input name="cardLetters"></label></p>
        </fieldset>
    </fieldset>
</form>
```

If the radio button is not selected, everything inside the nested `fieldset` will be disabled.

Selecting a radio button removes the `disabled` attribute on that `fieldset` to make the associated input field editable and adds the `disabled` attribute to the `fieldset` associated with the other radio button.

Discussion

While there are other ways to dynamically enable form fields, this method is one future possibility that takes advantage of the new `disabled` attribute added for `fieldset`s in HTML5.

Depending on how user agents support the `disabled` attribute, you may need to add scripts that dynamically set the `disabled` attribute on the `fieldset` instead of hardcoding the attribute.

See Also

The W3C's HTML5 Edition for Web Authors draft on forms at *http://dev.w3.org/html5/spec-author-view/forms.html*.

7.8 Identifying Required Form Fields

Problem

You want to indicate to users visually and programmatically which form fields are required.

Solution

If every field is required, include text instructions at the top of the form informing users that everything's required. This works fine if the form is short.

Write out required

If you need to accommodate internationalization (IL8N) or users with low vision, place the label on a separate line. Include (`Required`) within each `label` element for required fields:

```
<p><label for="fName">First Name (Required)</label></p>
<p><input type="text" id="fname"></p>
```

If the design dictates that the label and field must be on the same line, add an image icon within the `label` element. Set the value of the image `alt` attribute as `Required`:

```
<label for="fName">
    <img src="required-icon.jpg" alt="Required">
    First Name
</label>
<input type="text" id="fname">
```

Using ARIA

If the design dictates that the label and field must be on the same line, add an image icon within the `label` element. Set the value of the image `alt` attribute as `Required`, set the value of the image `role` attribute as `presentation`, and add the `aria-required="true"` attribute to the input field.

The required icon images can be left-aligned to make visual scanning easier for sighted users:

```
<label for="fName">
    <img src="required-icon.jpg" role="presentation" alt="Required">
    First Name
</label>
<input type="text" id="fname" aria-required="true">
```

Newer assistive technologies that support ARIA ignore the image icon because elements with the `presentation` role are intentionally ignored by (and not mapped to) accessibility APIs. However, they should recognize the `aria-required` attribute and announce that the field is required.

This solution also works for older assistive technologies that do not support ARIA, which ignore all of the ARIA attributes and instead provide the `alt` attribute of `Required` on the icon image.

Discussion

It may take a while until browsers and assistive technologies support the HTML5 `required` attribute on the `input` element.

The meaning of the `strong` element is changing in HTML5, though not substantially. It would still be appropriate to use it around the asterisk that represents a required field because typically required fields must contain values before the user proceeds.

The required attribute

What you probably wanted to see was the HTML5 `required` attribute on the `input` element, but browsers and assistive technologies do not currently support this. For sighted users, you could use CSS to style the appearance of the field, or you could add a styled asterisk so they can visually scan the screen for required fields:

```
<label for="fName">
    <strong>*</strong>
    First Name
</label>
<input type="text" id="fname" required>Discussion
```

See Also

"ARIA and Progressive Enhancement" by Derek Featherstone at *http://www.alistapart .com/articles/aria-and-progressive-enhancement* and "Future Web Accessibility: HTML5 `input` Extensions" at *http://webaim.org/blog/future-web-accessibility-html5-input-extensions*.

7.9 Using ARIA Live Regions to Announce When Dynamic Content Is Updating

Problem

You want to notify users when parts of the web page are dynamically updating.

Solution

First, assign the `aria-live` attribute to the HTML element where a content change or update may occur and decide on the urgency of communicating the update.

Then, select a standard live region role. Assign the role to the parent HTML element that contains the content that may change. If the default behaviors for the role are appropriate, you won't need to specify attributes:

```
<div role="alert">
```

The standard live region roles include:

alert
> Use this for a single, time-sensitive notification. It will be handled as an assertive live region and the update will appear immediately. An alert cannot receive focus, and therefore cannot be closed by the user.

alertdialog
> This type of alert message can receive focus. When the alert appears, you must automatically set focus on an active element in the alert dialog, such as an "OK" button. Include the `aria-describedby` attribute on that active element to point to the message in the dialog.

log
> Use this for things like message history or error logs: new information is added to the end of the log, and the oldest information may disappear.

marquee
> Use this for things like stock tickers or ad banners. This is similar to a log because the information presented may change frequently.

status
> Use this for a minor notification that does not warrant use of an alert. It will be handled as an assertive live region. A status should not receive focus. If a different part of the page drives the status changes, use the `aria-controls` attribute to identify the relationship.

timer
> Use this to display time elapsed or remaining. Update the timer at fixed intervals, unless the timer is paused or has reached the end of its count.

If you need something other than the standard ARIA live region roles and behaviors, you can create a custom live region.

Custom live regions

First, identify where a content change or update may occur and decide how urgently the update needs to be communicated.

Next, assign the `aria-live` attribute to the parent HTML element that contains the content that may change. The value for the `aria-live` attribute will reflect how quickly the update will be communicated to users. The available values are:

- `aria-live="off"`, where the update is not announced
- `aria-live="polite"`, where the update is announced when the user is idle or finishes with his current activity
- `aria-live="assertive"`, where the update is announced as soon as possible, even if it means interrupting the user's current task

Avoid using `aria-live="assertive"` unless it's critical to communicate the change immediately. Users may consider the disruption jarring and rude.

As in a polite conversation where people wait until there is a pause to chime in, the `aria-live="polite"` indicates a change when there is a break in the user experience.

So, let's start with fleshing out a `div` element:

```
<div aria-live="polite">
```

Then we need to decide how much context is required for the user to understand the update. If the entire live region must be presented for the change to make sense, assign the `aria-atomic` attribute with the value of `true` to the HTML element.

Repeating unchanged information may become redundant or make it harder to distinguish what portion has changed. If you want to communicate *only* the change and that change makes sense on its own, assign the `aria-atomic` attribute with the value of `false` to the HTML element:

```
<div aria-live="polite" aria-atomic="false">
```

Finally, identify the type of update. Assign the `relevant` attribute to the HTML element. The types of update are:

- `relevant="additions"`, where new nodes are added to the DOM
- `relevant="removals"`, where nodes are removed from the DOM
- `relevant="text"`, where changes occur to the text within existing nodes

You may assign multiple values to the relevant attribute by adding a space between values:

```
<div aria-live="polite" aria-atomic="false" relevant="additions removals text">
```

In fact, the default behavior should be `relevant="additions text"`. This reflects the most common type of changes.

Discussion

ARIA live regions provide a standardized way to alert assistive technology that a DOM change has occurred and tell it how to handle the change.

You may also prevent updates from being announced until all of the changes in a live region finish updating by changing the live region's state. You do this by dynamically setting the attribute state (`aria-busy="true"`) and then clearing it when the updates are ready to be announced. This might be useful when multiple updates in a live region need to be announced together to make sense.

See Also

You can find the WAI-ARIA 1.0 Roles Model at *http://www.w3.org/WAI/PF/aria/roles*, the WAI-ARIA 1.0 Authoring Practices 5.2.1. Live Region Properties and How to Use Them at *http://www.w3.org/WAI/PF/aria-practices/#liveprops*, and some ARIA live regions test examples at *http://test.cita.illinois.edu/aria/live/live1.php*. The Juicy Studio Accessibility toolbar for Firefox to examine ARIA live regions is available at *https://addons.mozilla.org/en-US/firefox/addon/juicy-studio-accessibility-too/*.

CHAPTER 8

Geolocation

Christopher Deutsch and Marc Grabanski

8.0 Introduction

The W3C Geolocation API allows for scripted access to geographical location information associated with a device's browser. In this chapter we'll first cover how to access this API and then dive into some examples of what you can do with this data using Google Maps and other third-party libraries like SimpleGeo.

All of the examples in this chapter use jQuery (see *http://jquery.com*), which can easily be included using a `script` tag in one of two ways. There is no need to download the *jquery.js* file; your web page can use the version hosted on Google's Content Delivery Network (CDN):

```
<script src="//ajax.googleapis.com/ajax/libs/jquery/1.6.4/jquery.js"></script>
```

And, just in case a call to the file across the Internet isn't available, a fallback to a local copy of the jQuery file can come right afterward in a second `script` element that checks for the previous copy's successful inclusion:

```
<script src="//ajax.googleapis.com/ajax/libs/jquery/1.6.4/jquery.js"></script>
<script>window.jQuery || document.write("<script
    src='js/libs/jquery-1.6.4.min.js'>\x3C/script>")</script>
```

8.1 Getting Basic Geolocation Data

Problem

You want to find the location of the user's Internet device.

Solution

Use the new HTML5 Geolocation API to get the user's location when she clicks a button and output the values to the web page, as shown in Figure 8-1.

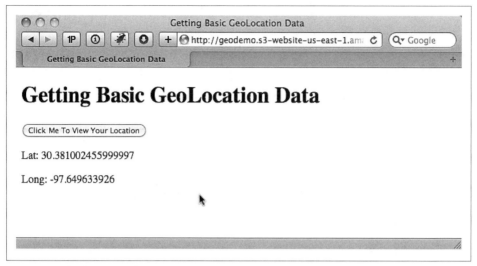

Figure 8-1. The latitude and longitude coordinates determined natively through the browser

Start by adding an input button to the page:

```
<input type="button" id="go" value="Click Me To View Your Location" />
```

Next, add the following JavaScript to handle the button's click event, access the Geo-location API, and output the results:

```
<script>
$(document).ready(function () {
    // wire up button click
    $('#go').click(function () {
        // test for presence of geolocation
        if (navigator && navigator.geolocation) {
            navigator.geolocation.getCurrentPosition(geo_success, geo_error);
        } else {
            error('Geolocation is not supported.');
        }
    });
});

function geo_success(position) {
    printLatLong(position.coords.latitude, position.coords.longitude);
}

// The PositionError object returned contains the following attributes:
// code: a numeric response code
// PERMISSION_DENIED = 1
// POSITION_UNAVAILABLE = 2
// TIMEOUT = 3
// message: Primarily for debugging. It's recommended not to show this error
// to users.
function geo_error(err) {
    if (err.code == 1) {
        error('The user denied the request for location information.')
```

```
        } else if (err.code == 2) {
            error('Your location information is unavailable.')
        } else if (err.code == 3) {
            error('The request to get your location timed out.')
        } else {
            error('An unknown error occurred while requesting your location.')
        }
    }

    // output lat and long
    function printLatLong(lat, long) {
        $('body').append('<p>Lat: ' + lat + '</p>');
        $('body').append('<p>Long: ' + long + '</p>');
    }

    function error(msg) {
        alert(msg);
    }
    </script>
```

Discussion

The `navigator` object gives us access to the new `geolocation` object. The `geolocation` object has the following methods:

- `getCurrentPosition()` returns the user's current position.
- `watchPosition()` returns the user's current position, but also continues to monitor the position and invoke the appropriate callback every time the position changes.
- `clearWatch()` ends the `watchPosition()` method's monitoring of the current position.

When determining the location of the Internet device, first check that the user's browser supports the Geolocation feature natively. If it does, call the `getCurrentPosition()` method:

```
if (navigator && navigator.geolocation) {
    navigator.geolocation.getCurrentPosition(geo_success, geo_error);
} else {
    error('Geolocation is not supported.');
}
```

Since this method executes asynchronously, pass it two callback functions: `geo_suc cess` and `geo_error`. The error callback is passed a **position error** object that contains a `code` and a `message` property. The `code` can be one of the following:

0   Unknown

1   Permission Denied

2   Position Unavailable

3   Timeout

The success callback is passed a `position` object that contains a `coordinates` object and a timestamp. The `coordinates` object contains the following:

- `latitude`, which is specified in decimal degrees
- `longitude`, which is specified in decimal degrees
- `altitude`, which is specified in meters above the ellipsoid
- `accuracy`, which is specified in meters
- `altitudeAccuracy`, which is specified in meters
- `heading`, which is the direction of travel specified in degrees
- `speed`, which is specified in meters per second

Of those seven, only three are guaranteed to be there: `latitude`, `longitude`, and `accuracy`.

For the solution, take the `latitude` and `longitude` and append them to the body of the web page using jQuery:

```
function printLatLong(lat, long) {
    $('body').append('<p>Lat: ' + lat + '</p>');
    $('body').append('<p>Long: ' + long + '</p>');
}
```

See Also

The W3C Geolocation specification at *http://dev.w3.org/geo/api/spec-source.html*.

8.2 Getting Basic Geolocation Data with a Fallback

Problem

You want to determine a user's Internet location when that user's browser does not support the HTML5 Geolocation API natively.

Solution

Perform an IP-to-location lookup as a fallback. It's certainly not as accurate as latitude and longitude coordinates, but it's far better than not having any location data at all.

Google versus MaxMind

Google offers the `google.loader.ClientLocation` object in its Google Maps API v3 library, but it does not work for many US IP addresses.

The MaxMind GeoIP JavaScript Web Service seems more accurate and up-to-date. Also, it's free as long as you link back to the *http://www.maxmind.com* website. Alternatively, MaxMind offers a JavaScript attribution-free license that can be purchased for $250/year.

Coding the solution

Modify our previous example to use MaxMind as a fallback. Start by adding the Java-Script library to the page:

```
<script src="http://j.maxmind.com/app/geoip.js"></script>
```

Then add the MaxMind fallback:

```
$(document).ready(function () {
    // wire up button click
    $('#go').click(function () {
        // test for presence of geolocation
        if (navigator && navigator.geolocation) {
            // make the request for the user's position
            navigator.geolocation.getCurrentPosition(geo_success, geo_error);
        } else {
            // use MaxMind IP to location API fallback
            printLatLong(geoip_latitude(), geoip_longitude(), true);
        }
    });
});

// output lat and long
function printLatLong(latitude, longitude, isMaxMind) {
    $('body').append('<p>Lat: ' + latitude + '</p>');
    $('body').append('<p>Long: ' + longitude + '</p>');
    // if we used MaxMind for location, add attribution link
    if (isMaxMind) {
        $('body').append('<p><a href="http://www.maxmind.com" target="_blank">IP
            to Location Service Provided by MaxMind</a></p>');
    }
}

function geo_error(err) {
    // instead of displaying an error, fall back to MaxMind IP to location library
    printLatLong(geoip_latitude(), geoip_longitude(), true);
}
```

> When calling `printLatLong()` using MaxMind, pass in an extra `true`
> parameter.

Discussion

Instead of showing an error if `navigator` or `navigator.geolocation` is undefined, use the `geoip_latitude()` and `geoip_longitude()` functions that the MaxMind JavaScript library provides to retrieve the user's latitude and longitude.

If you look at the source of the MaxMind *geoip.js* file, you'll see that it has already translated your IP address into location data. MaxMind creates a dynamic JavaScript file by reading the IP address that made the HTTP request, doing the IP-to-location translation on the server side, and then outputting the results.

In addition to latitude and longitude, the location data shown in Table 8-1 is available.

Table 8-1. Location data examples from MaxMind geoip.js

Method	Description	Example data
geoip_country_code()	Country Code	US
geoip_country_name()	Country Name	United States
geoip_city()	City	Minneapolis
geoip_region_name()	Region	MN
geoip_region_name()	Region Name	Minnesota
geoip_postal_code()	Postal Code	55401
geoip_area_code()	Telephone Area Code	612
geoip_metro_code()	Metro Code	613

The free version of MaxMind requires attribution in the form of a link back to the website, so the `isMaxMind` parameter has been added to the `printLatLong()` function to indicate that MaxMind was used to get the location:

```
function printLatLong(latitude, longitude, isMaxMind) {
    $('body').append('<p>Lat: ' + latitude + '</p>');
    $('body').append('<p>Long: ' + longitude + '</p>');
    // if we used MaxMind for location, add attribution link
    if (isMaxMind) {
        $('body').append('<p><a href="http://www.maxmind.com" target="_blank">IP
            to Location Service Provided by MaxMind</a></p>');
    }
}
```

 Another scenario to be mindful of is if the user denies your request for location information or something else goes wrong. To handle this eventuality, set up the geo_error handler to also fall back to using IP-to-location translation, as shown in the next recipe.

Because we've added MaxMind as a fallback, this solution is able to handle a larger percentage of browsers and devices without having to rely on native geolocation support in the browser.

See Also

MaxMind provides free/open source geolocation solutions for city, country, and IP lookups at *http://www.maxmind.com/app/ip-location*.

8.3 Reverse Geocoding an Address with Latitude and Longitude

Problem

You want to convert latitude and longitude coordinates into a human-friendly address.

Solution

Use the Google Maps JavaScript API to turn latitude and longitude into an address, as shown in Figure 8-2.

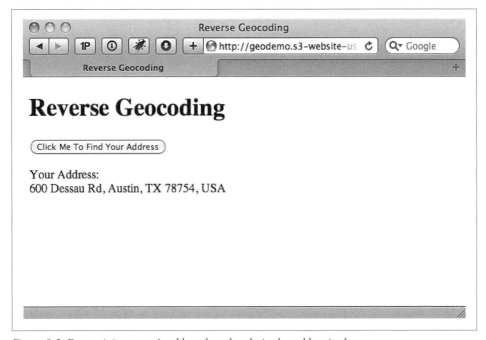

Figure 8-2. Determining a user's address based on latitude and longitude

The process of turning geographic data like a street address and zip code into geographic coordinates such as latitude and longitude is called *geocoding* (we'll get to this in the next recipe). Doing the opposite, turning coordinates into an address, is called *reverse geocoding*.

Begin by adding the needed scripts to your web page:

```
<script src="http://ajax.googleapis.com/ajax/libs/jquery/1.6.2/jquery.js">
</script>
<script src="http://j.maxmind.com/app/geoip.js"></script>
<script src="http://maps.google.com/maps/api/js?sensor=false"></script>
```

Add a button to trigger getting the user's coordinates and looking up the address:

```
<input type="button" id="go" value="Click Me To Find Your Address" />
```

and then add the JavaScript to handle the button click and getCurrentPosition() success callback:

```
$(document).ready(function () {

    // wire up button click
    $('#go').click(function () {
        // test for presence of geolocation
        if (navigator && navigator.geolocation) {
            // make the request for the user's position
            navigator.geolocation.getCurrentPosition(geo_success, geo_error);
        } else {
            // use MaxMind IP to location API fallback
            printAddress(geoip_latitude(), geoip_longitude(), true);
        }
    });


    function geo_success(position) {
        printAddress(position.coords.latitude, position.coords.longitude);
    }

    function geo_error(err) {
        // instead of displaying an error, fall back to MaxMind IP to location library
        printAddress(geoip_latitude(), geoip_longitude(), true);
    }

    // use Google Maps API to reverse geocode our location
    function printAddress(latitude, longitude, isMaxMind) {
        // set up the Geocoder object
        var geocoder = new google.maps.Geocoder();

        // turn coordinates into an object
        var yourLocation = new google.maps.LatLng(latitude, longitude);


        // find out info about our location
        geocoder.geocode({ 'latLng': yourLocation }, function (results, status) {
            if (status == google.maps.GeocoderStatus.OK) {
                if (results[0]) {
                    $('body').append('<p>Your Address:<br />' +
                        results[0].formatted_address + '</p>');
                } else {
                    error('Google did not return any results.');
                }
            } else {
                error("Reverse Geocoding failed due to: " + status);
            }
        });

        // if we used MaxMind for location, add attribution link
        if (isMaxMind) {
```

```
            $('body').append('<p><a href="http://www.maxmind.com" target="_blank">IP
                to Location Service Provided by MaxMind</a></p>');
        }
    }

    function error(msg) {
        alert(msg);
    }
```

Discussion

Get the coordinates from `getCurrentPosition()` and pass them to a `printAddress()` function, which uses the Google Maps API to do the reverse geocoding.

The `printAddress()` function begins by creating a new Google `Geocoder` object. The `Geocoder` object gives us access to the `geocode()` method, which can take in a variety of options and return information based on them.

In our case, we're using the `google.maps.LatLng()` method to create a new Google `LatLng` object that is passed into `geocode()` in order to get the address. The `geocode()` method is asynchronous, just like `getCurrentPosition()`, so we define an inline Java-Script function to handle the callback.

The callback's response contains two parameters, one for the results and the other for the `status` code. If the `status` is `OK`, then it's safe to parse the array of `GeocoderRe sults` objects stored in the `results` variable. The `results` variable is an array since `Geocoder` may return more than one entry.

Next, check for a `GeocoderResults` object in the first position of the array and, if it exists, append the `formatted_address` property to the web page's body.

See Also

For more information about reverse geocoding, see *http://code.google.com/apis/maps/documentation/javascript/services.html#ReverseGeocoding*.

8.4 Converting an Address into Latitude and Longitude

Problem

You want to turn an address into latitude and longitude coordinates.

Solution

Use the Google Maps JavaScript API V3 to turn an address into latitude and longitude, as shown in Figure 8-3. This is called *geocoding*.

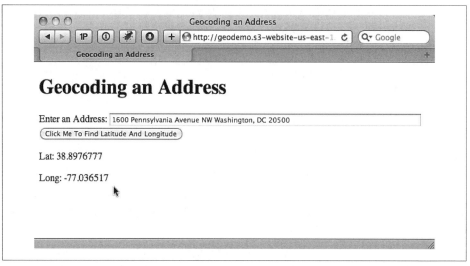

Figure 8-3. Determining latitude and longitude based on a human-friendly address

To begin, include 1.6.4 and the Google Maps JavaScript API V3 in the web page:

```
<script src="http://ajax.googleapis.com/ajax/libs/jquery/1.6.2/jquery.js">
</script>
<script src="http://maps.google.com/maps/api/js?sensor=false"></script>
```

The HTML5 Geolocation API can only return the user's location in coordinates, so let the user enter his address via an input text field:

```
<div>
    <label for="address">Enter an Address:</label>
    <input type="text" id="address" />
</div>
<div>
    <input type="button" id="go" value="Click Me To Find Latitude And Longitude"/>
</div>
```

The JavaScript below handles the button click, reading the input from the user, and calls the Google API to geocode the address:

```
$(document).ready(function () {

    // wire up button click
    $('#go').click(function () {
        // get the address the user entered
        var address = $('#address').val();
        if (address) {
            // use Google Maps API to geocode the address
            // set up the Geocoder object
            var geocoder = new google.maps.Geocoder();
            // return the coordinates
            geocoder.geocode({ 'address': address }, function (results, status) {
                if (status == google.maps.GeocoderStatus.OK) {
```

```
                    if (results[0]) {
                        // print results
                        printLatLong(results[0].geometry.location.lat(),
                            results[0].geometry.location.lng());
                    } else {
                        error('Google did not return any results.');
                    }

                } else {
                    error("Reverse Geocoding failed due to: " + status);
                }
            });
        }
        else {
            error('Please enter an address');
        }
    });

});

// output lat and long
function printLatLong(lat, long) {
    $('body').append('<p>Lat: ' + lat + '</p>');
    $('body').append('<p>Long: ' + long + '</p>');
}

function error(msg) {
    alert(msg);
}
```

Discussion

When the user clicks the button, use jQuery to read the value and validate that it's not blank. Next, create an instance of the `Geocoder` object. In order to do so, call the `geo code()` method, but pass an `address` option instead of latitude and longitude:

```
// set up the Geocoder object
var geocoder = new google.maps.Geocoder();
// return the coordinates
geocoder.geocode({ 'address': address }, function (results, status) {
    ...
```

Then access the `geometry` property of the `GeocoderResults` object. The `geometry` property contains a `location` property that can then be used to call the `lat` and `lng` methods to get our address's coordinates, which are then appended to the web page body in our `printLatLong()` function:

```
// print results
printLatLong(results[0].geometry.location.lat(), results[0].geometry.location.lng());
```

See Also

For more information about geocoding, see *http://code.google.com/apis/maps/documen tation/geocoding/*.

8.5 Getting Directions from the Current Location

Problem

You want to get directions from the user's current location to a specific address.

Solution

Use the Google Maps API to display the route the same way the Google Maps website would, and give the user the option to output the distance in miles or kilometers, as shown in Figure 8-4.

Figure 8-4. Determining the directions from a location

Use the jQuery and Google Maps JavaScript API V3 libraries:

```
<script src="http://maps.google.com/maps/api/js?sensor=false"></script>
<script src="http://j.maxmind.com/app/geoip.js"></script>
```

```
<script src="http://ajax.googleapis.com/ajax/libs/jquery/1.6.2/jquery.js">
</script>
```

The HTML is similar to the geocoding example in the previous recipe, with the addition of a drop-down box to select miles or kilometers. Also, instead of appending our results to the page body, we'll add a `div` to hold the calculated distance and a `div` to hold the Google Map:

```
<div class="field">
    <label for="address">Enter a Destination Address:</label>
    <input type="text" id="address" />
</div>

<div class="field">
    <label for="units">Units:</label>
    <select id="units">
        <option value="IMPERIAL">Miles</option>
        <option value="METRIC">Kilometers</option>
    </select>
</div>

<div>
    <input type="button" id="go" value="Get Directions" />
</div>

<div id="distance"></div>

<div id="map"></div>
```

We now need some JavaScript to do the following:

- Display a map of the United States on page load
- Handle the button click
- Get the user's current location
- Read the address input
- Pass the current location and address to the Google API to get the driving distance between the two locations
- Update the Google Map with the suggested driving route

The code looks like this:

```
// Google Maps globals:
var directionRenderer;
var directionsService = new google.maps.DirectionsService();
var map;

$(document).ready(function () {

    // Set up map starting point for Google Maps.
    // Set initial coords to latitude -92 and longitude 32, which is somewhere
    // around Kansas City in the center of the US, and then set the zoom to 4
    // so the entire US is visible and centered.
    var kansas = new google.maps.LatLng(32, -92);
```

```
            var myOptions = {
                zoom: 4,
                mapTypeId: google.maps.MapTypeId.ROADMAP,
                center: kansas
            }
            map = new google.maps.Map(document.getElementById("map"), myOptions);
            directionsRenderer = new google.maps.DirectionsRenderer();
            directionsRenderer.setMap(map);

            // wire up button click
            $('#go').click(function () {
                // Use our new getLatLng with fallback and define an inline function to
                // handle the callback.
                getLatLng(function (latitude, longitude, isMaxMind) {
                    // set the starting point
                    var start = new google.maps.LatLng(latitude, longitude);

                    // get the address the user entered
                    var address = $('#address').val();
                    if (address) {
                        // set end point
                        var end = $('#address').val();

                        // set the request options
                        var request = {
                            origin: start,
                            destination: end,
                            travelMode: google.maps.DirectionsTravelMode.DRIVING
                        };

                        // make the directions request
                        directionsService.route(request, function (result, status) {
                            if (status == google.maps.DirectionsStatus.OK) {

                                // Display the directions using Google's Directions
                                // Renderer.
                                directionsRenderer.setDirections(result);

                                // output total distance separately
                                var distance = getTotalDistance(result);
                                // output either miles or km
                                var units = $('#units').val();
                                if (units == 'IMPERIAL') {
                                    $('#distance').html('Total Distance: <strong>' +
                                        metersToMiles(distance) + '</strong> miles');
                                } else {
                                    $('#distance').html('Total Distance: <strong>' +
                                        metersToKilometers(distance) + '</strong> km');
                                }

                            } else {
                                error("Directions failed due to: " + status);
                            }
                        });
```

```
            }
            else {
                error('Please enter an address');
            }

            // if we used MaxMind for location, add attribution link
            if (isMaxMind) {
                $('body').append('<p><a href="http://www.maxmind.com"
                    target="_blank">IP to Location Service Provided by
                    MaxMind</a></p>');
            }
        });
    });

});

function getLatLng(callback) {
    // test for presence of geolocation
    if (navigator && navigator.geolocation) {
        // make the request for the user's position
        navigator.geolocation.getCurrentPosition(function (position) {
            // success handler
            callback(position.coords.latitude, position.coords.longitude);
        },
        function (err) {
            // handle the error by passing the callback the location from MaxMind
            callback(geoip_latitude(), geoip_longitude(), true);
        });
    } else {
        // geolocation not available, so pass the callback the location from
        // MaxMind
        callback(geoip_latitude(), geoip_longitude(), true);
    }
}

// return total distance in meters
function getTotalDistance(result) {
    var meters = 0;
    var route = result.routes[0];
    for (ii = 0; ii < route.legs.length; ii++) {
        // Google stores distance value in meters
        meters += route.legs[ii].distance.value;
    }
    return meters;
}

function metersToKilometers(meters) {
    return Math.round(meters / 1000);
}

function metersToMiles(meters) {
    // 1 mile = 1609.344 meters
    return Math.round(meters / 1609.344);
}
```

```
function error(msg) {
    alert(msg);
}
```

Discussion

To build out the solution, start by defining three global variables that are used to communicate with the Google API and to update our map div.

When the document loads, set the map of the US to be displayed. The Google Map object represents a map on your web page (you can have more than one).

Create a Map object by calling new google.maps.Map(document.getElementById("map"), myOptions), passing in the HTML element where you want to display the map and a Map options object.

There are many options that can be set, but the three used for this solution are zoom, mapTypeId, and center. The options are fairly descriptive as to their purpose. Set zoom to 4 to allow the user to see the entire US. For the mapTypeId, use ROADMAP, which displays the normal, default 2D tiles of Google Maps. The other options are SATELLITE, HYBRID, and TERRAIN. The center option indicates the location that is displayed in the center of the map.

The latitude and longitude of Kansas, which is a central location in the US, are hardcoded to create a LatLng object that can be used to set the center parameter. When the Map object is created using the new keyword it, automatically updates our map div.

The next line, directionsRenderer = new google.maps.DirectionsRenderer();, creates a new DirectionsRenderer object that can automatically update Maps for us. The line directionsRenderer.setMap(map); doesn't do anything yet, but it tells the user to enter an address and click the button.

In this example, refactored logic does a geolocation fallback in order to be a little more compact and reusable:

```
function getLatLng(callback) {
    // test for presence of geolocation
    if (navigator && navigator.geolocation) {
        // make the request for the user's position
        navigator.geolocation.getCurrentPosition(function (position) {
            // success handler
            callback(position.coords.latitude, position.coords.longitude);
        },
        function (err) {
            // handle the error by passing the callback the location from MaxMind
            callback(geoip_latitude(), geoip_longitude(), true);
        });
    } else {
        // geolocation not available, so pass the callback the location from
        // MaxMind
        callback(geoip_latitude(), geoip_longitude(), true);
    }
}
```

The getLatLng() function takes a single callback parameter that returns the latitude, longitude, and isMaxMind variables.

We check for the existence of navigator.geolocation just like we did before, but this time we define the navigator.geolocation callback handlers inline to call our common callback function. That returns either the results of getCurrentPosition() or the Max-Mind latitude and longitude.

For the button-click handler in the main example, we start by using the new get LatLng() function to collect the user's current location, which then is used to create a new LatLng object that we store in the start variable.

Next, we collect the address and store the text as a string in the end variable. To get the directions, we use the DirectionsService object that was created and stored into the global variable directionsService. The route() method of the DirectionsService object takes a DirectionsRequest object parameter and a callback method. The Direc tionsRequest object supports many options, but for this solution we only need to set the origin, destination, and travelMode options.

> We could make an API request to geocode the address and get its coordinates, but the Google API handles that automatically in the next step.

The origin and destination options can be either strings like the end variable, or the LatLng values. We set the travelMode option to DRIVING (the other options are WALKING or BICYCLING).

The route() method executes asynchronously, so we define a callback function that is passed a DirectionsResult object and a status code. We check the status variable to make sure the route() method finished successfully and then pass the result object to the DirectionsRenderer object, which updates the map with a highlighted driving route between our start and end locations.

To give you an idea of what is contained in the result variable, we pass it to the getTotalDistance() function, which is responsible for totaling the distance of the driv- ing route. The result object contains a routes property, which is an array of Direc tionsRoute objects. Each route indicates a way to get from the start to the end location. Usually only one route is returned, unless you set the provideRouteAlternatives option to true.

Our getTotalDistance() function only looks at the first route. Each DirectionsRoute object contains multiple properties, but the property needed is legs, which is an array of DirectionsLeg objects that defines a single leg of the journey between the start and end locations.

If the route does not contain any `waypoints`, it only has a single leg. Since waypoints were not defined here, the results should have a single leg, but for good measure we loop through each leg anyway.

Like the `route` object, the `leg` object also contains multiple properties, but the only one we need to access is the `distance` property, which contains a `DirectionsDistance` object. The `value` property of the `DirectionsDistance` object gives the total distance of the leg in meters. The loop adds up the distance of each leg and returns the total in meters.

Finally, we check the value of the units drop-down to find out if the user wanted the total distance in miles or kilometers. Then we call one of our helper functions `meter sToKilometers()` or `metersToMiles()` to convert meters into kilometers or miles, respectively, and output the value to the `distance div` element.

See Also

For more about getting directions from the Google Maps API, see *http://code.google .com/apis/maps/documentation/javascript/services.html#Directions*.

8.6 Example: Starbucks to Starbucks

Problem

You want to get directions from the nearest Starbucks to the next closest Starbucks.

Solution

Use SimpleGeo's Places API to find the closest Starbucks to the user's current location and then, once that location is set, make a second API call to SimpleGeo to find the next closest Starbucks location. Then use the Google Maps API to give directions from the first Starbucks to the second Starbucks.

To begin, add the SimpleGeo API to the collection of JavaScript libraries:

```
<script src="http://maps.google.com/maps/api/js?sensor=false"></script>
<script src="http://j.maxmind.com/app/geoip.js"></script>
<script src="http://ajax.googleapis.com/ajax/libs/jquery/1.6.2/jquery.js">
</script>
<script src="http://cdn.simplegeo.com/js/1.2/simplegeo.places.jq.min.js">
</script>
```

SimpleGeo is free, but it does require you to sign up to get an API key (see *http:// simplegeo.com*). Once you've signed up, you can find the API key by clicking the Tokens menu and then the JSONP Tokens submenu, as shown in Figure 8-5.

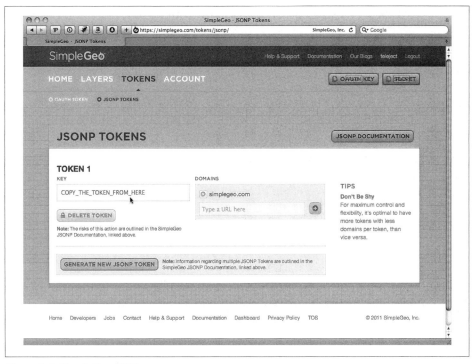

Figure 8-5. SimpleGeo API key

Add your website domain(s) to the allowed domains list. This prevents other people from using your API key. Now copy the key and replace the placeholder at the top of our sample's JavaScript:

```
// SimpleGeo globals:
var geoclient = new simplegeo.PlacesClient('REPLACE WITH YOUR API KEY');

// Google Maps globals:
var directionRenderer;
var directionsService = new google.maps.DirectionsService();
var map;

$(document).ready(function () {

    // Set up map starting point for Google Maps.
    // Set initial coords to latitude -92 and longitude 32, which is somewhere
    // around Kansas City in the center of the US, and then set the zoom to 4
    // so the entire US is visible and centered.
    var kansas = new google.maps.LatLng(32, -92);
    var myOptions = {
        zoom: 4,
        mapTypeId: google.maps.MapTypeId.ROADMAP,
        center: kansas
    }
    map = new google.maps.Map(document.getElementById("map"), myOptions);
```

```
        directionsRenderer = new google.maps.DirectionsRenderer();
        directionsRenderer.setMap(map);

        // wire up button click
        $('#go').click(function () {
            // Use our new getLatLng with fallback and define an inline function
            // to handle the callback.
            getLatLng(function (latitude, longitude, isMaxMind) {
                // use SimpleGeo to get closest Starbucks
                var query = "Starbucks";
                geoclient.search(latitude, longitude, { q: query, radius: 20,
                        num: 1 }, function (err, dataStart) {
                    if (err) {
                        error(err);
                    } else {
                        // We only asked for one result and SimpleGeo returns results
                        // based on distance so the closest is first, so make sure we
                        // got a result.
                        if (dataStart.features.length == 1) {
                            // save start coordinates and address
                            var startLat =
                                dataStart.features[0].geometry.coordinates[1];
                            var startLng =
                                dataStart.features[0].geometry.coordinates[0];
                            var startAddress =
                                dataStart.features[0].properties['address'];
                            // save in Google LatLng as well
                            var start = new google.maps.LatLng(startLat, startLng);

                            // look up the closest Starbucks to the one we just found
                            geoclient.search(startLat, startLng, { q: query, radius:
                                    20, num: 2 }, function (err, dataEnd) {
                                if (err) {
                                    error(err);
                                } else {
                                    // This time we asked for two results; the first
                                    // result should be the starting Starbucks,
                                    // so this time access the second result.
                                    if (dataEnd.features.length == 2) {
                                        // save end coordinates and address
                                        var endLat =
                                          dataEnd.features[1].geometry.coordinates[1];
                                        var endLng =
                                          dataEnd.features[1].geometry.coordinates[0];
                                        var endAddress =
                                          dataEnd.features[1].properties['address'];
                                        // save in Google LatLng as well
                                        var end = new google.maps.LatLng(endLat,
                                          endLng);

                                        // Now add directions from starting Starbucks
                                        // to ending one.
                                        // Set the request options:
                                        var request = {
                                            origin: start,
```

```
                    destination: end,
                    travelMode:
                      google.maps.DirectionsTravelMode.DRIVING
                };

                // make the directions request
                directionsService.route(request, function
                    (result, status) {
                    if (status ==
                      google.maps.DirectionsStatus.OK) {

                        // Display the directions using
                        // Google's Directions Renderer.
                        directionsRenderer.
                            setDirections(result);

                        // output info separately
                        $('#info').html('Closest Starbucks:
                            <strong>' + startAddress
                            + '</strong><br />' + 'Next
                            Starbucks: <strong>' + endAddress
                            + '</strong>');

                    } else {
                        error("Directions failed due to: " +
                            status);
                    }
                });
            }
            else {
                error('Could not find a Starbucks near ' +
                    startAddress);
            }
        }
    });

        }
        else {
            error('Could not find a Starbucks near you.');
        }
    }
});

// if we used MaxMind for location, add attribution link
if (isMaxMind) {
    $('body').append('<p><a href="http://www.maxmind.com"
        target="_blank">IP to Location Service Provided by
        MaxMind</a></p>');
}
    });
});

});
```

```
function getLatLng(callback) {
    // test for presence of geolocation
    if (navigator && navigator.geolocation) {
        // make the request for the user's position
        navigator.geolocation.getCurrentPosition(function (position) {
            // success handler
            callback(position.coords.latitude, position.coords.longitude);
        },
        function (err) {
            // handle the error by passing the callback the location from MaxMind
            callback(geoip_latitude(), geoip_longitude(), true);
        });
    } else {
        // geolocation not available, so pass the callback the location from
        // MaxMind
        callback(geoip_latitude(), geoip_longitude(), true);
    }
}

function error(msg) {
    alert(msg);
}
```

Discussion

Other than the call to `simplegeo.PlacesClient()` to set up SimpleGeo, the code starts off the same as the previous example.

In the click handler, we get the user's current location using the `getLatLng()` function and we use the resulting latitude and longitude to call the SimpleGeo `geoclient.search()` function to find the closest Starbucks to us. The `geoclient.search()` function takes in latitude and longitude parameters, our query options, and a callback function.

We set the query options to a search term (`q` param) of `Starbucks` within a 20-kilometer radius (`radius` param), and indicate that only one result (`num` param) is required.

The callback returns a `features` collection, which contains various information about each search result (including latitude and longitude). In the callback, we save the latitude, longitude, and address in variables as our starting location.

Then we make a second `geoclient.search()` call using the starting location as the reference point. This time it returns two results, since the first result is still the starting location. We store the second `feature` item's latitude, longitude, and address in the ending location variables.

Now that the start and end locations are set, we can use the same Google Maps API call as in the last example to display the driving directions between the two locations. To finish off the example, we display the starting and ending addresses above the map.

See Also

Create dynamic maps with datasets with a free JavaScript library at *http://polymaps.org*.

<canvas>

CHAPTER 9

Kyle Simpson

9.0 Introduction

One of the most exciting additions to web pages to be standardized by HTML5 is the canvas element:

```
<canvas id="mycanvas"></canvas>
```

This simple element allows users to draw graphics such as lines, circles, and fills directly into a rectangle-shaped block element that appears on the web page.

There are numerous features associated with the canvas element. For example, in addition to drawing images manually, browsers can take raw image data from an external image file and "draw" it onto the canvas element.

You can also erase and redraw all or a portion of the canvas image. The ability to edit canvas images lends itself to the creation of animations, where you appear to move elements around by drawing and redrawing them in varying positions.

In addition, canvas elements can have transparency, which means they can be layered or stacked on top of each other to create more sophisticated graphical images/effects. There are also a number of transformations and effects that you can apply to your canvas drawings. In essence, a canvas image is a dynamic image, unlike a static PNG or JPEG file.

In much the same way that you might draw an image using a graphics program like Adobe Photoshop, save it to a file, and load it into a web page, with canvas you can automate the drawing commands through code and immediately see the results on the page, without the need for loading an external file.

This capability allows you to do many sophisticated things that were once difficult or impossible to do, such as dynamically creating preview images.

While it is very helpful to understand the nuts and bolts of working with the canvas API, which this chapter will help expose you to, most practical projects use libraries that automate the usage of canvas for various tasks. As you will see, some of the tasks can be quite tedious, so using a helper library can be the key to keeping you productive and sane.

9.1 Drawing on a <canvas>

Problem

You want to draw graphic elements on your page rather than including them in as an external image with the img element.

Solution

Use the canvas element in your markup:

```
<canvas id="mycanvas"></canvas>
```

The canvas element can have "fallback" content inside the tag, which the browser will render only if canvas itself is not supported. While not a strong feature for accessibility purposes, this does provide a modest mechanism for alternate content that screen readers can make available to the user. (For more on accessibility, see Chapter 7.) Another approach would be to insert the canvas element inside figure element and provide alternative text through the figcaption (See Recipe 1.15). For more information on providing fallback content for canvas, see *http://www .w3.org/TR/2dcontext/#focus-management*.

Alternatively, you can create a canvas element dynamically, append it to the page, and then use CSS to position it where you need it:

```
var mycanvas = document.createElement("canvas");
mycanvas.id = "mycanvas";
document.body.appendChild(mycanvas);
```

To draw into the canvas element, first get a reference to the canvas element's context and then issue drawing commands against that reference:

```
var mycanvas = document.getElementById("mycanvas");
var mycontext = mycanvas.getContext("2d");

mycontext.beginPath();
mycontext.moveTo(10, 10);
mycontext.lineTo(35, 35); // draw a line path from (10,10) to (35,35)

mycontext.strokeStyle = "#000";
mycontext.stroke(); // draw the line
```

```
mycontext.beginPath();
mycontext.arc(35, 35, 10, 0, Math.PI * 2, true); // draw a circle

mycontext.fillStyle = "#f00";
mycontext.fill(); // fill the circle solid
```

Figure 9-1 shows the result of this code.

Figure 9-1. A <canvas> element on the page, with a black line and a red circle drawn on it

 In canvas, the order of how you draw things is important, as the last drawing operation for any pixel is the one that is visible. Here, we drew the line first and the circle second.

The canvas API

Here are some commonly used drawing commands in the canvas API:

beginPath()
> Start a path segment definition, to be used by a rendering operation like stroke() or fill().

closePath()
> Close the path by adding a line segment from the end of the path back to the beginning of the path.

moveTo(x, y)
> Move the registration point for the next relative drawing operation.

`lineTo(x, y)`
> Create a line path from the current registration point to (*x,y*).

`rect(x, y, width, height)`
> Create a rectangle path where (*x,y*) is one corner, and the diagonally opposite corner is (*x+width,y+height*).

`arc(x, y, radius, startAngleRadians, endAngleRadians, antiClockwiseDirection)`
> Create a circular arc path (up to a full circle), where (*x,y*) is the center of the arc and the arc starts and ends at the given angles (in radians) and moves in either a clockwise or counter-clockwise direction.

`fill()`
> Fill in the most recently defined path segment.

`stroke()`
> Stroke (i.e., render, make visible) the most recent path segment.

`drawImage(image, ...)`
> Draw an image into the `canvas` area.

`strokeText(text,...)`
`fillText(text,...)`
> Add text to the `canvas`.

`clearRect(x, y, width, height)`
> Clear a rectangular portion of the `canvas` from (*x,y*) to (*x+width,y+height*).

`strokeStyle=[string|object]`
`fillStyle=[string|object]`
> Set the color/style attributes for strokes or fills, respectively.

Discussion

The `canvas` API for 2D drawing is standardized in HTML5 (see *http://dev.w3.org/html5/2dcontext/*). In large part, `canvas` works the same way across all the modern browsers, which all now support it. However, be aware that there are some subtle differences between the browsers' implementations.

> Because these quirks in behavior between different browsers/versions are generally outside the specification and are more implementation-specific, detailing or predicting them is futile.
>
> As such, we do not cover those quirks in depth; instead, the reader is implored to carefully test the usage of `canvas` and its API in all relevant browsers to avoid pitfalls.

The `canvas` element is specified to have a couple of *rendering contexts*, which is basically a fancy way of saying "coordinate systems." At this time, the only useful (implemented) rendering context is *2d*, which defines a flat, two-dimensional Cartesian coordinate system with (0,0) at the top-left corner (thereby matching the coordinate system style in web pages). Practically all **canvas** API calls are made against the context, rather than the **canvas** itself.

Assuming you have a reference to a **canvas** element, to get a reference to its 2d **con text**, use:

```
var mycontext = mycanvas.getContext("2d");
```

Once you have the **context**, the **canvas** API commands listed in the previous section are all available to be called. The shape-drawing commands in the **canvas** API are all path-based. This means that you first "draw"—or define, but not visibly—a *path* (one or more straight or curved edges) that represents the shape (line, arc/curve, rectangle, etc.), and then you specify what you want done to the path.

Typically, you *stroke* the path, drawing a line along its boundary edges, and/or *fill* the path, filling its interior with a color or pattern.

Because you essentially render a path only after that path is defined, you will often end up needing to create many separate path segments in your drawing, and you will apply different strokes/fills/etc. to render each of the segments as you define them.

The first step in defining a path segment is always to call **beginPath()**:

```
mycontext.beginPath();
mycontext.moveTo(10, 10);
mycontext.lineTo(30, 30);
```

 If you call **closePath()** before you call a rendering command like **stroke()** or **fill()**, the path literally is "closed," in that the beginning point of the path is automatically joined with the end point of the path, with a final line segment.

After defining your path segment, call a rendering command, such as **stroke()** or **fill()**. Those commands act upon that most recently defined path segment—whatever has been defined since the most recent **beginPath()** call—and then subsequently that path is no longer active or available:

```
mycontext.beginPath();
mycontext.moveTo(10, 10);
mycontext.lineTo(30, 30);
mycontext.stroke();
```

Keep in mind that if you draw more than one shape in the same path segment, generally speaking, the **canvas** interprets the paths as being connected. In this sense, "connected" means that there is an edge from the end of one shape to the beginning of the next. This is not always true, though; some shape definition commands imply their own independent or not-relative segments.

Again, it's best practice to explicitly define your path segments, to avoid such pitfalls. One explicit way to avoid segments being connected is to use moveTo(...), which conceptually "picks up the pen" and moves it to a new location before setting it down, rather than acting like the pen has drawn a connecting line from the previous location to the new location.

Vectors versus bitmaps

You may be familiar with the concept of *vector* drawing as opposed to *bitmap* drawing. Vector drawing is essentially describing an image as a series of shapes using equations, such that the shapes (the vectors) can be modified (rotated, scaled, transformed, etc.) without any loss of quality.

Bitmap drawing, on the other hand, is specifically constrained to painting a color into one or more individual pixel locations. Transformations against bitmaps are "lossy" in that you get some fuzzy or blurry artifacts along color boundaries as you make the transformations, because what might have been a clear color boundary from one pixel to the adjacent pixel in the original orientation of the drawing is now not a clear boundary between two pixels, but a mix of colors between the two pixels.

It is important to keep vector and bitmap ideas clear and separate in your mind as you work with the canvas element. The paths that you draw with API commands like lineTo(...) are like vectors: they can be defined and then modified using various transformations, without any loss of quality. Once you have the path in the state that you want, you then render that path, which creates visible pixels in the bitmap output of your canvas element. If you were to then apply more transformations to your bitmap, such as rotating the entire element, you would be subject to potentially "lossy" transformations, as described above.

To put it more plainly, think of your path definitions as vector equations—which are invisible and, until rendered, can be changed at will—and think of the stroke and fill operations that you perform against a path as pixel bitmap rendering. In principle, this is no different from how a vector image editing program would operate.

 If you draw a shape (or modify a shape's location or dimensions) where it overlaps only part of a pixel, such as a line from (10.5,20) to (10.5,50), each half-pixel will be partially rendered (anti-aliasing), which may produce fuzzy line effects.

There are, of course, operations that you explicitly *want* to perform only against the final rendered output (such as color mutations), but these operations are bitmap-based, as opposed to the geometric transformations you perform against paths.

See Also

For more information on how to use canvas, see this canvas tutorial on MDC: *https://developer.mozilla.org/en/Canvas_tutorial.*

9.2 Using Transparency

Problem

You want to draw shapes in the canvas element which have some transparency, so they allow content from beneath to show through.

Solution

The canvas element is, by default, transparent, which means that it will show any content that is stacked beneath it. You can control what pixels are transparent or not simply by what you draw onto the canvas element.

If we position a red circle drawing (like the one from the previous recipe) over the top of some text, the portions of the canvas element not drawn on by the circle will remain transparent, and the text from beneath will show through, as illustrated in Figure 9-2.

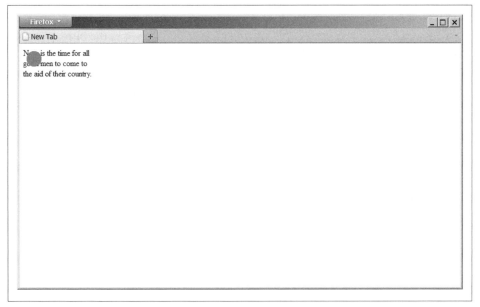

Figure 9-2. Drawing a circle on top of text in a page, with transparency showing the not-covered text from beneath

Further, you can ensure that a pixel you have drawn on the canvas element retains partial transparency by manipulating the alpha channel of the color used to draw the pixel. *Partial transparency* means that what the user sees for each pixel is the combination of the color at that location *below* the canvas element and the color shown for that pixel *in* the canvas element.

For example, if we were to make the red circle from the previous example partially transparent, it would appear as shown in Figure 9-3.

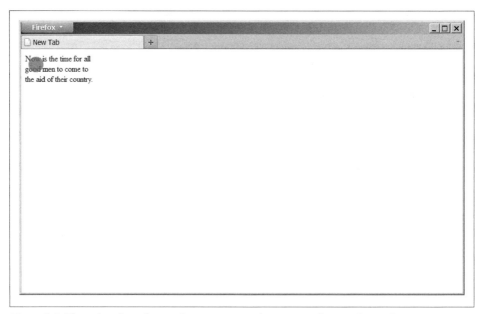

Figure 9-3. The red circle with partial transparency, showing text from underneath

The partially transparent color is useful not only for content that appears on the page beneath the canvas element, but also for content that has already been drawn onto the canvas element itself:

```
mycontext.beginPath();
mycontext.arc(40, 40, 25, 0, Math.PI * 2, true); // draw a circle
mycontext.closePath();

mycontext.fillStyle = "#f00";
mycontext.fill(); // fill the circle solid

mycontext.beginPath();
mycontext.arc(70, 40, 25, 0, Math.PI * 2, true); // draw a circle
mycontext.closePath();

mycontext.fillStyle = "rgba(0,0,255,0.75)";
mycontext.fill(); // fill the circle solid;
```

In the above code snippet, we draw a partially transparent blue circle overlapping part of a red circle. The portion of the circles that overlaps will produce the color purple from the mixing of the blue with the red, as seen in Figure 9-4.

Figure 9-4. Applying partial transparency to the blue circle so its color mixes with that of the red circle in the overlap

Discussion

In general, a `canvas` element starts out with all its pixels being completely transparent. Any pixel that is drawn with a fully opaque color will no longer have any transparency, whereas any pixel that is drawn with a partially opaque color will retain partial transparency. The default is fully opaque with no transparency. You generally define the alpha transparency of a color with `"rgba"`, in the same way that you specify CSS3 color values (see *http://www.w3.org/TR/2003/CR-css3-color-20030514/#numerical*), like so:

```
mycontext.fillStyle = "rgba(255,0,0,0.5)";
```

Here, the `0.5` specifies a 50% opacity for the red color, meaning all pixels that are drawn with that color style will have 50% transparency and thus that the content from beneath will partially show through, as shown in Figure 9-5.

The other way to affect the transparency of rendered pixels is to set the `globalAlpha` property, with a value ranging from `0.0` to `1.0`.

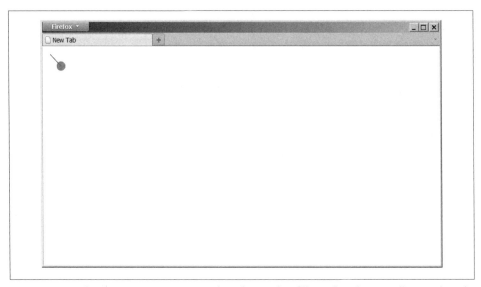

Figure 9-5. Applying 50% transparency to the color used to fill a red circle, partially revealing the previously drawn black line below it

When a pixel is drawn with partial transparency, the default composite operation is to take that pixel's existing rendered color definition, if any, and combine it with this new color definition to produce the new pixel color. That's how the black line appears to be below the partially transparent red dot in Figure 9-5.

Keep in mind, though, that there are not two actual layers of shapes here (as you might be used to with digital imaging software), even though it appears that way. The pixels that were rendered were composited together, combining what was already there in the first path with what's drawn by the second path. The final result is still one single-layer bitmap rendering in your **canvas** element. This means that once these two shapes have been rendered on top of each other, they cannot be moved or changed independently, since there's just one bitmap.

However, since pixels in a **canvas** element can have transparency, it is possible to emulate separate layers by simply stacking **canvas** elements, and drawing different shapes into each. In this case, there is not really **canvas**-level compositing going on between the two independent layers (they are separate elements, although obviously your browser, operating system, and computer screen are doing the compositing), so the two elements can be moved, modified, erased, etc., independently of each other. See Recipe 9.10, for more on this subject.

See Also

For more information on transparency, see this **canvas** "styles and colors" tutorial on MDC: *https://developer.mozilla.org/En/Canvas_tutorial/Applying_styles_and_colors.*

9.3 Setting <canvas> Dimensions

Problem

You want to explicitly specify the width and height of your canvas element to be different than the default dimensions.

Solution

Add the width and height attributes, and their corresponding values, to your canvas element:

```
<canvas id="mycanvas" width="200" height="200"></canvas>
```

You may also want to change the width and/or height of your canvas element with JavaScript. If you want to change how much width or height (i.e., pixels for rendering) is available in your canvas element, you must change the *attributes* of the canvas element (not the CSS style properties of width and height, as you might assume):

```
mycanvas.setAttribute("width", "200"); // will change the bitmap dimensions
mycanvas.setAttribute("height", "200");
```

You can also set the width and height properties directly on the element:

```
mycanvas.width = 200; // will change the bitmap dimensions
mycanvas.height = 200;
```

Either approach will allow your canvas element to use 200 pixels in the horizontal direction and 200 pixels in the vertical direction.

By contrast, controlling the size of your canvas element with CSS—either with CSS rules or by directly setting CSS properties in JavaScript— does not affect the bitmap dimensions of your canvas element, but rather takes the existing canvas element (at its existing bitmap dimensions) and stretches or shrinks its physical dimensions, as necessary:

```
mycanvas.style.width = "200px";  // will shrink the horizontal rendering
mycanvas.style.height = "200px"; // will stretch the vertical rendering
```

Discussion

The default dimensions of a canvas element are 300 pixels wide by 150 pixels high. In practice, you'll usually want to define different dimensions for your canvas element.

> As with all block-level HTML elements, if you make your canvas absolutely positioned, it does not necessarily default to having any physical dimensions to render. You need to explicitly define the physical rendering dimensions via CSS, in addition to the bitmap pixel dimensions. To keep a consistent rendering ratio, make sure the physical dimensions match the bitmap pixel dimensions.

You can specify the bitmap pixel dimensions using attributes on the `canvas` element, either in the markup or with a `setAttribute(...)` call. You can also resize the `canvas` element by using CSS styling on the width/height, but this has the effect of shrinking or stretching the `canvas` element while keeping the existing pixel dimensions, rather than actually changing them.

For instance, let's say you wanted a full-page `canvas` element that resized itself with the window. If you want that sizing to be achieved by stretching or shrinking the `canvas` element while maintaining the same pixel dimensions, use CSS, like this:

```
#mycanvas { width:100%; height:100%; }
```

However, if you want a `canvas` element that keeps resizing its bitmap pixel dimensions along with the dimensions of the browser window, you need to use JavaScript:

```
window.onresize = function() {
    mycanvas.width = document.documentElement.clientWidth;
    mycanvas.height = document.documentElement.clientHeight;
};
```

You can resize the `canvas` element as often as you like. However, each time you resize it, the drawing space will be cleared. This is actually a useful trick, as you can quickly clear the `canvas` by simply setting its `width` to be the same as its current width:

```
function clear(mycanvas) {
    mycanvas.width = mycanvas.width;
}
```

See Also

For more information on how to use `canvas`, see this `canvas` tutorial on MDC: *https://developer.mozilla.org/en/Canvas_tutorial*.

9.4 Using Gradients, Patterns, and Line Styles

Problem

You want to create gradients and other drawing styles.

Solution

Each time you render a path to the `canvas` element, the color and style for that drawing are picked up from the currently set stroke and fill styles.

For instance, to vary the way that line segments are drawn on paths, you can control the stroke styles with `lineWidth`, `lineCap`, and `lineJoin`:

```
mycontext.lineWidth = "12";
mycontext.lineJoin = "round";
mycontext.moveTo(20, 20);
mycontext.lineTo(50, 50);
mycontext.lineTo(20, 70);
mycontext.stroke();
```

The result is shown in Figure 9-6.

Figure 9-6. Applying the lineWidth and lineJoin stroke styles

To vary what is painted inside the paths you draw, you can control the fill styles to create gradients or image patterns (Figure 9-7):

```
var lingrad = mycontext.createLinearGradient(20,20,40,60);
lingrad.addColorStop(0.3, "#0f0");
lingrad.addColorStop(1, "#fff");
mycontext.fillStyle = lingrad;

mycontext.moveTo(20, 20);
mycontext.lineTo(50, 50);
mycontext.lineTo(20, 70);
mycontext.closePath();
mycontext.fill();
```

Figure 9-7. Linear gradient filling a shape

Discussion

There are several different ways to control the style of how your paths are rendered. For instance, for lines (strokes), you can set the `lineWidth` property to vary the width of the lines used to stroke. In addition, the `lineCap` property controls how the cap/end of a line segment is rendered (squared off, rounded, etc.), and the `lineJoin` property controls how the connection (or joint) between two line segments is drawn. Figure 9-8 shows a few different line styles.

In addition to line styles, you can define custom color styles for both lines and fills. There are two options: gradients and patterns.

Gradients are a gradual progression from one color to another color (or colors). They can be *linear* (progressing in a straight line) or *radial* (progressing radially/circularly from a central point). To use them, you create a gradient object, set one or more *color stops* on it, and then use that object as the `strokeStyle` or `fillStyle`.

Patterns are essentially created by taking an existing image (even another `canvas` element) and using that as the "color" for a line or fill, repeating the image in question as necessary to fill the space required of the color. To use them, you create a pattern object, specifying which image to use and how to repeat it, and then use that object as the `strokeStyle` or `fillStyle`. Figure 9-9 shows the results of a few different fill gradients and patterns.

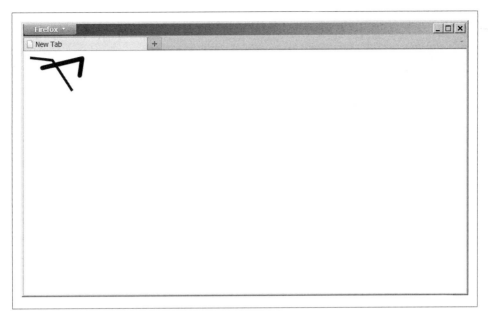

Figure 9-8. Various line styles

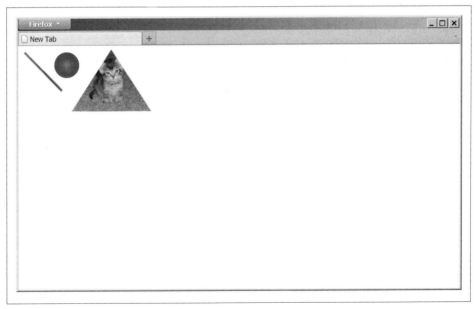

Figure 9-9. Various fill gradients and patterns

Pattern fills also allow you to tile (or repeat) an image. The `canvas` API command `createPattern(...)` takes as its second parameter a string value to control the tiling. For no tiling, use `no-repeat`. Currently, the only tiling value supported consistently is `repeat`, which defaults to repeating the image both horizontally and vertically, as shown in Figure 9-10:

```
var img = document.getElementById("my_fish_image");
var imgfill = mycontext.createPattern(img, "repeat");
mycontext.fillStyle = imgfill;
mycontext.fillRect(0, 0, 200, 200);
```

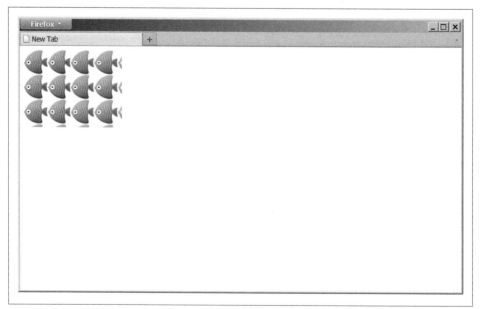

Figure 9-10. Tiling an image using a fill pattern

See Also

For more information on line styles, gradients, and pattern fills, see this `canvas` "styles and colors" tutorial on MDC: *https://developer.mozilla.org/En/Canvas_tutorial/Applying_styles_and_colors*.

9.5 Pulling External Images into a `<canvas>` Drawing

Problem

You have an existing image (graphic, icon, photo, etc.) in an external file that you want to put into a `canvas` element, so that you can then manipulate or embellish it with `canvas` API drawing commands.

Solution

First, either load the image in question using an `img` tag in your markup and get a reference to it, or create an `Image` element dynamically in your JavaScript code:

```
var img = new Image();
img.src = "http://somewhere/to/my/image.jpg";
```

Next, once the image is loaded, draw the image onto a `canvas` element:

```
var img = new Image();
img.onload = function() {
    // note: we're calling against the "2d" context here
    mycontext.drawImage(img, 0, 0); // draw the image at (0,0)
};
img.src = "http://somewhere/to/my/image.jpg";
```

 The image object you pass as the first parameter to `drawImage(...)` can actually be a real image, another element, or a `video` element (achieved by capturing a frame of video into your `canvas`).

This assumes that your `canvas` element is already properly sized to be able to handle the image that you're trying to draw into it. If it's too small in either dimension, *clipping* occurs, with the image being cut off on the right or bottom edge, respectively.

Discussion

The `canvas` API gives you the `drawImage(...)` command to let you capture image bitmap data from another source (an image, another `canvas` element, or a `video` element) and draw it directly into your `canvas` element.

There are three ways to call `drawImage(...)`. The simplest form, shown above, takes an element to capture the bitmap image data from and two coordinates, the (X, Y) location inside your `canvas` element at which to place the top-left corner of the image.

The second form takes an additional two parameters, (dw, dh), which are the width and height of the area from the original image that you want to capture and copy to your `canvas` element.

The third form of the call takes quite a few more parameters than the second form. The first four numeric parameters, (sx, sy, sw, sh), specify the top-left location and the width/height of the area from the original source image data to capture, and the last four parameters, (dx, dy, dw, dh), represent the top-left location and the width/height of the area where the image data will be copied to in your `canvas` element:

```
function createCanvas(id, width, height) {
    var canvas = document.createElement("canvas");
    canvas.id = id;
    canvas.setAttribute("width", width);
    canvas.setAttribute("height", height);
```

```
    document.body.appendChild(canvas);
    return canvas;
}

var small_canvas = createCanvas("small", 100, 100);
var large_canvas = createCanvas("large", 300, 300);
var small_context = small_canvas.getContext("2d");
var large_context = large_canvas.getContext("2d");

var img = new Image();
img.onload = function() {
    // note: using different (sw,sh) and (dw,dh) dimensions here shrinks the image
    small_context.drawImage(img, 0, 0, 300, 300, 0, 0, 100, 100);
    // just grab the top-left 300x300 area from the image
    large_context.drawImage(img, 0, 0, 300, 300);
};
img.src = "http://somewhere/to/my/image.jpg";
```

Figure 9-11 illustrates these parameters.

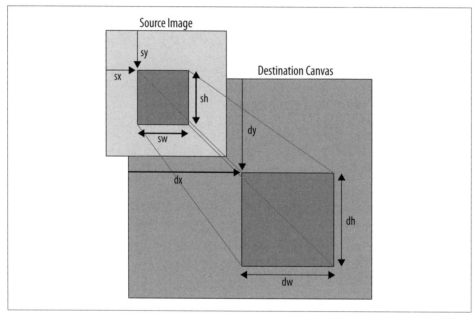

Figure 9-11. Explaining the (dx,dy,dw,dh) and (sx,sy,sw,sh) parameters of drawImage(...)

Once you've drawn an image into your element, that image data is no different from any other bitmap image data that you could draw. This means that you can easily draw over the top of your drawn image, using all the same capabilities as previously discussed.

See Also

Tutorial on pulling an image into canvas with Ajax: *http://www.html5canvastutorials .com/advanced/html5-canvas-load-image-data-url/*.

9.6 Setting Color Transformations

Problem

You want to apply a color transformation (like grayscale or invert) to an existing canvas drawing.

Solution

The canvas API provides a command called getImageData(...) that grabs all the pixel color data from the canvas element, handing it to you in one long array:

```
var drawing = mycontext.getImageData(0, 0, 200, 200);
```

 The array you get from getImageData(...) is not in quite the format you'd generally expect. First, it's not a two-dimensional array, with width and height dimensions. Instead, it is a linear single-dimension array, where the values wrap from one line to the next, like a big long string of text that you paste into a text editor.

Second, there are four consecutive entries in the array for each pixel, each entry corresponding to a color component for a pixel. So, each pixel takes up four entries in the array, in the form of [..., *red, green, blue, alpha,* ...].

Once you have the image data captured, you can manipulate that data using any transformations you please and then write it back to the canvas element.

To grayscale the drawing, the simplest algorithm is to take the average of the red, green, and blue color components and set all three to that average value:

```
var avg;
// skip 4 entries (1 px) at a time
for (var i = 0; i < drawing.data.length; i = i + 4) {
    avg = (drawing.data[i] + drawing.data[i+1] + drawing.data[i+2]) / 3;
    drawing.data[i] = drawing.data[i+1] = drawing.data[i+2] = avg;
}
```

To color-invert the drawing, the simplest algorithm is to take each color component value, subtract it from 255, and set that color value back:

```
// skip 4 entries (1 px) at a time
for (var i = 0; i < drawing.data.length; i = i + 4) {
    drawing.data[i] = 255 - drawing.data[i]; // invert red
    drawing.data[i+1] = 255 - drawing.data[i+1]; // invert green
```

```
        drawing.data[i+2] = 255 - drawing.data[i+2]; // invert blue
}
```

Now that the data has been modified, we simply write it back to the `canvas` element, using the `putImageData(...)` command:

```
mycontext.putImageData(drawing, 0, 0); // put the image data back at (0,0)
```

Discussion

As we discussed in Recipe 9.1, the image that is rendered visible on the page is the bitmap data rendering of the paths and styles (or vectors) that you defined while drawing your image.

Fortunately, the `canvas` element allows us to access and modify some or all of the pixel color data in the element. This means that any manner of sophisticated bitmap transformations can be accomplished. In addition to applying color transformations, as we did here, you could apply algorithms to blur the image, pixelate it, zoom it, etc. Those various algorithms are beyond the scope of this chapter (and this book), but the process would always be the same as that outlined in this recipe: first get the bitmap image data array, then process the individual color component (red, green, blue, alpha) entries for each pixel, and then write some or all of that data back to your `canvas` element.

 If you write an external image to a `canvas` element that comes from a different domain than the page's domain, the `canvas` is marked as "unclean" (meaning it's not abiding by the same-origin security policy), and thus you are not able to call `getImageData(...)` to retrieve that data.

You can always write to the `canvas` element, but you can only read data from it if *all* the data in the `canvas` originated from the page's domain.

See Also

This recipe only briefly touched on basic ways to manipulate the colors in your can vas images and drawings. For much more complex effects that you can apply to your `canvas` element, check out PaintbrushJS: *http://mezzoblue.github.com/PaintbrushJS/ demo/*.

9.7 Working with Geometric Transformations

Problem

You want to apply some transformations to your drawing commands, such as scaling, rotation, skewing, etc.

Solution

The `canvas` API provides several commands for transforming your `canvas` drawing actions:

translate(*x*, *y*)
> Move/skew the location of the origin point for the coordinate system from (0,0) to (*x*,*y*).

scale(*x*, *y*)
> Scale the units of the coordinate system in the *x* and *y* directions, independently.

rotate(*angle*)
> Rotate the coordinate system about the origin point, (0,0), by the angle (moving in a clockwise direction) specified in radians.

When you start combining multiple transformations, it is often easier to manage the state of the `canvas` element on a stack, where you can simply revert back one level to undo all transformations (and other state, like style/color settings) with one command. The `canvas` API provides two commands for managing your state stack, `save()` and `restore()`:

```
mycontext.save();               // save the current state of the canvas
mycontext.translate(10, 10);    // move the origin point to (10,10)
mycontext.arc(0, 0, 10, 0, Math.PI * 2, true); // draw a circle
mycontext.stroke();
mycontext.restore();

mycontext.save();
mycontext.rotate(Math.PI / 4); // rotate 45 degrees clockwise
mycontext.moveTo(0, 0);
mycontext.lineTo(10, 0);
mycontext.stroke();
mycontext.restore();
```

In both these transformations, the action taken could easily be reversed. That is, we could easily translate back to our original origin point with `translate(-10, -10)`, or back to our original rotation with `rotate(Math.PI / -2)`.

However, as soon as you start combining multiple translations at once, or nesting translations into multiple steps or layers, stack management becomes quite necessary. It is best practice to always use stack management for your `canvas` element's state as you make style changes or transformations.

Discussion

The concept of using transformations to adjust your drawing commands is probably going to be a bit strange to you at first. Most developers are initially a little confused by this idea. Don't worry, though; after you've done it a few times you'll get more comfortable with this new mindset, and it won't seem quite so foreign.

To get started, here's what you need to know: transformations do not actually affect your drawing commands or what's currently in the canvas element. Instead, transformations affect the coordinate system, so that all the coordinates that you use in your subsequent drawing commands are automatically interpreted in the transformed coordinate system, instead of the original coordinate system.

Say what?! Okay, let's try a different approach. Think of these transformations as keeping your pen in the same location, but (without the pen touching the paper) moving the paper underneath your pen to a different location or rotating it at an angle, then drawing what you planned as if the paper hadn't moved, and then moving the paper back to its starting position on the desk.

Re-read that last paragraph again, to make sure you understand how coordinate system transformations affect how you draw into the canvas element.

If you translate (or move) the coordinate system 10 pixels to the right and draw a shape at (0,0) relative to the now-moved coordinate system, the shape actually appears at (10,0) in the absolute coordinates *relative* to your canvas element container.

So, translating the coordinate system 10 pixels to the right and drawing a shape at (0,0) is basically the same as not translating the coordinate system at all and simply drawing the shape at (10,0):

```
mycontext.save();
mycontext.translate(10, 0); // move coordinate system 10 pixels right
mycontext.moveTo(0, 0);
mycontext.lineTo(50, 0);    // line actually appears from (10,0) to (60,0)
mycontext.stroke();
mycontext.restore();

mycontext.moveTo(10, 0);
mycontext.lineTo(60, 0);    // same line, basically
mycontext.stroke();
```

The same goes for rotation, although the math is a little trickier. If you rotate the canvas by 30 degrees clockwise and draw a shape at (50,0), it's actually drawn at a relative location that appears to be 30 degrees down from its horizon:

```
mycontext.save();
mycontext.rotate(Math.PI / 6); // rotate 30 degrees clockwise
mycontext.moveTo(0, 0);
mycontext.lineTo(50, 0); // line actually angles 30 degrees down from horizontal
mycontext.stroke();
mycontext.restore();
```

At first, you may wonder why translations and rotations are even necessary. After all, can't you just draw your line or circle at the proper location and in the proper orientation, and not worry about complexity of the transformations?

For some tasks, yes. But again, for more complicated tasks, it's almost imperative that you transform your coordinate system so that your use of the drawing commands (and, in particular, which numbers you use for the parameters) is more sensible and semantic.

How would you draw a rectangle at an angle? Well, you could calculate the vertices using geometric calculations and then manually draw the four sides as individual lines. But who wants to do it that way? Instead, rotate the coordinate system and call the rect(...) command; it's as simple as that.

Scaling is another example of something that almost always requires transformations to work properly, specifically because scaling can be done independently in both the *x* and *y* directions. What scaling amounts to is saying that if you scale the *x* direction of your coordinate system to twice as large, and you draw a line that is supposed to be 50 units (pixels) long, it actually is rendered as twice as long (100 pixels):

```
mycontext.save();
mycontext.scale(2, 1);    // scale x direction units by a factor of 2
mycontext.moveTo(0, 0);
mycontext.lineTo(50, 0);  // line actually appears to extend to (100,0)
mycontext.stroke();
mycontext.restore();

mycontext.moveTo(0, 0);
mycontext.lineTo(100, 0); // same line, basically
mycontext.stroke();
```

Other tasks—rotating an image, for instance—also beg for transformations, because it would be very difficult (and certainly, performance-wise, impractical) to manually transform the raw bitmap image data array yourself. Instead, you simply rotate the coordinate system and draw the image into it, and the **canvas** element does the hard work for you:

```
mycontext.save();
mycontext.rotate(Math.Pi / 4);   // rotate 45 degrees clockwise
mycontext.drawImage(img, 0, 0);  // draw the image at (0,0)
                                 // in the rotated coordinate system
mycontext.restore();
```

Finally, let's take a look at nesting transformations, to reinforce why transformations and stack management of the **canvas** element's state are helpful (as shown in Figure 9-12):

```
mycontext.beginPath();
mycontext.strokeStyle = "#f00"; // red color
mycontext.translate(20, 20);    // move the coordinate system to (20,20) origin
mycontext.moveTo(0, 0);         // actually (20,20)
mycontext.lineTo(80, 10);       // actually (100,30)
mycontext.stroke();

mycontext.save();               // save <canvas> state

mycontext.beginPath();
mycontext.strokeStyle = "#00f"; // now blue color
mycontext.rotate(Math.PI / 4);
mycontext.moveTo(0, 0);
mycontext.arc(0, 0, 52, Math.PI / 3, Math.PI / 6, true);
mycontext.closePath();          // connects back to the start of the path
```

```
mycontext.stroke();

mycontext.restore();              // back to previous <canvas> state

mycontext.beginPath();
mycontext.moveTo(80, 10);
mycontext.lineTo(14, 50);
mycontext.stroke();
```

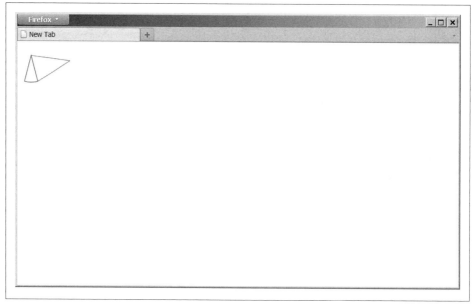

Figure 9-12. Coordinate system transformations and stack management of the canvas state

See Also

See the W3C specification for **canvas** transformations at *http://www.w3.org/TR/2dcon
text/#transformations*.

9.8 Placing Text on a <canvas>

Problem

You want to include text directly in your **canvas** drawing.

Solution

The **canvas** API provides two commands for rendering text in your drawing: fill
Text(...) and strokeText(...). Both commands take the same parameters: (*stringTo
Render, x, y*[, *maxWidth*]). The only difference is whether the text is filled in or simply
outlined.

To set the font style (font face, size, etc.), use the `font` property:

```
mycontext.font = "25pt Arial";
```

Now, simply call the appropriate text command:

```
mycontext.fillText("Hello World", 0, 25);
mycontext.strokeText("Hello World", 0, 75);
```

The result of this code snippet is shown in Figure 9-13.

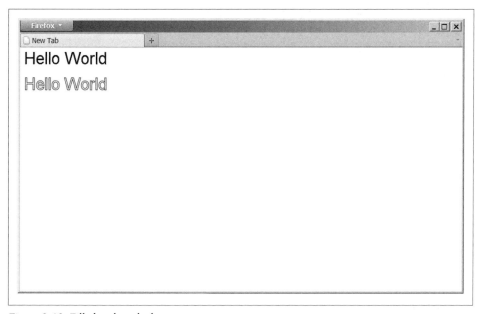

Figure 9-13. Filled and stroked text

Discussion

The `fillText(...)` and `strokeText(...)` commands use the font styling specified in the `font` property. The available settings (font face, style, size, etc.) are defined to be the same as what would be available to CSS font style rules. The colors used are, of course, controlled by the `fillStyle` and `strokeStyle` properties, respectively. The same goes for the stroke line width.

See Also

For more on drawing text on a `canvas`, see *https://developer.mozilla.org/en/drawing_text _using_a_canvas*.

9.9 Clipping <canvas> Drawings

Problem

You want to use a drawing command, but you want to clip the drawing by some other shape that you define.

Solution

The `canvas` API provides the command `clip(...)`, which will take the currently defined path and use that as a *clipping mask* for subsequent drawing commands. This means the `canvas` element will only draw inside the defined clipping mask boundaries and will discard any drawing outside the path.

To add the text of the letter "H" but clip it by a circle, you would do this:

```
mycontext.beginPath();
mycontext.arc(50, 50, 25, 0, Math.PI * 2, true); // circle path
mycontext.clip(); // make the path our clipping mask

mycontext.fillStyle = "#f00";
mycontext.font = "50pt Arial";
mycontext.fillText("H", 25, 75);
```

The result of the circle-clipped "H" is shown in Figure 9-14.

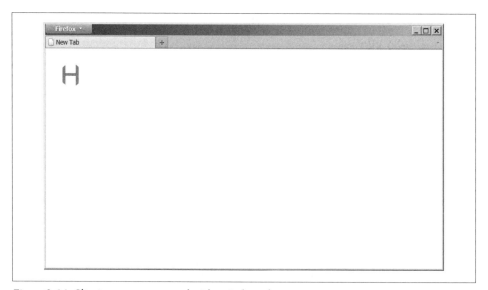

Figure 9-14. Clipping a text command with a circle path

As you can see, the circle itself was not drawn; instead, it was used as the clipping path for the subsequent `fillText` drawing command.

Discussion

The canvas element's state defaults to a clipping mask that comprises the entire visible area of the canvas element. Once you define a clipping mask using the clip(...) command, that clipping mask will remain in effect for all future drawing commands, until you change or reset it.

Just as we saw in Recipe 9.7, you can use stack management of the element's state to make a temporary clipping mask change, and then roll it back to the default (entire element), as shown in Figure 9-15:

```
mycontext.save();
mycontext.beginPath();
mycontext.arc(50, 50, 25, 0, Math.PI * 2, true); // circle path
mycontext.clip(); // make the path our clipping mask

mycontext.fillStyle = "#f00";
mycontext.font = "50pt Arial";
mycontext.fillText("H", 25, 75);
mycontext.restore(); // back to default <canvas> state (including clipping)

mycontext.font = "25pt Arial";
mycontext.fillText("ello World", 70, 70); // black text, not clipped
```

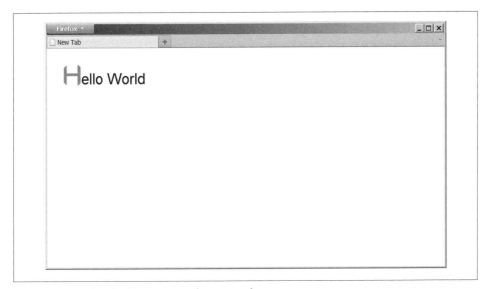

Figure 9-15. Rolling back to previous clipping mask state

See Also

The W3C specification on clipping at *http://www.w3.org/TR/2dcontext/#clipping-re gion*.

9.10 Animating <canvas> Drawings

Problem

Drawing static shapes into the canvas element is fine, but now you want to make the shapes move around.

Solution

Animation with the canvas element boils down to drawing a frame of your animation and then, a few milliseconds later, erasing that drawing and redrawing the next frame, probably with some elements slightly moved or otherwise changed. If you animate by showing the frames fast enough—around 20–30 frames per second—it generally looks like a smooth animation of your shapes.

In this chapter, we've already covered how to draw various things into your canvas element. We also briefly mentioned one way to clear your canvas element (resetting the width). To fire up some animation, all we need to do is put those two concepts together.

Here's a basic example of a moving red dot (which is shown in Figure 9-16):

```
function draw_circle(x, y) {
    mycontext.fillStyle = "#f00";
    mycontext.beginPath();
    mycontext.arc(x, y, 10, 0, Math.PI * 2, true);
    mycontext.fill();
}

function erase_frame() {
    mycanvas.width = mycanvas.width;
}

var ball_x = 50;
var ball_y = 50;
var delta = 3;

draw_circle(ball_x, ball_y);

setInterval(function(){
    if (ball_x > 100 || ball_y < 15 || ball_x < 15 || ball_y > 100) {
        delta *= -1;
    }
    ball_x += delta;
    ball_y += delta;
    erase_frame();
    draw_circle(ball_x, ball_y);
}, 35);
```

Figure 9-16. Animating a red circle in the canvas

Discussion

Depending on the setup of your animation frame, you may need to employ various methods to get the most efficient drawing (and erasing) of your shapes and/or images. We'll now cover several different approaches to drawing and erasing to accomplish animations with the **canvas** element.

If you have a transparent background and one shape (like a circle) bouncing around in your **canvas**, as in the example code above, you don't need to erase the whole **canvas** element before drawing the next frame; you only need to erase the small portion of the element that has something drawn in it (i.e., the circle).

That is, all you need to do is erase the part of the **canvas** element that you drew onto in the previous frame. Especially for larger dimensions, this technique can enhance performance significantly.

To erase only part of the **canvas** element, use the **canvas** API command `clearRect(...)`:

```
function draw_circle(x, y) {
    mycontext.fillStyle = "#f00";
    mycontext.beginPath();
    mycontext.arc(x, y, 10, 0, Math.PI * 2, true);
    mycontext.fill();
}

function erase_circle(x, y) {
    mycontext.clearRect(x-10, y-10, 20, 20);
}
```

```
var ball_x = 50;
var ball_y = 50;
var delta = 3;

draw_circle(ball_x, ball_y);

setInterval(function(){
    if (ball_x > 100 || ball_y < 15 || ball_x < 15 || ball_y > 100) {
        delta *= -1;
    }
    erase_circle(ball_x, ball_y);
    ball_x += delta;
    ball_y += delta;
    draw_circle(ball_x, ball_y);
}, 35);
```

This technique of drawing the entire frame and then erasing it and redrawing it with some things moved or changed works fine, but in certain circumstances, it's not ideal. For instance, if you are animating a shape like our red circle on top of a static drawing (or an image/photo/etc.), it's quite a waste of resources to redraw the unchanging background image 30 times per second, simply because the foreground shape (the red circle) has moved and needs to be redrawn.

One solution to this problem is to use two canvas elements, stacked on top of each other. In the background canvas element, you draw your static scene image, and in the foreground canvas element you do your animation of the red circle, as above. This way, the background image is only drawn once, not every time you redraw the layer with the moving red circle, as shown in Figure 9-17.

In this example, drawing and redrawing the entire canvas just to show the same red circle in different positions doesn't seem strictly necessary. However, in practical cases, you may be animating more than just the position. For instance, you may animate an object by moving its position and rotating it at the same time. In such cases, the draw/redraw method of animation is most appropriate.

For this simple case, another option would have been to have a canvas element in the foreground that was only big enough to contain the red circle (20×20 pixels), and simply to move that element itself around, using CSS positioning on the page. Especially for that case, having the red circle separate from the background image is quite helpful, so that the two elements can be positioned independently.

See Also

Basic canvas animation tutorial at *https://developer.mozilla.org/en/Canvas_tutorial/Basic_animations*.

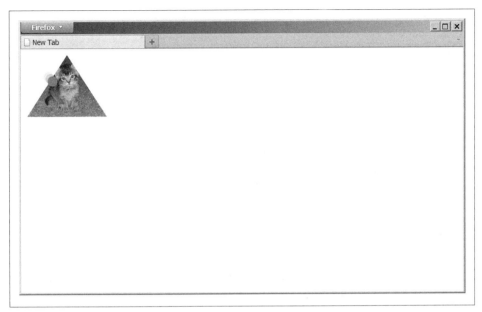

Figure 9-17. A background canvas with an image and, stacked on top of it, a foreground canvas with the animated red circle

9.11 Drawing Graphs with <canvas>

Problem

You have some data that you want to plot in a graph using a canvas element.

Solution

All of the canvas API commands discussed in this chapter, plus other advanced commands (for complex curves, etc.), can be combined to create very nice-looking graphs that visualize data, either as line, pie, or other types of charts.

As you can probably imagine, the complexity of such a task is quite high. So, we will not discuss specifically how to draw your own graphs, but will instead show how to use a simple, free graphing library (which does the hard work for you!) called *flot*.

The flot library uses jQuery, so you need to load a recent version of jQuery first, and then the latest release of the flot library:

```
<script src="jquery.js"></script>
<script src="jquery.flot.js"></script>
```

Next, you need to create a placeholder element in your page, into which flot will render the canvas graph. The flot library will automatically match the bitmap rendered dimensions of the canvas element to the size of the placeholder element that you specify:

```
<div id="my_graph" style="width:600px; height:300px"></div>
```

Now, you need to set up the data that you will plot onto your graph. You can either load this data dynamically, using Ajax, or include the data inline in your script code, as shown here:

```
var graph_data = [[0, 3], [4, 8], [8, 5], [9, 13]];
```

The format of the data is an array of [X,Y] pairs for each data point, representing values for the x- and y-axes for each point, respectively.

Once you have the graph data, if the default graphing options are acceptable, simply call the flot graphing API directly, passing it your data:

```
var my_graph = $("#my_graph"); // get a reference to the placeholder
$.plot(my_graph, [graph_data]); // pass the graph data as one data series
```

You will notice that we passed the graph data inside [], meaning we actually passed an array wrapped around our graph data. The flot graphing API supports graphing multiple data series at a time on one graph. In our example, our graph data was only one such data series, but you could pass other data series as desired. The default options and styles will result in a nice-looking graph, as shown in Figure 9-18.

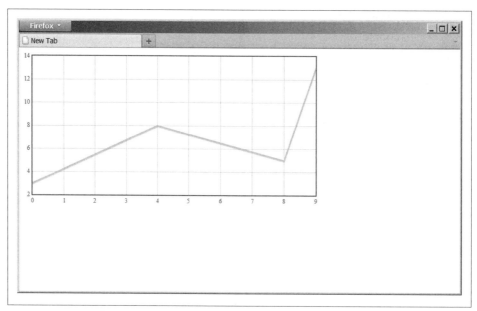

Figure 9-18. Using flot to graph some data with a <canvas> element

As you can see, with just a few lines of code we were able to leverage the power of the flot library to generate a professional-looking graph, instead of having to write hundreds of lines of our own canvas API code.

 As an interesting exercise, take your knowledge of the canvas API from this chapter's recipes and see if you can reproduce the same graph without using the flot library.

The flot library API allows you to manually generate and display labels for the x- and y-axes, control the minimum and maximum range for each axis, manually define the grid step size for each axis, control colors and line styles, and much more.

Discussion

The flot library is very flexbile and powerful. It has a multitude of options for controlling how graphs are drawn. We will not cover the details of the flot API here, but you're encouraged to explore the API and configuration options here: *http://people.iola.dk/olau/flot/API.txt*.

In addition to the built-in graph options, flot features a plug-in system that allows others to create extensions to its capabilities. This makes flot a very capable browser graphing solution for your sites. Several useful plug-ins are included with the flot distribution, and many others are available for optional usage.

There are, of course, dozens of other canvas graphing libraries available as well, some free and some for license. These options have a wide range of capabilities, so be sure to explore what's available.

See Also

For more information on using flot to plot graphs in a canvas element, see the flot home page at *http://code.google.com/p/flot*.

9.12 Saving a <canvas> Drawing to a File

Problem

You want to save the current drawing in a canvas element to a file.

Solution

The canvas API provides the command toDataURL(...), which will extract the image data from the canvas element into the specified image format. For instance, to extract the image data for a graph generated by flot (see Recipe 9.11) as a PNG format file, you would do this:

```
var canvas = $("canvas", my_graph)[0];
var image_data = canvas.toDataURL("image/png");
```

Now that you have the raw image data, you can save the image data as you please.

For instance, to send the image data to a server via Ajax, using jQuery, you might use:

```
$.post("http://location/path/to/upload", {data: image_data});
```

Discussion

The easy part is extracting the raw image data from the element. The hard part is saving that raw data to an actual file.

If you want to save the file back to a server, you can easily send the data to the server as a string value using Ajax. Once the data arrives on the server, you have to parse out the dataURI format, base64-decode the image data, and save that information to a file.

If you wanted to then let a user save that file to his computer, you could tell the browser to download the file you just created, which would then prompt the user to save the file on his system.

Some very recent releases of browsers are supporting local file access, so that you can (in theory) allow a user to save the image to his own computer without needing to first upload it to a server and then re-download it.

Because the process of actually handling these files in this way is rather complex (and beyond the scope of this chapter), you may want to instead use a tool like Canvas2Image, which takes care of much of this difficult stuff for you: *http://www.nihilogic.dk/labs/canvas2image/*.

See Also

For more information on saving **canvas** images to a server (using PHP) and then making them available for users to download and save, see this blog post: *http://blog.kevinsoo kocheff.com/saving-canvas-data-to-an-image-file-with-java-61171*.

CHAPTER 10

Advanced HTML5 JavaScript

Kyle Simpson

10.0 Introduction

HTML5 has dramatically broadened its scope from previous revisions. Whereas HTML4 was primarily focused on markup, HTML5 is focused not only on markup but also on a variety of advanced JavaScript APIs that help bring new features to life. However, most of these new technologies actually have their own specifications, working groups, etc., so it can be confusing to refer to the entire group of technologies under one umbrella term like "HTML5." It is for this reason that, as a way of being more precise, the trend has become to discuss such APIs as *companions* to HTML5—or, as some have put it, "HTML5 and friends." So, in this chapter, we get familiar with several friends of HTML5.

We've already covered the JavaScript APIs behind several markup-anchored elements, such as `canvas`, `audio`, and `video`. Here, our focus is on some other companion APIs, which notably are not necessarily tied to a particular markup element. You can think of the recipes in this chapter as being the meat on the bones of what it takes to create a truly interactive web application.

It's important to note that the technologies discussed in this chapter are in varying degrees of standardization and implementation. They are not universally agreed upon or built into browsers yet, so using them requires some caution and planning. For some things, there are ways to fall back to older or less-capable functionality in non-supporting browsers, but in other cases you have to build a workflow into your application that will handle when certain features are simply not present.

Because work on these particular sets of technologies is happening so rapidly, and what we know at the time of writing may be outdated by the time of reading, this chapter does not cover directly what things are supported where. You are encouraged to test these features in your target browser environments to get the most updated information.

10.1 Local Storage

Problem

You want to store some data (like user preferences or partially entered form data) persistently on a user's system, so that it's available on a subsequent visit.

Solution

HTML5 introduced two new APIs for in-browser persistent data storage: `sessionStorage`, which stores data only for the lifetime of the browser instance/session, and `localStorage`, which stores data persistently "forever" (which in this case means, "until either the code or the user clears it out").

Both interfaces have the same API. The difference between the two is basically how long the browser persists the data.

 Data stored in these containers must be strings. If you need to store complex data objects, one good option is to serialize the object into JSON, using `JSON.stringify()`.

To test if a browser supports either of the storage APIs, use the following feature-detect:

```
var storage_support = window.sessionStorage || window.localStorage;
```

To store some data for only the current browser instance (i.e., so it goes away when the user closes the browser), use `sessionStorage`:

```
var user_id = "A1B2C3D4";
var user_data = {
    name: "Tom Hanks",
    occupation: "Actor",
    favorite_color: "Blue"
    // ...
};

sessionStorage.setItem(user_id, JSON.stringify(user_data));
```

To store some data for a longer period of time, use `localStorage`:

```
var user_id = "A1B2C3D4";
var user_prefs = {
    keep_me_logged_in: true,
    start_page: "daily news"
    // ...
};

localStorage.setItem(user_id, JSON.stringify(user_prefs));
```

These code snippets look almost identical because the APIs are identical.

To pull data (if available) from the storage container, use code like this:

```
var user_id = "A1B2C3D4";
var user_data = { /* defaults */ };
var user_prefs = { /* defaults */ };

if (sessionStorage.getItem(user_id)) {
    user_data = JSON.parse(sessionStorage.getItem(user_id));
}
if (localStorage.getItem(user_id)) {
    user_prefs = JSON.parse(localStorage.getItem(user_id));
}
```

These storage APIs allow you to very simply set and retrieve key/value data, where the value is a string but can represent anything you want, including the string serialization of a complex data object.

> The localStorage and sessionStorage APIs are synchronous in design, which makes them easier to use but can result in slower performance. Be careful using these APIs in performance-sensitive code.

Discussion

The solution for storing data client-side that most likely first popped into your head is cookies. However, cookies have a number of problems that make them less than ideal for storing user data. In this chapter we explore a new alternative: the HTML5 storage (also known as "DOM storage") APIs.

sessionStorage and localStorage share the same API; the difference, as belied by their names, is in how long they persist the data. For data that you only need to persist for the lifetime of a browser session—things such as user login data, shopping cart contents, etc.—the sessionStorage API is probably your best option. For more long-lived data—things such as application preferences—localStorage may be a better option.

> Many browsers even persist sessionStorage data across browser crashes. This makes it a great container to temporarily mirror data being entered into form fields: if the browser crashes, you can restore what the user was typing.

The APIs for sessionStorage and localStorage are as follows:

getItem(*key*)
  Returns an item of data from the storage container, referenced by its key

setItem(*key*, *item*)
  Adds an item of data to the storage container, referenced by its key

key(*index*)

Returns the key for an item of data at the numerical index specified

removeItem(*key*)

Removes an item from the storage container, referenced by its key

clear()

Clears out all data in the current storage container

length

Identifies how many items of data are in the storage container

Most browsers give up to 5 MB of space for these storage containers. For most practical applications, this is more than enough. Be prepared to detect and handle errors, though, if you are writing more data than the browser allows.

Unlike cookies (which have explicit expirations) and sessionStorage (which has implicit expiration at the end of the browser instance/session), the localStorage API has no expiration at all. This has both good and bad consequences.

The benefit is that data stays around as long as you need it to unless the user explicitly clears it herself, but the downside is that the 5 MB limit may be reached more quickly than anticipated, especially if old data is abandoned and left forever to sit idle in the storage container.

One common solution is to implement a custom expiration mechanism, by storing a timestamp with each piece of data and then checking manually on each page load to see if any old data needs to be removed.

For instance, your ecommerce site might keep a record of all items the user has viewed across various visits, so it can display that in a "Previously Viewed" area. However, you don't want the application to remember those items forever, so you might manually expire entries that are older than, say, 21 days:

```
// first, store the currently viewed item in the history
var current_item = {
    id: "ABCD0123",
    data: "Mens' Running Shoes",
    ts: new Date() // current timestamp, used for expiration check later
};
localStorage.setItem(current_item.id, JSON.stringify(current_item));

// then manually "expire" all old entries
var key, data;

for (var i=0; i<localStorage.length; i++) {
    key = localStorage.key(i);
    data = localStorage.getItem(key);
    if (data.ts < ((new Date()) - 60*60*24*21)) { // more than 21 days old
        localStorage.removeItem(key);
    }
}
```

Both APIs restrict access to reading and writing data to the exact same page domain (domain, subdomain, schema, port, etc.) as the hosting page, meaning that you cannot share data across different domains with either of them. This is both a helpful and frustratingly restrictive reality: the benefit is that data is well protected privacy-wise (i.e., from other snooping sites), but the downside is that your application's different services on different domains cannot share their data through this interface.

See Also

For more information on the DOM storage APIs, see this MDC entry: *https://developer .mozilla.org/en/dom/storage*.

10.2 Application Caching

Problem

You want to make your web application (including all its resources) available to users even in an offline state, without relying on the normal browser cache.

Solution

HTML5 defines a special application cache, commonly called the appcache, that allows you to instruct the browser to cache certain resources—images, CSS, JS, etc.—in a way that makes them available to the application even if the user's browser is offline and not connected to the public Internet.

To test if the browser supports appcache functionality, use the following feature-detect:

```
var appcache_support = !!window.applicationCache;
```

To utilize appcache in your application, first you need to create a manifest file listing the resources you want in the appcache. This file might look like:

```
CACHE MANIFEST

CACHE:
index.html
help.html
style/default.css
images/logo.png
images/backgound.png
```

The appcache manifest file should include a CACHE section for listing the resources you want to include in the appcache. You can also specify a NETWORK section for URLs that need to be dynamically called (e.g., via Ajax) and should never be cached, and a FALL BACK section that lists local (cached) file fallbacks for any remote URL requests that fail (such as default content in an offline scenario for a normally online call to a server API).

Applications executing in the `appcache` context are not allowed to connect to remote URLs unless those URLs are listed within the `NETWORK` section of the manifest. This is to provide an additional layer of security to applications, preventing them from contacting servers that aren't known and whitelisted.

Once you have the manifest file—in this example we've named it *cache.manifest*—tell the browser about the file by adding a property to the `html` element in your markup, like so:

```
<html manifest="cache.manifest">
```

The cache manifest file must be served with the MIME type `text/cache-manifest`.

That's it! Now your application is offline-capable via `appcache`. The browser persistently caches the listed resources and does not re-request them on subsequent page loads, unless the cache manifest file changes.

Updating the appcache

Simply changing a file that is stored in a user's `appcache` is *not* enough to get that new version of the file delivered to the user. The browser will only check for updated versions of files in its `appcache` (and subsequently download any changes) if the manifest file changes.

However, you may not have any changes to make to the manifest file itself if, for example, there are no new resources to list and none to remove.

So, one easy approach is to include in your file a comment that you can update with a new value whenever you change one or more files and want the browser to update its `appcache`:

```
CACHE MANIFEST
# cache version: 1257

CACHE:
index.html
help.html
style/default.css
images/logo.png
images/backgound.png
```

Each time you update a resource that is in the `appcache`, simply bump up the version number in the comment. The next time a user loads the page, the browser will see this new cache manifest file and update the `appcache` contents.

There's a catch, however. Even if the browser sees during page load that the manifest file has changed, it still lets the current page load continue immediately, with the now out-of-date appcache contents; it then asks for the updated files to be loaded in the background, to be ready for the *next* page load.

Fortunately, the browser provides a JavaScript API to help: the applicationCache interface. Using this interface, you can detect that a new set of appcache contents has been fetched and is now available, and force them to be applied to the appcache right away, rather than on the next page load:

```
var cache = applicationCache;
cache.addEventListener("updateready", function(){
    if (cache.stats == cache.UPDATEREADY) {
        cache.swapCache(); // swap in the new cache items
    }
}, false);
```

This makes the new appcache items available for any further uses during the current page lifetime.

However, any places where the resources were already used on the page are not updated. That can result in a strange user experience, depending on the situation.

The cleanest way to force the entire page to be updated with the new resource versions is to simply reload the page. However, be kind to the user, and first ask if he wants to reload the page, like this:

```
var cache = applicationCache;
cache.addEventListener("updateready", function(){
    if (cache.stats == cache.UPDATEREADY) {
        if (confirm("This site has been updated. Do you want to reload?")) {
            location.reload();
        }
    }
}, false);
```

So far, we've only seen how to respond to cases where the appcache is marked for updating during a page load. However, some sites are designed to be long-lived, with few or no page reloads. In this case, getting updates requires special handling.

To force the browser to do a check for an updated *cache.manifest* file and fetch the appcache contents if the file has been modified, you can call the update() API method:

```
function updateAppcache(){
    var cache = applicationCache;
    cache.update(); // check to see if the cache manifest file has been updated

    cache.addEventListener("updateready", function(){
        if (cache.stats == cache.UPDATEREADY) {
            if (confirm("This site has been updated. Do you want to reload?")) {
                location.reload();
            }
        }
    }
```

```
        }, false);
    }
```

Typically, you would wire up such a check to happen either on an automatic time interval, such as every 24 hours, or in response to a specific application action, such as the user clicking a button in your page.

 If you perform appcache updates at an automatic time interval, prompting the user before a reload is probably the friendliest approach. However, if the user initiates the update you can probably safely reload the page without prompting, as soon as the appcache is updated.

Discussion

We mentioned that the appcache is special, and the reason for that assertion is that, unlike with the browser cache, resources that are in the appcache never expire (this is similar to the localStorage interface we discussed in Recipe 10.1).

Practically speaking, this means any resources listed in the cache manifest are cached permanently. More specifically, the browser does not re-request any of those resources on subsequent page loads.

The persistent caching of resources definitely improves performance on subsequent page views, especially on bandwidth-limited mobile devices. However, it's sometimes necessary to be able to update one or more items in that persistent cache.

There are two ways to go about forcing the browser to discard its cache and update the resources listed in the manifest. One technique is useful for subsequent page loads, while the other is useful for updates during the lifetime of a single page view.

It's important to understand that if an appcache already exists for a page at the time of page load, even if it's determined to be out of date by virtue of finding an updated cache manifest file, the browser still uses the current appcache to render the page; any updates to the appcache contents are available only on the *next* page load.

However, using JavaScript via the UPDATEREADY event, as shown above, you can detect that the current page was rendered with out-of-date cache items and force an update of the appcache during that page view. This allows any subsequent uses of resources in the page lifetime to use the updated versions of the files. You can also just reload the entire page to use the new appcache contents everywhere, as long as this is okay with the user.

The appcache is considered to be more reliable for offline application resource caching than the normal browser cache. It also provides a JavaScript API for interacting with updates—something the regular browser cache doesn't provide.

See Also

The beginner's guide provides an introduction to `applicationCache` functionality at *http://www.html5rocks.com/en/tutorials/appcache/beginner/*. For more in-depth information on the `applicationCache` API, see this MDC entry: *https://developer.mozilla.org/en/offline_resources_in_firefox*. In addition, *http://appcachefacts.info* has a great discussion of important nuances of `appcache` behavior.

10.3 Drag and Drop

Problem

You want to implement native drag-and-drop functionality without managing mouse events manually or using a complex library.

Solution

Recognizing how common drag-and-drop interaction is in today's complex web applications, HTML5 now defines a direct API for handling drag and drop ("D&D").

To test if the browser supports native D&D functionality, use the following feature-detect:

```
var dnd_support = 'draggable' in document.createElement('span');
```

Now, let's build a simple D&D demo. We'll begin by setting up some visual styles for our D&D elements:

```
<style>
#foobar { background-color:yellow; width:100px; height:100px; cursor:move; }
#catcher { background-color:blue; width:150px; height:150px; padding:5px;
    margin-bottom:5px; }
</style>
```

The first step in enabling native D&D is to put the `draggable` attribute on the element you want to be drag-enabled:

```
<div id="catcher">...</div>
<div id="foobar" draggable="true">...</div>
```

Next, we need to use the JavaScript API and D&D events to tell the browser where the element can be dragged to and what to do once it's dropped there.

For example, we can listen for the `dragstart` event, and style the element differently when it's being dragged (e.g., putting a border around it or making it partially transparent):

```
var foobar = document.getElementById("foobar");
foobar.addEventListener("dragstart", function(evt) {
    this.style.border = "3px dotted #000"; // black dotted-line border
}, false);
```

Now let's style an element that can receive the drop, so that when the dragged item is over it, it is obvious that you can drop the element there (as opposed to just dropping it in any location):

```
var catcher = document.getElementById("catcher"); // catch the dropped element
catcher.addEventListener("dragenter", function(evt) {
    this.style.border = "3px solid red"; // give the catcher a red border
}, false);

catcher.addEventListener("dragleave", function(evt) {
    this.style.border = ""; // remove the border from the catcher
}, false);

catcher.addEventListener("dragover", function(evt) {
    if (evt.preventDefault) evt.preventDefault();
    return false;
}, false);
```

In the preceding snippet, we added event listeners to the element that catches our dropped element for the dragover, dragenter, and dragleave events. The dragenter and dragleave events simply toggle on and off a red border for our target element, to make it clear that you can drop the element there (as shown in Figure 10-1).

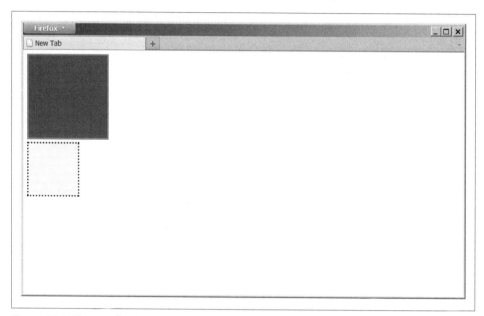

Figure 10-1. Showing the drag event in progress, dragging the yellow box into the blue box

The dragover event is fired continuously while dragging the element around on top of the target, so we do not want to toggle on the red border in that handler (doing so would create unnecessary work for the browser). However, we do need to prevent that event's default behavior, depending on the type of element being dragged. This is why we use preventDefault() and return false.

Lastly, we need to wire up a dataTransfer object with data that the browser needs for handling the D&D actions. So, we'll modify our dragstart event handler like so:

```
foobar.addEventListener("dragstart", function(evt) {
    this.style.border = "3px dotted #000"; // black dotted-line border

    evt.dataTransfer.effectAllowed = "move";
    evt.dataTransfer.setData("Text", this.id);
}, false);
```

The effectAllowed property controls what visual feedback—generally the mouse cursor—the browser gives on the type of drag event that is occurring (move, copy, etc.).

The setData(...) method tells the D&D mechanism in the browser which data from the element being dragged should be dropped into the target element, otherwise known as the *drop catcher*. Here we specify that only the id property of the original element, which is used later to actually move the element, is transferred.

Now we need to define a dragend event handler to clear up the visuals and a drop event handler to actually do the moving of our element:

```
foobar.addEventListener("dragend", function(evt) {
    this.style.border = ""; // remove the border
}, false);

catcher.addEventListener("drop", function(evt) {
    if (evt.preventDefault) evt.preventDefault();
    if (evt.stopPropagation) evt.stopPropagation();

    this.style.border = ""; // remove the border from the catcher

    var id = evt.dataTransfer.getData("Text"); // get the id
    var elem = document.getElementById(id);
    elem.parentNode.removeChild(elem); // remove the element
    this.appendChild(elem); // add the element back into our catcher

    return false;
}, false);
```

In the drop event handler, we first get the data that was transferred in the drop, which in this case was the id property of the original source element that we dragged. Next, we remove that element from its current location, and finally add it back into the new location inside our catcher container. The result is shown in Figure 10-2.

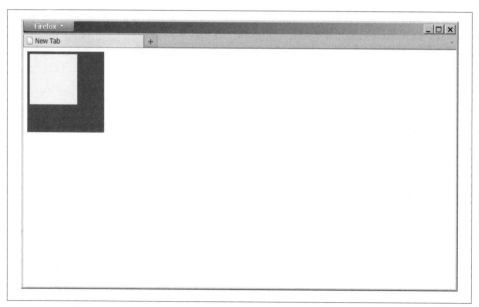

Figure 10-2. Showing the results of dragging the yellow box into the blue box

Discussion

The native HTML5 drag-and-drop API is both useful and quite complex. As you can see from the previous code snippets, it doesn't require an entire complex library to enable D&D on your site, but it's not particularly trivial either. With that complexity, though, comes lots of flexibility.

The first and most obvious thing you'll notice when attempting to run the above code yourself (it's not entirely obvious just from the screenshots) is that the yellow box itself doesn't move while you are holding down the mouse button and moving the mouse.

Different browsers render this experience slightly differently, but in general, the yellow box stays put during the drag; what shows is a different icon for the mouse cursor, to let the user know that a D&D event is in progress.

It may seem a bit counterintuitive that dragging an element doesn't actually move the element itself. You might expect it to work the same as if you drag a window around on your desktop—the window tracks along directly under the mouse cursor as you move.

On the other hand, if you drag an icon around on the Windows OS desktop, the icon doesn't move with the mouse—it only moves once you let go of the mouse button and stop the drag (this is the drop). This latter experience is more closely aligned with how native D&D works in HTML5.

Consider that native D&D is designed so you can drag all sorts of different things, not all of which have visual representations like our yellow box does. As such, native D&D

does not necessarily imply actually visually moving any element on the page. Instead, D&D is about dragging a reference from one object to another and connecting the two in a D&D event, whereby you can then decide what that connection means and how to respond.

The events associated with native D&D are:

dragstart
> Called when the "draggable" element first starts being dragged

dragend
> Called at the end of a drag event, successful or canceled

dragenter
> Called on a target drop container when the drag first moves over the target

dragleave
> Called when the drag moves off the target

dragover
> Called continuously while the drag is over the target

drop
> Called when the drag event is completed by dropping the element onto the target drop container

Sometimes, you might just be copying invisible attributes from one element to another. Other times, you might be initiating some action like deleting, by moving an element onto a trash icon. In our example, we are repositioning the yellow box inside the blue box, so once the D&D event finishes, we actually move the yellow box.

Since the yellow box is visible, it seems to make sense that we might want to move it around as we drag (like when dragging a window). However, the typical JavaScript approach to this does not work, because the mousemove event does not fire during a D&D action. The global drag event does fire on the document, but cross-browser it doesn't reliably have coordinates we can use to position the element.

If you need to actually move an element around during the drag, it's best not to use native D&D... for now, anyway. Hopefully this shortcoming will be addressed eventually. Until then, use established patterns and/or libraries for emulating D&D with mouse events.

Another very advanced usage of the native D&D functionality that is on the horizon is the ability to drag items between windows, or between your browser and the desktop, and vice versa. For instance, you can drag a file from your desktop and drop it onto a target on a web page. You respond to the drop the same way as in the code snippets above; the only difference is that you don't need an element on your page with the draggable attribute to be the thing that you dragged. For example:

```
catcher.addEventListener("drop", function(evt) {
    if (evt.preventDefault) evt.preventDefault();
    if (evt.stopPropagation) evt.stopPropagation();
```

```
    this.style.border = ""; // remove the border from the catcher

    var files_array = evt.dataTransfer.files;
    // Now you have a reference to the file(s) that the user dragged
    // onto your page. Do something cool with them!

    return false;
}, false);
```

As you can see, the native D&D functionality is focused on data transfer between two elements, rather than on moving an element from one position to another. This helps us out here big time. We receive in the `dataTransfer.files` property a list of references to the file(s) that the user chose to drag onto our application. There is nothing visual about this operation—it is entirely about dragging data (file references) from the desktop to an element on our page!

 Once we have a reference to a file on the user's system, what can we do with it? We address that in Recipe 10.7.

There are likely to be a lot of changes to this advanced functionality before it settles and is standardized across all browsers. But it's exciting to know that it's coming soon!

See Also

For more information on native HTML5 drag and drop, see this tutorial: *http://www .html5rocks.com/en/tutorials/dnd/basics/*.

10.4 Web Workers

Problem

You want to run a complex, long-running JavaScript task without locking up the UI in the browser.

Solution

You need to run the JavaScript task in a separate thread, and the way to do this is with the `Worker` API, otherwise known as Web Workers.

Web Workers create a special environment for JavaScript code to run in that occurs in a separate thread from the main UI of your page. This means that your page's UI won't be locked up if you have particularly long-running JavaScript code.

To test if the browser supports Web Workers, use the following feature-detect for the `Worker` API:

```
var webworkers_support = !!window.Worker;
```

Now let's build a simple Web Workers demo. We'll initialize a large two-dimensional array with random numbers, a task that may take long enough to cause a noticeable UI delay. (You might use such a 2D array of random numbers to represent random pixels in a `canvas` element; see Chapter 9.) Two nested `for` loops do the trick:

```
var data = [];
for (var i=0; i<1500; i++) {
    data[i] = [];
    for (var j=0; j<1500; j++) {
        data[i][j] = Math.random();
    }
}
```

There's nothing particularly exciting going on here. Such an array, with 2.25 million (1500 × 1500) operations to initialize it, may very well lock up the UI for anywhere from 2 to 30 seconds, depending on browser and device capability.

A more graceful way to handle this, without locking the UI, is to put such an operation into a separate thread—a Web Worker—and simply wait to be notified of it finishing before continuing.

To do this, put the above code into a separate file (called, for instance, *init_array.js*) and wrap the code in an `onmessage` event handler:

```
self.onmessage = function(evt) {
    var data = [];
    for (var i=0; i<1500; i++) {
        data[i] = [];
        for (var j=0; j<1500; j++) {
            data[i][j] = Math.random();
        }
    }

    self.postMessage(data);
    data = null; // unassign our copy of the data now, to free up memory
};
```

This is the code for the Web Worker. The code first tells the worker to listen for the `message` event, which lets the worker know when to start. Once started, the worker performs the long-running computation. Finally, the worker sends back a message (the data array in our example), using `postMessage(...)`, to the main page. Workers can also be started by other workers, and the communication works exactly the same.

Unlike in normal JavaScript operations, where passing an object around is done by reference, the data passed in worker messages is *copied*, which means that double the memory is consumed during the transmission. For most types of data, this is not an issue to be concerned with.

But in our example with the large array, the considerable memory usage is something to watch out for as it may cause issues on memory-limited mobile devices. To conserve memory, only keep variables with large amounts of data in them around for the shortest amount of time necessary.

In the main page of our UI, we create the worker, pointing it at the appropriate file. Then we set up a listener for the `message` event, to receive the message (the initialized array) from the worker when it finishes its job. Finally, we start the worker by sending it an empty message using `postMessage()`:

```
var worker = new Worker("init_array.js");

worker.onmessage = function(evt) {
    alert("Data array initialization finished!");
    var data = evt.data;
};

worker.postMessage(); // tell our worker to start its task
```

Discussion

Web Workers are very useful for offloading complex or long-running tasks to another thread, something that JavaScript itself cannot do.

If Web Workers are not supported in a particular browser, you'll need to just run your code in the main JavaScript thread, and deal with the delays it may cause. In some circumstances, you can break up your long-running code into smaller chunks and run one chunk at a time, pausing briefly in between to let the UI update before resuming. For example:

```
function doNextChunk() {
    var done_yet = false;
    for (var i=0; i<500; i++) { // do 500 iterations at a time
        // do something
        // when done, set done_yet = true
    }
    if (!done_yet) setTimeout(doNextChunk,0);
    else alert("All done finally!");
}

doNextChunk();
```

Using a `setTimeout(...,0)` pattern, we do 500 iterations of a long-running loop, pause for a brief moment (just long enough for the UI to update), then resume and do another 500 iterations, and so on. This technique has better performance than letting a long-running piece of code tie up the UI indefinitely, but it is still far less efficient than if Web Workers can be used.

By creating a Web Worker, you are creating a bridge between the main JavaScript in your page and a sandboxed piece of JavaScript running in another thread. The two sides of the bridge communicate with each other by asynchronously sending and receiving messages, using `postMessage(...)` and listening for the `message` event.

 An asynchronous Ajax call using `XMLHttpRequest` ("XHR") to a server is quite similar to sending and receiving asynchronous messages to/from a Web Worker.

The Web Workers communication interface also allows errors to be sent and received. To signal an error from inside a worker, simply `throw` a JavaScript error, like so:

```
self.onmessage = function(evt) {
    var data = [];
    for (var i=0; i<1500; i++) {
        data[i] = [];
        for (var j=0; j<1500; j++) {
            data[i][j] = Math.random();
            if (data[i][j] == 0) {
                throw "I don't like zeros in my array!";
            }
        }
    }

    self.postMessage(data);
    data = null; // unassign our copy of the data now, to free up memory
};
```

To receive an error message from a worker, listen for the `error` event:

```
var worker = new Worker("init_array.js");

worker.onerror = function(err) {
    alert("An error occurred in the initialization of the array.");
    throw err; // optional
};

worker.onmessage = function(evt) {
    alert("Data array initialization finished!");
    var data = evt.data;
};

worker.postMessage();
```

A Web Worker is sandboxed away from the main page, and basically can only communicate with the page using these messages. That means the worker cannot access the DOM to read or modify any information. Also, UI-centric tasks like calling an `alert(...)` dialog are not allowed.

However, a worker does have several helpful things available to it. For example, it can access the `navigator` object, to identify the user agent (browser) running it, and it can load scripts into itself using the `importScripts(...)` command:

```
if (navigator.userAgent.test(/MSIE/)) { // UA sniffing is *bad* practice!!
    importScripts("ie_helper.js");
}
self.onmessage = function(evt) {
    /* ... */
};
```

 `loadScripts(...)` loads one or more scripts in parallel, but always executes them in the order requested. Also, `loadScripts(...)` executes synchronously, meaning it blocks the rest of the worker until it finishes loading and executing the scripts.

A worker may spawn another worker, as we've just seen. The code that created a worker may also terminate it, by calling `terminate()` on the worker instance.

Finally, workers may use timeouts and intervals, including `setTimeout(...)`, `clearTimeout(...)`, `setInterval(...)`, and `clearInterval(...)`. This would be useful if, for instance, you wanted to have a worker running in the background every so often, notifying the page each time it runs:

```
self.onmessage = function(evt) {
    setInterval(function(){
        self.postMessage(Math.random()); // send a random number back
    }, 60*60*1000); // execute once per hour
};
```

See Also

The W3C specification for Web Workers at *http://dev.w3.org/html5/workers/*.

10.5 Web Sockets

Problem

You want to create persistent, two-way communication between your web application and the server, so that both the browser and the server can send and receive data to and from each other as needed.

Solution

Most browsers now have the native ability to establish a bidirectional socket connection between themselves and the server, using the `WebSocket` API. This means that both sides (browser and server) can send and receive data. Common use cases for Web Sockets are live online games, stock tickers, chat clients, etc.

To test if the browser supports Web Sockets, use the following feature-detect for the WebSocket API:

```
var websockets_support = !!window.WebSocket;
```

Now, let's build a simple application with chat room–type functionality, where a user may read the current list of messages and add her own message to the room.

We'll have a text entry box where new messages are written before being sent, and we'll have a list of messages in the chat room. We don't need features such as login or authentication here, only simple chat room message sending and receiving:

```
<!DOCTYPE html>
<html>
<head>
<title>Our Chatroom</title>
<script src="chatroom.js"></script>
</head>
<body>
<h1>Our Chatroom</h1>

<div id="chatlog"></div>

<input id="newmsg" /><br />
<input type="button" value="Send Message" id="sendmsg" />
</body>
</html>
```

Now, let's examine the JavaScript in *chatroom.js*:

```
var chatcomm = new WebSocket("ws://something.com/server/chat");

chatcomm.onmessage = function(msg) {
    msg = JSON.parse(msg); // decode JSON into object

    var chatlog = document.getElementById("chatlog");
    var docfrag = document.createDocumentFragment();
    var msgdiv;

    for (var i=0; i<msg.messages.length; i++) {
        msgdiv = document.createElement("div");
        msgdiv.appendChild(document.createTextNode(msg.messages[i]));
        docfrag.appendChild(msgdiv);
    }

    chatlog.appendChild(docfrag);
};

chatcomm.onclose = function() {
    alert("The chatroom connection was lost. Refresh page to reconnect.");
};

document.getElementById("sendmsg").addEventListener("click", function(){
    var newmsg = document.getElementById("newmsg");

    chatcomm.send(newmsg.value); // send the message to the server
```

```
        newmsg.value = ""; // clear out the message entry box
    }, false);
```

Let's break down that code just a little bit. First we create the socket and point it at a location on our server. The server URL in our example uses the "ws://" protocol, as opposed to the more common "http://" you're familiar with. This signals the special protocol that Web Sockets use between client and server.

Next, we set up two event listeners on our socket object: `onmessage` and `onclose`. The `onclose` handler is self-explanatory—it is fired when the connection is closed.

 The server-side implementation of this chat room demo is beyond the scope of this chapter, but there are lots of tutorials and software projects that make this very easy to implement in any of your favorite server-side languages, including PHP, JavaScript (*node.js*), Java, etc.

Such a chat room server just needs to implement basic send and receive actions, much like the JavaScript you see here for the client. As a basic implementation, the server doesn't even need to persist the messages; it can just publish each message out to the socket stream as it is received, meaning that all clients that are currently connected see it.

Our `onmessage` handler receives a string of data (which in our example we expect to be JSON) and parses it into a message object. The message object contains an array of one or more messages (each one is just simple text). The handler loops through each message, adding it to the chat log in the order received.

Lastly, the code sets up a `click` event handler on the "Send Message" button. When clicked, the handler takes whatever has been typed into the text entry input and sends it to the server, using the `send(...)` method.

Discussion

Admittedly, this type of functionality is not at all new. Since the advent of Ajax, using the `XMLHttpRequest` ("XHR") object, developers have been sending and receiving data between browser and server. Other approaches have included instantiating an invisible Flash object and using Flash's socket communication capabilities.

However, it's quite inefficient in the XHR approach to establish a whole new connection for each piece of data you need to send from browser to server. It's similarly undesirable to instantiate a memory-heavy Flash instance to use socket communication. So, Web Sockets are understandably a welcomed addition to the "HTML5 & Friends" family of technologies.

The message sending and receiving in Web Sockets is like a sensible mix between XHR and Web Workers, which we looked at in the previous recipe.

Web Sockets require both the browser and the server to speak a standardized and agreed-upon protocol (much like HTTP is for normal web pages). However, this protocol has undergone quite a lot of experimentation and change as it has developed over the last couple of years.

While things are beginning to stabilize, Web Sockets are still quite volatile, and you have to make sure that your server is speaking the most up-to-date version of the protocol so that the browser can communicate properly with it.

The `WebSocket` object instance has, similar to XHR, a `readyState` property that lets you examine the state of the connection. It can have the following constant values:

`{worker}.CONNECTING (numeric value 0)`
 Connection has not yet been established

`{worker}.OPEN (numeric value 1)`
 Connection is open and communication is possible

`{worker}.CLOSING (numeric value 2)`
 Connection is being closed

`{worker}.CLOSED (numeric value 3)`
 Connection is closed (or was never opened successfully)

The events that a `WebSocket` object instance fires are:

`open`
 Called when the connection has been opened

`message`
 Called when a message has been received from the server

`error`
 Called when an error occurs with the socket (sending or receiving)

`close`
 Called when the connection is closed

For each of these events, you can add an event listener using `addEventListener(...)`, or you can set a corresponding handler directly on the worker object instance, including `onopen`, `onmessage`, `onerror`, and `onclose`.

If Web Sockets are not supported, you'll need to provide some fallback functionality for your application, or at least gracefully notify the user that his browser doesn't support the required functionality. Fortunately, there's a very easy way to do that.

Because consistent browser support for Web Sockets has been elusive, the best practice suggestion for using Web Sockets is to use a library like Socket.io (*http://socket.io*), which attempts to use Web Sockets if available, and falls back to a variety of other techniques for communication if Web Sockets are not present.

You should also be aware of how Web Sockets usage scales in terms of server resources. Traditional web requests only take up dedicated resources from the server for a split second at a time, which means you can serve a lot of web traffic from your server without having too much overlap and thus running out of resources.

Sockets, on the other hand, tend to be more dedicated, so there can be issues with resource availability under high load. Your server setup and architecture will vary greatly with your application's needs and are a big factor in how well you are able to utilize Web Sockets.

See Also

For more information about Socket.io, see the project home page at *http://socket.io*.

10.6 History

Problem

For your web application, you want fine-grained control to manage the forward/backward button history queue, as well as the displayed URL in the address bar of the browser.

Solution

HTML5 brings us several important enhancements to the browser's `window.history` object, commonly referred to as the `History` API.

To test if the browser supports the enhanced `History` API, use the following feature-detect:

```
var history_support = !!(window.history && window.history.pushState);
```

Normally, when you change the URL in the address bar, the browser initiates a new request to the server for that new page. But today's complex web applications more commonly use Ajax to load only new information, without full-page refreshes. This leads to a disconnect, where web applications can't update the address bar URL because they don't want a browser page refresh.

To change the URL in the address bar without forcing a new page load, use the `history.pushState(...)` method. This method updates the URL in the address bar and creates a special state-oriented entry in the browser's history. This means that if a user then clicks the back button in her browser, instead of doing a reload of the previous page, the browser fires the new `popstate` event, which your application can respond to by setting the page back to that previous state.

The new URL you pass to pushState() or replaceState() must have the same origin (domain, etc.) as the current page, or the API throws an error. You can change the path, filename, query string, and hash portions of the URL, just not the protocol/schema, domain, or port.

It would make no sense, and indeed would be a security risk, to allow mixing of URL origins in the state queue. Use normal location/history manipulation if you need to navigate across different origins.

Let's take a look at an example of how these two additional functionalities work together to allow you to handle forward/backward navigation with only state changes (and not separate page loads), as well as keeping the displayed URL in the address bar up-to-date.

Our example keeps track of whether an element is visible or not, and maintains this state in the browser's forward/backward navigation stack—as well as reflecting that state in the browser address bar URL—so that the current state can be copied and pasted or bookmarked:

```
<html>
<head>
<title>History Exmaple</title>
<script>
function showText(updateHistory) {
    document.getElementById("long_desc").style.display = "block";
    if (updateHistory) history.pushState(null, null, "?show");
}
function hideText(updateHistory) {
    document.getElementById("long_desc").style.display = "none";
    if (updateHistory) history.pushState(null, null, location.href.replace(/\?show/, ""));
}
function toggleText() {
    var elem = document.getElementById("long_desc");
    if (elem.style && elem.style.display == "none") showText(true);
    else hideText(true);
}
function manageText() {
    if (location.href.match(/\?show/)) showText();
    else hideText();
}

window.addEventListener("popstate", manageText, false);
window.addEventListener("DOMContentLoaded", function(){
    document.getElementById("toggle").addEventListener("click", function(e){
        toggleText();
        e.preventDefault();
        return false;
    }, false);

    manageText();
}, false);
</script>
```

```
  </head>
  <body>
  <p>Here's a short description.</p>
  <a id="toggle" href="#">toggle</a>
  <p id="long_desc">Here's a longer description, which can be shown or hidden.</p>
  </body>
  </html>
```

If you run this demo and click successively on the "toggle" link, you'll see that the longer text description paragraph is indeed toggled on and off. You'll also notice that when the paragraph is visible, the URL has "?show" in it, and when it's hidden, this parameter is removed. Finally, you will notice the forward/backward navigation cycles through these states, showing and hiding the paragraph as appropriate.

Try copying the URL while the "?show" is visible and pasting it into a new browser tab, and you'll see that indeed the paragraph is visible—the state really was preserved in the URL, as we wanted.

The above example keeps track of the state changes in the forward/backward queue of the browser. For some applications, this is desirable. For other applications, polluting the forward/backward queue with lots and lots of intermittent state changes is not appropriate.

In this case, instead of using pushState(...) you can use replaceState(...), which (as the name implies) replaces the current state entry in the forward/backward navigation with the new desired state. If we do that for our example above, it looks like this:

```
// ...

function showText(updateHistory) {
    document.getElementById("long_desc").style.display = "block";
    if (updateHistory) history.replaceState(null, null, "?show");
}
function hideText(updateHistory) {
    document.getElementById("long_desc").style.display = "none";
    if (updateHistory) history.replaceState(null, null, location.href.replace(/\?show/, ""));
}

// ...
```

Running that updated demo, you'll see that the toggling and the URL behave the same. The only difference is that there's no forward/backward queue state to cycle through.

Discussion

Browsers have long supported a History API. The difference that HTML5 brings is the enhanced functionality of pushState(...), replaceState(...), and popstate.

Before the HTML5 History API enhancements were added to browsers, the only way to emulate the functionality described above was using the URL's "hash" (the end of a URL that looks like "#some|stuff|here").

In terms of behavior, most browsers agree in that if you change the current page's hash, the browser saves that state in the forward/backward queue, updates the displayed URL, and does not request a new page from the server. On the surface, that sounds just like what we're looking for. However, there are several browser quirks (race conditions, etc.) that make it hard to get consistent and reliable results when dealing with hash changes.

In particular, older browsers don't all support the hashchange event, which is very helpful in monitoring the state of the URL hash in case a user copies and pastes a URL into the address bar. Without that event, you must poll the URL hash using a timer.

Fortunately, all this mess is generally taken care of by various helper libraries. One particularly useful library is History.js (*https://github.com/balupton/history.js*), which attempts to use the new HTML5 History API enhancements and falls back to URL hash management automatically.

The above code example stores a simple state in the URL ("?show"). This is good for the copy/paste (or bookmarking) use case, as the entirety of the state is in the URL and thus restorable.

If you have a more complex set of states to manage, and copy/paste or bookmarking is not important, you can actually store a much richer and more complex set of states with each entry. This complex state is saved with an entry, and then retrieved and sent back to your application via the popstate event handler as the user navigates back with the back button.

The first parameter to pushState(...)/replaceState(...) is the state object, which can be any arbitrarily complex object that you need, as long as it's serializable to a string value. For example:

```
window.addEventListener("popstate", function(e){
    alert("Current state data: " + JSON.stringify(e.state));
}, false);

window.pushState({foo:"bar"}, null, "?foobar");
window.pushState({bar:"baz"}, null, "?barbaz");
history.back(); // triggers popstate to go back to the "?foobar" page/state
```

 Browsers currently don't support the second parameter, which is a "title" for the new state, so just pass null or an empty string for that parameter.

See Also

For more information about using the API, see the following MDC entry: *https://devel oper.mozilla.org/en/DOM/Manipulating_the_browser_history*. For more information about History.js, see the github repo at *https://github.com/balupton/history.js*.

10.7 Local Files

Problem

You want users to be able to read an image file from their local filesystem and do something with it in the web page, such as previewing or uploading it.

Solution

Prior to HTML5, the only interaction users could have with their local filesystem was through the `<input type="file">` element. This functionality was opaque as far as the page's JavaScript was concerned, because the page couldn't see anything about the file selected, or interact with it in any meaningful way.

HTML5 gives us the `FileReader` API, which lets us take a reference to a local file and read its contents directly into the web page. To test if the browser supports the enhanced `FileReader` API, use the following feature-detect:

```
var history_support = typeof FileReader != "undefined";
```

We saw in Recipe 10.3, how to get a reference to a local file or files using the native drag-and-drop functionality. In a very similar way, we can now get a reference to the local file(s) selected by the user in an `<input type="file">` element:

```
<p>Pick an image file:</p>
<input type="file" id="file_selector" />

<script>
var file_selector = document.getElementById("file_selector");
file_selector.addEventListener("change", function(){
    var files_array = this.files;
    // Now you have a reference to the file(s) that the user selected.
    // Do something cool with them!
}, false);
</script>
```

Either way, once you have a reference to a local file, such as an image file, you can read the contents of that file using a `FileReader` instance:

```
function read_image_file(file) {
    var reader = new FileReader();
    reader.onload = function(e){
        var image_contents = e.target.result;
        // now you have the contents of the file
    };
    reader.readAsDataURL(file);
}
```

Now that you have the file contents—in this case, as a *data URI* (base64 encoding of the file)—you can display the contents in an `img` element. The code all put together looks like this:

```
<p>Pick an image file:</p>
<input type="file" id="file_selector" />

<script>
var file_selector = document.getElementById("file_selector");
file_selector.addEventListener("change", function(){
    var files_array = this.files;
    // we only allowed one file to be selected
    if (files_array[0].type.match(/image/)) { // it's an image file
        read_image_file(files_array[0]);
    }
}, false);

function read_image_file(file) {
    var reader = new FileReader();
    reader.onload = function(e){
        var image_contents = e.target.result;
        var img = document.createElement("img");
        img.src = image_contents;
        document.body.appendChild(img);
    };
    reader.readAsDataURL(file);
}
</script>
```

This code snippet assumes only one file has been selected, but the <input type="file"> element now supports the multiple attribute, which allows the user to select more than one file at a time. This is why we receive an array of file references, rather than a single file reference.

If you also want to let the user upload the selected image file, you simply need to send the file's contents to the server via an XHR Ajax call:

```
<p>Pick an image file:</p>
<input type="file" id="file_selector" />
<input type="button" id="upload" value="Upload Image" disabled />

<script>
var file_selector = document.getElementById("file_selector");
file_selector.addEventListener("change", function(){
    var files_array = this.files;
    // we only allowed one file to be selected
    if (files_array[0].type.match(/image/)) { // it's an image file
        read_image_file(files_array[0]);

        file_selector.disabled = true; // disable the file selector now
        var upload = document.getElementById("upload");
        upload.disabled = false;
        upload.addEventListener("click", function(){
            upload_file(files_array[0]);
        }, false);
    }
}, false);
```

```
function upload_file(file) {
    var xhr = new XMLHttpRequest();
    xhr.setRequestHeader("Content-Type", "multipart/form-data");
    xhr.setRequestHeader("X-File-Name", file.fileName);
    xhr.setRequestHeader("X-File-Size", file.fileSize);
    xhr.setRequestHeader("X-File-Type", file.type);
    xhr.open("GET", "image_upload.php");
    xhr.send(file);
}

function read_image_file(file) {
    var reader = new FileReader();
    reader.onload = function(e){
        var image_contents = e.target.result;
        var img = document.createElement("img");
        img.src = image_contents;
        document.body.appendChild(img);
    };
    reader.readAsDataURL(file);
}
</script>
```

Notice that you now have access to the file's name, size, and type, so you send that data along to the server with the file's contents. Other than that, we're not doing much extra here that's particularly HTML5y—we're just using standard XHR to upload the file.

Discussion

HTML5 gives us the FileReader API, so we can read the contents of a user's local file and use those contents in our web pages.

The example above shows how to use the contents of an image file to display a preview, and how to send (i.e., upload) those file contents to a server using Ajax. Of course, there are a variety of other things you might want to do with the file's contents. For instance, the FileReader API provides a readAsBinaryString(...) method that gives you a binary string representation of the file's contents. If you know the format of the file you are reading, you can perform various operations on this data.

As another example, if you put the image data into an img element (as shown above), you could use what you learned in Recipe 9.5, to render that image to a canvas element, where you can then perform various color and geometric transformations (see Recipes 9.6 and 9.7).

At this time, access to local files is restricted to read-only, and it must be initiated by a user action, such as dragging a file onto the web page or selecting one or more files from the <input type="file"> element. This is probably for the best, safety-wise, as allowing pages to write to the local filesystem, while cool, could be quite dangerous!

Also, keep in mind that local file access is still heavily evolving in browsers, so it's very important to test the functionality you want in your target browser environments and to provide fallback behavior if it isn't present or doesn't work the way you need it to.

See Also

For more information about interacting with local files from the web page, see this MDC entry: *https://developer.mozilla.org/en/Using_files_from_web_applications*.

HTML5 Resources

Comparison of HTML5 Layout Engines (http://en.wikipedia.org/wiki/Comparison_of _layout_engines_(HTML_5))

> Not all browsers are equal. Check with this page for a breakdown of how different engines handle HTML5.

Comparison of JavaScript frameworks (http://en.wikipedia.org/wiki/Comparison_of _JavaScript_frameworks)

> A Wikipedia entry serving as a feature comparison between the different JavaScript libraries that make web building easier. Included in the comprehensive listing are entries on how well each library handles basic accessibility and ARIA support.

Dive into HTML5 (http://diveintohtml5.info/)

> Written in the public domain and codified in *HTML5: Up and Running*, Mark Pilgrim breaks down the HTML5 specification and browser support in exquisite detail.

HTML5 Boilerplate (http://html5boilerplate.com/)

> The title is a bit of misnomer as it includes more than HTML5, but the misnomer is the only complaint. The entire HTML5 Boilerplate is a thesis project on how to set up and run an efficient web page template.

HTML5 id/class name cheat sheet (http://oli.jp/2008/html5-class-cheatsheet/)

> When creating a template, it's good to draw on previous work. Take a look at this survey of common values for `id` and `class` attributes.

HTML5 Implementations in Web Browsers (http://wiki.whatwg.org/wiki/Implementa tions_in_Web_browsers)

> This wiki page contains a centralized listing of which browsers support the different parts of HTML5.

HTML5 Demos (http://html5demos.com/)

> A collection of demos put together by JavaScript developer Remy Sharp.

HTML5 Doctor (http://html5doctor.com/)
> Before there was IE9 or Chrome, the HTML5 Doctor was in explaining the specification, testing what worked and what didn't. Continuously updated, covering the latest issues facing web designers building with HTML5.

HTML5 Reset (http://html5reset.org/)
> A basic set of HTML and CSS files to code a project with HTML5 for various browsers including older versions of Internet Explorer.

HTML5 Rocks (http://www.html5rocks.com/)
> HTML5 Rocks is a playground of HTML5 examples and tutorials produced by Google.

HTML: The Markup Language Reference (http://dev.w3.org/html5/markup/spec.html)
> This is the W3's home of the HTML5 specification.

Modernizr (http://www.modernizr.com/)
> The act of detecting which browser a site visitor is using is '90s thinking. In this new millennium, web builders check to see if the feature is present in the browser instead. A JavaScript library allows for checking the availability of HTML5 features like GeoLocation, WebSockets and even CSS3 properties.

When Can I Use (http://caniuse.com/)
> When you need to know if a browser supports a feature of HTML5 or not, When Can I Use is one of the easier, if not easiest, references to check.

Index

A

a element
    adding links to block-level content, 20
    draggable support, 29
.aac format, 97
abbr element
    about, 19, 145
    additional information, 19, 146
    styling, 145
    title attribute, 19
abbreviations
    defining, 19
    identifying to users, 144
    term definition, 145
accessibility
    additional information, 156
    ARIA live regions and, 157–159
    associating form fields with labels, 151
    enabling fieldset element dynamically, 154
    grouping form fields logically, 152–153
    identifying abbreviations, 144
    identifying acronyms, 144
    identifying required form fields, 155–156
    identifying sections of web content, 146–148
    multimedia, 99, 100
    navigation links and, 149–151
    published guidelines on, 140
    purpose of, 139
    text alternatives for images, 141–144
    workarounds for assistive technology bugs, 148
Accessible Rich Internet Applications (see ARIA)

acronym element, 19, 145
acronyms
    defining, 19
    identifying to users, 144
    term definition, 145
addresses
    geocoding, 169–171
    reverse geocoding, 167–169
alert role (ARIA), 157
alertdialog role (ARIA), 157
align attribute, 32
animating drawings, 210–212
application cache, 221–225
application role (ARIA), 147
applicationCache interface, 223
appointment scheduling sample form, 92–94
ARIA (Accessible Rich Internet Applications)
    about, 140
    identifying required form fields, 155
    landmark roles, 146–148
    live regions, 157–159
    multiple image references and, 142
aria-atomic attribute, 158
aria-describedby attribute, 142, 151
aria-labelledby attribute, 142, 151
aria-live attribute, 157–159
aria-required attribute, 156
article element
    about, 5
    main role, 148
    script element comparison, 9–11
    usage considerations, 7
aside element
    about, 5
    complementary role, 146

We'd like to hear your suggestions for improving our indexes. Send email to *index@oreilly.com*.

dragstart event, 225, 229
DRM (Digital Rights Management), 100
drop event, 227, 229
Dynamic Google Analytics Tagging application, 138
dynamic maps, 182

E

editable drop-down (combo box), 73–76
elements, 32
    (see also structural elements; specific elements)
    associating images with, 143
    mapping to ID and class names, 51–54
    obsolete, 32
em element, 14
embedded content, defined, 95
error event, 233, 237
event listeners, adding, 125
expanding text content natively, 23–25
explicit sectioning, defined, 11

F

fallback content
    canvas element and, 184
    creating, 98, 114
Featherstone, Derek, 156
fieldset element
    disabled attribute, 154
    enabling dynamically, 154
    grouping form fields logically, 152–153
figcaption element
    about, 21
    text alternatives for images and, 142, 144
figure element
    about, 21
    aside element and, 21
    text alternatives for images and, 142, 144
figures, marking up, 20
FileReader API
    about, 242–245
    readAsBinaryString() method, 244
flot library, 213–215
Foliot, John, 121
font element, 32
footer element
    about, 5
    contentinfo role, 147

Internet Explorer recognizing HTML5 elements, 36
    links and, 148
    usage considerations, 7
form element
    form role, 146
    search role, 147
form fields
    associating with labels, 151
    autofocusing on, 80
    contact information, 58–61
    creating editable drop-down, 73–76
    date and time, 62–65
    disabling autocomplete in, 82
    displaying placeholder text in, 80–81
    entering numbers, 66–69
    grouping logically, 152–153
    identifying required, 155–156
    requiring, 77
    restricting values in, 84–86
    search, 55–56
    selecting colors, 71–72
    selecting from range of numbers, 69–71
    user-friendly, 67
form role (ARIA), 146
forms
    about, 55
    additional information, 155
    appointment scheduling sample, 92–94
    best practices, 91
    making HTML5 work in older browsers, 86–90
frame element, 32
frameset element, 32
Friedl, Jeffrey, 84
fundamental syntax and semantics (see syntax and semantics)

G

geocoding
    additional information, 171
    addresses into coordinates, 169–171
    defined, 167
    reverse, 167–169, 167, 169
Geolocation API
    about, 161
    additional information, 164
    geocoding addresses, 169–171
    getting basic geolocation data, 161–164

VP8 codec, 116

W

W3C (World Wide Web Consortium)
about, ix
additional information, 2
Geolocation API, 161
on accessibility, 139–141
on canvas transformations, 206
on clipping, 209
on contenteditable attribute, 29
on forms, 155
on HTML4 and HTML5 differences, 5
on multimedia accessibility, 100
on ol element, 27
on range input type, 71
on small element, 18
on Web Workers, 234
RDFa specification, 127
Unicorn unified validator, 48
WAI (Web Accessibility Initiative), 140
WAI-ARIA specification, 7, 159
.wav format, 97
wave visualization of audio via canvas element,
103–106
WCAG (Web Content Accessibility
Guidelines), 140, 142
Web Accessibility Initiative (WAI), 140
web browsers (see browsers)
Web Content Accessibility Guidelines
(WCAG), 140, 142
web documents (see documents)
Web Hypertext Application Technology
Working Group (see WHATWG)
Web Workers (see Worker API)
.webm format, 97, 116
WebM Tools, 118
WebSocket API
about, 234–238
readyState property, 237
WHATWG (Web Hypertext Application
Technology Working Group)
about, ix
on abbr element, 19, 146
on draggable attribute, 30
on media element attributes, 97
width attribute, 32
Worker API
about, 230–234

additional information, 234
clearInterval() method, 234
clearTimeout() method, 234
postMessage() method, 232
setInterval() method, 234
setTimeout() method, 232, 234
terminate() method, 234
World Wide Web Consortium (see WC3
(World Wide Web Consortium))
WYSIWYG editors, 28

X

XFN (XHTML Friends Network), 127
XMLHttpRequest API, 233, 236

About the Authors

Christopher Schmitt has been working on the Web since 1993. He is the principal of Heatvision.com, Inc., a new-media design firm, and resides in Austin, Texas. He speaks frequently about web design and standards-based development at conferences including OSCON, SXSW Interactive, AIGA In Control, and CSS Summit. His books include *Adapting to Web Standards: CSS and Ajax for Big Sites* (New Riders), *Professional CSS: Cascading Style Sheets for Web Design* (Wrox), and *CSS Cookbook* (O'Reilly). His personal site is *http://christopherschmitt.com*.

Kyle Simpson is a UI architect from Austin, Texas. He is passionate about user experience, specifically optimizing the UI to be as responsive, efficient, secure, and scalable as possible. He considers JavaScript to be the ultimate language and is constantly tinkering with how to push it further. If something can't be done in JavaScript or web technology, he's bored by it. He has a number of open source projects, including LABjs, HandlebarJS/BikechainJS, and flXHR, and he also is a core contributor to SWFObject.

Colophon

The animal on the cover of *HTML5 Cookbook* is a common kestrel (*Falco tinnunculus*), a member of the falcon family. A more archaic name for this bird is "windhover," based on its unique hunting style. By facing into the wind and spreading its wings to catch and slow the air, the kestrel can hover in one place and scan for prey on the ground below.

The common kestrel is the most widespread bird of prey in Europe, and it can also be found in Asia and Africa. It prefers open habitats like fields, shrubland, and marshes, but it is very adaptable as long as there are places to perch and prey. Kestrels almost exclusively eat small mammals like shrews, mice, and most commonly, voles. Depending on the season and energy expended, each bird needs to eat the equivalent of 4–8 voles each day.

The plumage of the common kestrel is chestnut brown with black spots, with a lighter underside and black wings. The tails differ by sex; females have black bars, and the males have gray feathers with a black tip. Male kestrels also have gray heads. These birds measure 13–15 inches long, with a wingspan of 26–32 inches (making them somewhat smaller than other birds of prey). Kestrels can see in the ultraviolet spectrum, which helps them locate prey—voles mark their trails with urine, which reflects ultraviolet light. This leads the hunting bird to either the vole itself or its nest.

The cover image is from *Cassell's Natural History*. The cover font is Adobe ITC Garamond. The text font is Linotype Birka; the heading font is Adobe Myriad Condensed; and the code font is LucasFont's TheSansMonoCondensed.

Get even more for your money.

Join the O'Reilly Community, and register the O'Reilly books you own. It's free, and you'll get:

- $4.99 ebook upgrade offer
- 40% upgrade offer on O'Reilly print books
- Membership discounts on books and events
- Free lifetime updates to ebooks and videos
- Multiple ebook formats, DRM FREE
- Participation in the O'Reilly community
- Newsletters
- Account management
- 100% Satisfaction Guarantee

Signing up is easy:

1. **Go to: oreilly.com/go/register**
2. **Create an O'Reilly login.**
3. **Provide your address.**
4. **Register your books.**

Note: English-language books only

To order books online:
oreilly.com/store

For questions about products or an order:
orders@oreilly.com

To sign up to get topic-specific email announcements and/or news about upcoming books, conferences, special offers, and new technologies:
elists@oreilly.com

For technical questions about book content:
booktech@oreilly.com

To submit new book proposals to our editors:
proposals@oreilly.com

O'Reilly books are available in multiple DRM-free ebook formats. For more information:
oreilly.com/ebooks

O'REILLY®

Spreading the knowledge of innovators   oreilly.com

Have it your way.